A Commissioner's Primer to Economics of Competition Law in India

Geeta Gouri

A Commissioner's Primer to Economics of Competition Law in India

palgrave
macmillan

Geeta Gouri
Competition Commission of India
New Delhi, Delhi, India

ISBN 978-981-19-9475-3 ISBN 978-981-19-9476-0 (eBook)
https://doi.org/10.1007/978-981-19-9476-0

This Palgrave Macmillan imprint is published by the registered company Springer Nature Singapore Pte Ltd.
The registered company address is: 152 Beach Road, #21-01/04 Gateway East, Singapore 189721, Singapore

Dedicated to my mentors
Late Mr. T. L. Sankar
Dr. Y. Venugopal Reddy
&
my constant friend, support and confidante
Rajen Harshé

Contents

List of Figures

List of Tables

CHAPTER 1

Regulation and Competition

Open market functioning has many supporters as detractors biased in favor of regulation and competition rather than regulation and control. These divergent pulls frame the political economy of regulation and competition. Paradigm shifts in economic policies from regulation to competition is a layered process beset with distinguishing the process from regulating a sector to regulating markets for competitiveness. In India at least the processes are not sharply defined. Regulation has always been central to the industrial strategies adopted by the Government of India. Discussions on regulation per se contend with differing perspectives of welfare maximization of economic welfare and consumer harm. The underlying debates on industrial strategies preceding the shift to economic liberalization was on the opening of sectors to private investments and the sequencing of reforms at the macro-level of current account versus capital account liberalization and at the micro-level of the sectors that need regulation on account of their economic characteristics of natural monopoly such as power sector and telecom (Geeta, 2020, 2017). The debate in these sectors was on the balance of power in the structure of designated regulatory body or sector commissions.[1] The paradigm shift to an open economy and a market facilitator was much slower with the Competition Commission established a decade later. The debates were on agreements that result inappreciable effect on competition to entry barriers legally created or market created to abuse of market

G. Gouri, *A Commissioner's Primer to Economics of Competition Law in India*, https://doi.org/10.1007/978-981-19-9476-0_1

power through dominance. Having been associated with a sector regulator (Andhra Pradesh Electricity Regulatory Commission) and later with the Competition Commission of India (CCI), I am familiar with the layers of differences and in the overlaps in different forms of regulation that have been debated and legislated in India. The subject of regulation is a fascinating subject without a definitive conclusive ending. The debate continues. This chapter is an introduction to regulation and competition.

1 Regulation or a Regulated Controlled Economy

A simple rule to distinguish between regulation and a regulated economy is the difference in regulating sectors to regulating the entire economy through licensing and controls over foreign exchange, pricing, allocation of funds. The adopted strategy of mixed economy and import substitution was of regulating of controlling resource allocation in the economy. A web of licensing and controls emerged with emphasis on public sector rather than on competition and private initiative. There was no licensing for the public sector but their control, management and commercial activities were controlled by the government(s). Between the dominance of licensing to economic liberalization was the New Economic Policy (NEP) the half-way house that saw several Committees set up by the government to assess the efficacy and efficiency of licensing and control by the State.

These Committees in their assessment pointed that policies adopted during the period of closed economy or import substitution was less concerned with generating competition and more with preventing concentration of economic power. It is no surprise, therefore, that the aim of the first attempt at market regulation the Monopolies and Restrictive Trade Practices Act 1969 ("MRTP Act") was to prevent the concentration of economic power to common detriment, to regulate monopolies and to take action against monopolistic and restrictive trade practices and other matters connected or incidental thereto (Gouri and Pandiya, 2020).[2] The association of market power with monopolistic or oligopolistic structures of enterprises translated into a static understanding of competition in terms of the Competition Act, 2002 (CA02). Designed to regulate anti-competitive agreements with respect to production, supply, distribution, storage, acquisition or control of goods or provision of services; any abuse of dominant position as well as combinations that can cause, or are likely to cause, appreciable adverse effect on competition in the Indian economy CA02 was framed for a traditional product market economy.

Obsession with size and market power is a historical obsession of earlier regulations and control policies raising several uncomfortable questions in the assessment of emergent platform market or data markets and in the case of bundled patents. The unilinear approach to monopolization is changing slowly. Assessing the presence of competitive constraints, of identifying and weighing consumer benefits and the theory of harm is slowly emerging perhaps more keenly in the case of mergers than in AoD cases with a discernible shift from AAEC to investment and growth. Slip-ups occur in a reversion to the historic obsession in emergent markets obfuscating regulation and competition.

The importance of understanding the difference between regulation and regulated economy in implementation of the CA02 is the temptation to control the market.[3] In terms of decisions of the competition authority, the inclination to define the market rather than facilitating the market of market governance of control. Within regulation there is clear distinction between sector regulators, and the fair-trade regulator or competition regulator (CCI) in terms of regulatory functioning. Sector regulators are ex-ante regulators while CCI is an ex-poste regulator except in the case of combinations (mergers & acquisitions).

2 Distinctions in Regulation

The primary distinction between ex-ante and ex-poste defines the distinction in regulation. In the case of ex-ante regulation, the regulatory Commission fixes the tariffs to be charged to consumers. The simplest methodology is to fix a reasonable rate of return on the cost (operating or variable cost) of the enterprise which are mainly utilities that were in the public sector. Marginal cost pricing is not a very attractive proposition in pricing schedules of utilities. As there is no competition, there are no market benchmarks to arrive at the appropriate costs. The utilities submit their annual revenue requirements and through a process of negotiations the costs are decided. Clearly, power equations between the regulator and the regulated entity define the cost and the tariffs. The two major sector regulators electricity and telecom, emerged before the Commission was conceived, legislated and operationalized.

The oldest independent sector regulator is the Reserve Bank of India established in the 1930s. The lineage of RBI and the specialized nature of monetary policy as a major instrument of the RBI are outside the purview of CCI. Cases of competition among commercial banks relating to consumer complaints on uniform interest rates on loans and deposits few cases have filed with CCI. There have been complaints from the electricity sector and the telecom sector filed with the Commission. In a recent decision, the Supreme Court has passed an Order that complaints in the telecom sector can proceed only to CCI post-TRAI the telecom regulatory authority. This pertains to bidding for spectrum space where cartelization was alleged. The Monopolies and Restrictive Trade Practices Act (MRTP) the precursor to CCI was enacted in 1969 and continued till CCI became operational in 2009. The early sector regulators, the Telecom Regulatory Authority under TRAI Act in 1997, amended in 2000 with a minor modification in 2014; and the regulators in the electricity sector SERCs and CERC under the Electricity Act, 2003. In the electricity sector, the Indian Electricity Supply Act 1910 replaced by the Electricity Supply Act 1946 amended in 1991—generation was opened to the private sector and Regional Load Dispatch Centres. Telecommunications and electricity are known as public utilities. The segments regulated were natural monopolies. Wires, railways and grid networks are natural monopolies. Public utilities were unbundled as part of economic liberalization into two segments the natural monopoly segment and the competitive segments. Natural monopolies defined in terms of high fixed costs and low operating costs are monopolies in a given market. And in fixing tariffs by the regulatory commissions power equations tend to dominate between the appropriate regulation and the State visible in the unbundled public utilities or those privatized such as Discoms (distribution companies).[4] Economics of regulation of utilities is primarily in the design of tariffs and as of now these tariffs are not market determined. Several factors are taken into account for distributing the costs aimed ultimately at ensuring consumer benefits. Consideration of time of use, peak and off-peak hours, distance are important for fixing the tariff. Consumers are classified on the basis of 'contribution to peak' modified by categorization of large and small consumers. As a power game in politics at least in the electricity sector, the trade-offs are between subsidies from the government and cross-subsidies. There is, however, a time constraint and functional constraint with regard to regulation of the power sector. Technology has evolved to decentralized power systems. Small decentralized power generating solar units, wind mills bagasse-based generations and the scope for large generating stations to small units often as low as 1 MW.

In a sense, consumers have become generators and in the process changed the structure of tariff fixation. Similarly in the telecommunications field emergence of spectrum and radio waves allow for several players offering space at market determined prices are outcomes of technological developments. Multiple players at multiple levels are competition concerns and not of the sector regulator.

Competition policy applies to sectors where structural conditions are compatible with normal functioning of the market. The economics of competitive market structures is of oligopolistic markets where the presence of a few firms can result in anti-competitive effects by way of cartels, abuse of dominance in terms of exclusionary and extortionary outcomes.

3 Regulation and Competition—in the Market for the Market

There have been several cases on TRAI and ERCs which have centered around competition issues of choice for consumers, bidding and auctioning of spectrum and radio waves are overlapping areas between sector regulators and CCI bringing to the forefront that boundaries between sector regulator and competition authorities are hazy. The initial emphasis on natural monopoly and economies of scale is muted. Technology has softened the natural monopoly concept and the experience of regulation in utilities has affirmed that there cannot be a break between competition and regulation. At the center of the continuum between regulation and competition is a reversion to 'competition for the market' and 'competition in the market'. Antitrust tools for the former emphasize bidding and contracts, among competitors while in the case of the latter the emphasis is on barriers to entry, unfair pricing (predatory), leveraging et al. As boundaries narrow the best measurement of effective regulation is effective competition (Kahn, 1988). Public sector entities or para-statal organizations are exposed to the same competition rules as any other private enterprise devoid of the protectionist umbrella of the government. Public sector enterprises are statutorily created monopolies and not natural monopoles. Antitrust laws presumably are ownership neutral except the challenge stems from control exercised by a single shareholding entity namely the government.

Competition is on market functioning with appropriate benefits flowing from the pressure exerted on firms to perform. Consumers benefit from efficiency in production besides ensuring a variety of goods and servicing enhancing the consumption basket. The traditional approach was to define competition in terms of number of firms in the market or the size of the enterprise and capacity to assert market power replaced by defining competition in terms of prevalence of competitive constraints as the appropriate and preferred option. Competition authorities only need to be convinced on the presence of competitive constraints which is not always an easy exercise. A wider canvas than of only defining markets in terms of substitutes (Section 2r, CA02) prompts a review of decisions of CCI. It is not easy as it requires translating economic theory of efficient firm to be combined with welfare aspects. The analysis of competition is to promote competitive pricing and ensure allocative and productive efficiency. In a static framework, the argument that a dominant enterprise indulges in high pricing if price is not equal to marginal cost may fail to capture the dynamics business. It is also possible for prices to below marginal cost. In a dynamic competitive market pricing strategies are strategies for meeting competition. Emphasis shifts to consumer benefits and consumer welfare, to innovations that benefit consumers. The interplay between firms under conditions of free entry, competitive endeavors does suggest a utopian scenario. The competition authorities' job is to ensure competitive markets 'for the market' and 'in the market'. Complications arise if external policy conditions are imposed such as removal of inequality of income; generation of employment; concerns of privacy. It is possible to establish a connect but in a convoluted manner. On these matters, CCI is empowered under the Act to advice the government accordingly under Section 21A (Bhattacharjee et al., 2018). The government always has the right to give directions to the Commission under Section 55 or to exempt certain sectors under Section 54.

4 Raghavan Committee Report

The significance of competition and of an open trade-based economy and the credit of competition goes to the High Level Committee on Competition Policy and Law, 2000 more popularly known as the Raghavan Committee Report.[5] The Committee deliberated on the requirement of an open economy where trade and an open economy ensured greater efficiency in resource allocation and consumer welfare. In fact the approach of the Committee brought to focus the aspect of public interest from protecting competition to protecting consumers. The earlier industrial policy of import substitution defined welfare in terms of protecting domestic industrialists from competition represented by producer surplus. It changed with the Raghvan Committed Report which argued that the ultimate raison d'être of competition is the interest of the consumer. To quote:

> Consumer interest and public interest are considered synonymous. But they are not and need to be distinguished. In the name of public interest, many Governmental policies are formulated which are either anti-competitive in nature or which manifest themselves in anti-competitive behaviour. If the consumer is at the fulcrum, consumer interest and consumer welfare should have primacy in all Governmental policy form.

The extant laws of market the Monopolies Restrictive Trade Practices Act and the Consumer Protection Act would need redefinition of welfare in terms of consumer surplus and not just producer surplus. The Committee itself an outcome of the WTO round of negotiations of lowering tariffs, removal of Quantitative Restrictions (QRs) and encouraging trade among countries. The concept of competitive advantage underlying trade laws required domestic laws to match with international laws. An economy in transition is a complete overhaul of a regimen built on levels of controls and restrictions and as many advocated a competition policy was imminent to get all parties and States on board. In 2007 a Working Group on Competition Policy was instituted to outline the dimensions of an open economy.

Attention is drawn to three points emphasized by the Raghavan Committee. Firstly, a domestic competition law is important to prevent international cartels from asserting their anti-competitive practices in the country. Secondly, modern and technological industries where economies of scale define competition in monopolistic or oligopolistic market structures competition law ensure the retention of competitive market measures. Lastly, the primacy of consumers. All producers are consumers but all consumers are not producers. The present CA02 was detailed in the Report with one difference—ex-ante merger would not be within the purview of the Competition Law and the proposed Competition Commission. Instead a separate Merger Commission or a separate bench of the Competition Commission to avoid delays in merger clearance with clearance of 90 days period was proposed. Perhaps the partitioning was advocated to maintain the tradition of ex-ante regulation and ex-poste competition assessment.

5 Emergent Markets and Competition

The CA02 was operationalized in 2009 sans a Competition Policy despite the recommendations of the Working Group of the Planning Commission. [6] Framed in the economics of traditional product market as most competition Acts world over emergence of platform markets revealed the limits of CA02 and now with emergent data markets and market for ideas a major change in the approach of competition law is imminent. Two of these new markets are neural while the third relates to the aspect of technology and standard setting relating to the network and related patents. The review Committee of the Act staying within the traditional mold of product markets could not offer any understanding of competition issues in emergent markets with several issues of concern to economists and competition analysts. The jury is not yet out on the exact antitrust concerns suffice to state that the competition authorities are uncomfortable. A quick look at these markets and to the concerns raised.

5.1 *Platform Markets*

Platform markets are neural markets on the internet often referred to as online markets defined by the characteristic of having 2 (or multi) sides to the market sellers and buyers on one side and advertising firms on the other side. These spaces are created by tech firms that enable interactions between the two sides. Several firms also have their own web sites besides being listed on the platform of well-established tech firms. They are not classified as platform markets but nonetheless provide competitive constraints to the main platform. Radio taxi services using broad band are not considered as platform markets. Antitrust complaints have been raised against the high-tech firms. Network effects have made the high-tech firms large and dominant. The commonly followed model is for consumers to surf the net freely currently disputed while raising revenue from advertisements. The algorithms for surfing permit linking markets and creating network effects. Concerns have been raised on:

a. The deep discounts presumably offered by platforms as against prices offered by brick-and-mortar shops;
b. Price Parity Clauses;
c. Exclusive Agreements;

d. Platform to Business Contract terms;
e. Platform Neutrality
f. Algorithmic collusion
g. Privy to a large amount of consumer data and privacy concerns

In the review of CA02, an entire chapter has been devoted to platform markets with the acceptance that a lot more of cases are required to modify the present Act. The beginning of discomfort with a legal framework ensconced in the product market comes out sharply in the first platform case the Google. The dissent Order was skeptical of the evidence marshaled to prove allegations of favoritism in the ranking of advertisements on the search engine platform. Enquiry into Amazon and Flipkart on deep discounting may throw up valuable insights. Newspaper reports suggest that CCI is yet to come to terms of consumer welfare. Apps on phones in local language indicate a growing clientele of online shopping on apps even in rural areas. Competition is active and hot for big tech firms from small platforms and web sites. Shifting contours of relevant market defined by substitutability of Section 2(r) needs relooking for platform markets. The offline-online demarcation may be a mechanism to retain consumers through differential pricing schemes. Studies initiated by CCI are a beginning toward understanding the emergent markets. Restrictions of the Act, however, depend on a wider irreverential approach than hitherto followed.

Algorithmic collusion is again a completely new area that need exploration. Is this collusion deliberate or robotic? Earlier cases on hindsight of algorithmic collision were not well articulated for want of expertise. In areas of AI competition experts would have to lean on technical expertise.

5.2 *Data Markets*

Access to data which enables profiling of consumers and locking effects has seen the emergence of 'data markets'. Data becomes an asset that can be bought and sold or just rented out is emerging as a major area of business development. Monetizing data is a new concept to earlier data collection by individual firms. Reference to data in the context of platform markets is just one small part of data required for new business. A lot of valuable data is available from surveys especially of health and household consumption patterns. Beginnings of data market were noticed in the joint venture of Amazon and Cloudtail (Catamaran) now broken.

Antitrust interventions have concentrated on data portability, data sharing, platform neutrality addressing the market power of platforms markets and not of data markets. Emergence of data markets is a new phenomenon that has not caught attention. Issues pertaining to access to data are seen as among the major current antitrust concerns. Data is always the basis of successful business but Big Data of platforms of high-tech firms to many authorities represent market power. Consumers pay with their personal data in surfing these platforms, and the EU Commission is upbeat on this aspect placing privacy and rights of consumer to their data as primary to antitrust analysis of platform markets raises the fundamental question is data privacy a competition issue?

5.3 *Market for Ideas*

The core of digitalization is standard essential patents. These patents are a set of complementary patents bundled together and sold as a bundle. The package or bundle of patents to meet the standards fixed by SSOs (Standard Setting Organizations) as all telecommunication equipment including phone sets have to be interoperable and meet global standards be it 3G, 4G or 5G and the internet of things. The bundle of patents is required to be FRAND (or RAND) compliant. Ironically, traditional competition law frowns on tying and bundling which is the core of patents and SEPs. Several cases against Ericsson have been filed in CCI alleging the methodology of fixing royalty or license fee; authenticity of patents in the bundle; and the right to select patents from the bundle. Institutional structure of SEPs and of licensing fee are now in the arena of competition authorities.

Market of ideas is the emergent market of patents and of knowledge.

6 Conclusions

My intent was to capture the vast canvas of competition issues and the importance of understanding the context in terms of market structures. The analytic framework in terms of economics and of innovative approaches, the requirements of an irreverential approach and the requirements of a wider forum of discussion were synthesized in this chapter.

Notes

1. Aditya Chintapanti Professor of Competition law in Jindal University in his discussions with me on institutional structure and organization of regulatory commissions used the template of Hancher and Moran (1989).
2. Geeta Gouri and Kalyani Pandya, The Indian competition law experience—its history and its.
   (digital) future., INDIAN LAW REVIEW, https://doi.org/10.1080/24730580.2020.1843316.
3. Alfred E. Kahn, The Economics of Regulation -Principles and Institutions, MIT Press, 1988.
4. A comprehensive book on public utilities and of the public sector is Sankar, T.L and Venugopal Reddy, Editors, Privatisation, Diversification of Ownership of Public Enterprises. Book Links Enterprises, 1989. Dr. Y.V. Reddy in his seminal piece on State, Market and Privatization: Stalemate in State-Action in India maps out the inherent tensions in the shift from State dominated regulation to market-framed operations.
5. Report of High Level Committee on Competition Policy and Law (2000). S.V.S. Raghavan Committee. The Competition Commission has come out with a series of booklets on the history and details of the Act which is available on the web site.
6. REPORT OF THE WORKING GROUP ON COMPETITION POLICY, Planning Commission Government of India February 2007, Chairperson Vinod Dhall who later became the single Member of the non-operational Competition Commission of India.

References

Alfred E. Kahn. (1988). The Economics of Regulation Principles and Institutions. MIT Press.

Bhattacharjea, A., and Oindrilla D. (2018, June). Competition Law and Competition Policy in India: How the Competition Commission has Dealt with Anticompetitive Restraints by Government Entities. Online released.

Geeta Gouri & Kalyani Pandya. 2017. The Indian competition law experience–its history and its (digital) future. *Indian Law Review*, 276–300. http://ssrn.com/abstract=2787343

Geeta Gouri & Kalyani Pandya. 2020. Protecting Competition v/s Protecting Competitor: Assessing the Antitrust Complaints against Google. *The Criterion Journal of Innovation, 2*, 531–558.

CHAPTER 2

Basics of Economics of Competition and Markets in Product Markets

Economics of competition law incorporates concepts from microeconomic theory of the firm in assessing competition and markets. The tools of economics namely price, cost and quantity are the parameters for defining competition, monopoly and monopolistic or oligopolistic competition. The Competition Act, 2002 (CA02) and its clauses are framed in these parameters. This chapter is a primer on economics that sent out red flags to me as a Commissioner of the Competition Commission of India on the possibility of antitrust abuse. In writing this chapter, I pose the question what were the red flags that were picked up and those that got missed out. On hindsight the latter is equally important having had the time to think and ponder. The chapter, therefore, is not a replication of microeconomics textbook or a primer of economics. It is a primer to the economics of competition and markets as applied to product markets. It captures the insights of a Commissioner's experience with the vantage of time. In Chapter 3, we examine economics of competition in emergent market. In implementing the law fluidity of interpretation is permissible if the underlying economics of competition is robust. Econometrics and the use of regressions in estimating price-quantity fixation in cartel analysis often need the backing of game theory to strategize moves of dominant players in oligopolistic markets, to establish market power in instances of abuse of dominance or in mergers. CA02 itself is limiting designed for markets that are now considered traditional in the image of

G. Gouri, *A Commissioner's Primer to Economics of Competition Law in India*, https://doi.org/10.1007/978-981-19-9476-0_2

brick-and-mortar markets. Neural markets, algorithms, software, patents and access to data that emerged with digitalization and 'internet of things' pose challenges to competition authorities in the very basic assessment of anti-competitiveness. In this context markets as elaborated in the previous chapter are classified into four distinct categories defined in terms of the economics of each market. They are:

(i) conventional or *traditional product market* with a continuum from perfect competition to monopoly to monopolistic competition;
(ii) *platform markets* normally on the internet characterized by two sides with sellers and buyers on the one side and advertisers on the other—network effects and economies of scale result in the emergence of giant tech firms;
(iii) *data markets* emerging from access to data of platform markets to compiling and computing varied data that is anonymized and automized to find a niche in the monetizing of data—a quasi-public good;
(iv) *market for ideas* of patents and knowledge—Standard Essential Patents bundle of patents that define the capability of telecommunication systems of the service providers.

Business models are shaped by the market of reference.[1] Nuances of each market in its structure and competitive constraint unless reflected in the economics competition authorities employ antitrust analysis remains in a void—irrelevant.

The replacement of the first market regulation in India the Monopolies and Restrictive Trade Practices Act (MRTP) with CA02 was inevitable. Ground realities of economic liberalization policies initiated in 1991 were at variance with a structuralist MRTP designed for a protectionist industrial and trade policies. The new Act was envisaged as a proactive economic law for regulating markets appropriate to the industrial policies of economic liberalization. Enacted in 2002 the Act became operational in 2009, consequently it was dated even before it became operational. Rapid developments in technology and market structures in a short period (2002–2009) redefining the concept of competitiveness itself the Act were inadequate as a competition law for new and emergent market structures (Gouri, 2020).[2]

At the outset a few observations are helpful based as they are on my experience in presenting economics of antitrust to those more comfortable with legalese. Firstly, law is relatively black and white while economics has large areas of grey. In its application to antitrust arguments economic theories model and simulate market outcomes depending upon the values of select parameters. As a result, there is often no concrete economic evidence of definite outcomes of market behavior. This is more so in the case of platform markets and market for ideas. Evidence that law seeks is not available and at most reference is to counterfactuals. Secondly, dynamics of market and divergent business models have seen behavioral analysis treading into economic theory. Lawyers are more comfortable with conventional economics. Thirdly, tendency of economists to be highly technical with their own vocabulary prefaced with rigorous mathematical proofs is deterring. Communications with the larger audience are the objective of this primer and to stay with the simple diagrams. Lastly, the scope for blurring of distinction between competition law and other non-market policy instruments is common.[3] Objectives of competition law are to address market distortion rather than emphasize redress of inequities which perhaps are better addressed through interventions, such as duties, taxes. Lack of clarity on the objective of competition law and the limits of Competition Act blunt a powerful instrument without rectifying dysfunctional or distorted markets. In defining consumer welfare arguments that border on inequities can pose problems on the scope of competition analysis.[4]

In this chapter, we look at the economics of product market which gives the basic economic tools of analysis.

1 Product Market

The tools of an economist are seen with reference to demand, cost and price. CA02 to reiterate is framed in conventional economic analysis also referred to as the price-quantity framework of product markets. It is the basic model of interactions between demand, cost and price. Recent modifications to the Act retain the same structure with a limited attempt at incorporating dynamism of emergent markets such as that of platform markets. Bare market construct is of buyers (consumers) and sellers (producers, enterprises, firms) referred to as the traditional product market where competitive markets defined in terms of numbers of sellers and buyers in binaries of perfect competition or monopoly.

The Act leans to 'per se' approach to competition abuses rather than to an 'effects-based' economic analysis. Competition is not defined in the Act. Reference is to 'adverse effect on competition' applicable to horizontal or vertical agreements among enterprises. A market structure with a single firm (monopolist) or a dominant firm can be equally constrained in exerting market power in terms of fixing price or quantity drawing distinction between 'competition for the market' and 'competition in the market'. Antitrust economists have, therefore, preferred to use the phrase 'effective competition' meriting intervention by competition authorities only if there is harm to consumers. Attention is diverted from looking at mere number of firms in a market to outcomes assessed in terms of consumer harm from the lack of competition. The task is more complex and demanding for economic analysis. The European Commission and the Department of Justice and Federal Trade Commission of US refer to 'effective competition' which shifts the emphasis from static to dynamic analysis (Bishop and Walker, 2010).[5] Focusing on outcomes the importance of defining and measuring welfare gains and losses come to the forefront. It still leaves debatable issues at loose ends for instance of defining consumer and of defining harm.[6]

Demand, cost and price tools of economics at the disposal of competition authorities to assess anti-competitive outcomes are basic to modeling or scenario building. Use of game theory in modeling strategies of doing business expands a Commissioner's box of tools in providing insights into dynamics of markets. Cournot, Bertrand, Stackleberg and variants of monopolistic competition are models which lay emphasis on possible business strategies adopted by producers persuade posing questions of importance for economic analysis. Referred to as 'effects-based' analysis questions relate to the state of competitiveness in a defined market; presence of counterfactuals; the presence of competitive constraints to assess the evidence and ability of a firm to assert market power. The forces that generate market power and the presence of competitive constraints lay the foundations of competition economics.

(i) *Price, cost and demand-basic tools of competition*

The business model of any firm, enterprise or producer is based on the cost of producing a product, the price charged which depends on the cost and the demand for the product. Demand is a driving factor in deciding on what to produce, how much to produce and how to price a product. In the case of multiple products or where joint costs of production are involved the same factors apply with the difference that cost is spread among the products in terms of demand for each of the products. Most of us are familiar with the market description given in the figure below but it always helps to refresh basic concepts. What is amazing is the simplicity of basic economic tools and the scope it provides for valuable insights into business models of firms. On the vertical axis, price is shown and on the horizontal axis quantity. The two sets of curves used in Fig. 1a are the demand or the average revenue curve and the supply curve (average cost curve). The competitive price and quantity is where $P = \text{MR} = \text{MC}$. It could be at the point where the MC curve cuts the MR curve or where the MC curve cuts the demand (AR) curve. In Fig. 1b relationship between the marginal revenue (MR) curve and the marginal cost (MC) curves is shown. The underlying assumption is that a firms objective is of profit maximization while for consumers it is utility (satisfaction) maximization. A profit maximizing firm will expand his output as long as there is demand in the market. A utility maximizing consumer will continue to purchase a product until her utility (satisfaction) is reached. Reference in the figure is to market cost curves and market demand and not of the individual firm.

(i) *Cost and supply curves*

Marginal cost curve and its relation to the average cost are the two important curves. Both curves follow the shape of the total cost curve in terms of curvature. The curvature of the marginal cost curve is more steep than of the average cost curve. The average cost curves consist of two components—fixed cost and variable cost. There can be separate average cost curves for the two cost components. In the case of the marginal cost curve reference is only to the variable cost or operating cost. For antitrust analysis, marginal cost is more important than average cost. The standard cost curve is U-shaped denoting increasing costs after a threshold of production viability is reached. Further expansions to output add to costs rather than revenue causing the average cost curve to rise. The L-shaped MC is when total costs have been completely recovered, and there are

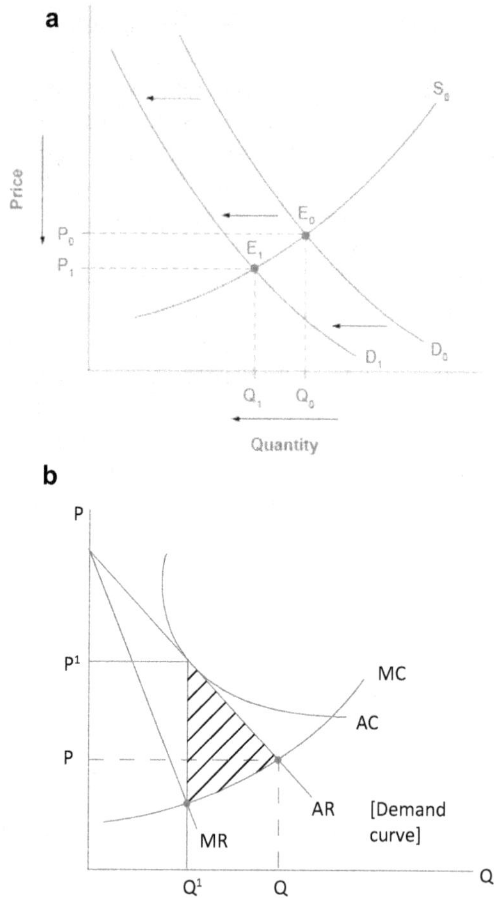

Fig. 1 (a) Simple pricing of demand and (b) Supply curve intersection

only operating costs suggesting that the firm is enjoying the benefits of economies of scale. In this case, MC curves are flat and asymptotic to the x-axis indicate that operating costs are minimal. Flattening of the cost curves are usually associated with natural monopolies and economies of network. A natural monopoly is a situation where only one firm is able to recover costs fully. They were largely associated with networks, such as railway lines, fixed lines of telephone networks and transmission lines on ground. Broadband and internet service providers (ISP) over spectrum and radio waves fall in the same category but are not categorized as natural monopolies despite high investment costs and minimal operating costs. Bandwidths are wide and can sustain several service providers. The low latency of transmission networks on spectrum support a wide range of services that reflects in the number of platform markets, search engines, web sites, etc.

In Fig. 1b, the average cost curve cuts than the marginal cost at the point where the MC curve starts rising. The average cost rises but lies below the marginal cost curve. The average cost is total cost divided by the number of units produced while the marginal cost is the cost of the incremental unit produced. The point of intersection between MR and MC is also shown. The curvatures and point of intersection are self-explanatory. In a simple product market, the two curves are 'U' shaped with a flat bottom to the 'U'. There are short run cost curves and long run cost curves. The long run average cost curve is the envelope of short run average cost curves including all the lower points of the short run cost curve. Technology fixes the capacity of plant. Rising cost curves are indicative for installation of new and additional capacity.

In Fig. 2, we have shown both the U-shaped marginal cost curve and the flat MC which is asymptotic to the origin. The latter as stated are typical to network markets on platforms. Price can be minimal or maybe zero as there are no operational costs to be recovered. To designate such pricing schemes as predatory on grounds that price is lower than the MC is to miss the nature of the industry. Antitrust analysis while it focuses on the spaces available for a dominant firm on pricing strategies the shape of cost curves flat, U-shaped, asymptotic is the leverage for a dominant firm to charge: (i) a low price lower than her marginal cost (predatory pricing); or (ii) to indulge in excess pricing; or (iii) to discriminate between consumers (price discrimination). Flexibility of pricing also permits a monopolist firm to appropriate the benefits or consumers surplus which under competitive conditions (MR = MC) would have been enjoyed by consumers in terms of lower price and larger availability of goods and services.

In terms of business and revenue strategies, a firm or enterprise can play around with price as long as its average cost is recovered from sales revenue. Price leveraging is, however, dependent on the demand for its product. A firm can reduce prices and entice consumers away from other firms as long as demand curve is downward sloping creating a piquant

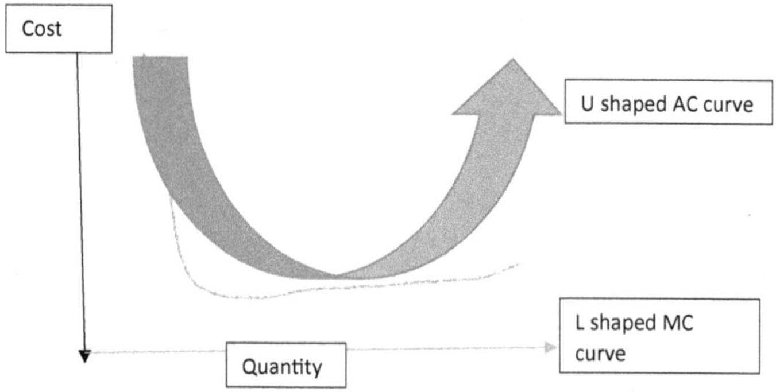

Fig. 2 Illustrative cost curves

situation for competition authorities. Price cuts benefit consumers. A dominant firm in lowering prices benefit consumers. In the process price cuts could create entry barriers that further limit the number of players by causing exit of firms that are unable to match the price cuts. The dilemma of 'harm to competitors versus harm to competition' is whether to worry about competition or about consumer benefits especially if price cuts are sustainable (Gouri, M. Salinger, 2017).[7] I shall keep returning to this dilemma faced by competition authorities.

Antitrust abuses associated with pricing strategies either as exploitative or exclusionary causing harm to competition require detailed analysis of cost structures. Data on cost are available from balance sheet or from investigation into the finances of the company. A point of clarification is necessary. Reference to a firms profit used in the balance sheet is an accounting concept. In economics a firms profit is already included in the cost of production as the return to capital employed and the risk taken in investing in the venture.

(ii) *Demand curve*

The other important curve in the price-cost-quantity relation is the demand curve. The demand curve which is also the Average Revenue (AR) curve provides insights into: (a) the extent of feasible competition; (b) consumer gain or consumer harm; and (c) an assessment of consumer welfare and producers' welfare. Reference is to the AR or demand curve unlike the emphasis on marginal costs. The marginal revenue curve has the same shape as the demand curve (AR curve) but lies below the AR curve. It is more of an indicator of how much revenue the last unit adds to the revenue of the company. In a competitive market structure MR = MC indicates zero profits. As stated earlier in monopolistic competition, reference is to the competitive price where MC curve cuts the AR curve or when AC curve is tangential to the AR curve.

The demand curve is the locus of price points at which consumers are '*willing-to-pay*' for the output defined on the x-axis. The slope of the demand curve reflects the responsiveness of consumers to price(s) and is the price elasticity of demand. A downward-sloping demand curve indicates consumer's response to price increase or price decrease. The shape of the curve suggests that as price increases consumers will consume less of the output or product while a price decrease consumers increase their consumption of the good. The slope of the curve depicts the response to a price change measured by calculating the elasticity of the curve at a point or over a range.

Figure 3 illustrates the different forms of the demand curve. These curves are drawn on the demand responses to changes in prices. There can also be backward-sloping demand curve when demand increases despite the increase in price.

The shapes of the demand curve estimated from price elasticity of demand are important indicators of the prevalence of competitive conditions in a market. A horizontal or flat demand curve suggests that there are several players in the market, and it is not possible for the price to fall anymore. This would be the closest approximation to a perfectly competitive market. A horizontal straight price line indicates that at a given price there is no limit to the quantity bought or consumed. If all producers sell at one price market conditions are highly competitive, no one producer can manipulate the price. The numbers of firms are large and all sell at the same price, leaving out the possibility of price manipulation. The price so fixed is a market price and competitive. These are conditions that are associated with the classical perfect competition market. The closest one comes to in everyday life is of the vegetable market.

It could also reflect a cartelized market when all firms cartelize and fix a single price. Price parallelisms confirmed through correlation of prices of goods of firms over a period of time are estimated to establish the presence of cartels. Conditions for perfect competition are: (i) large number

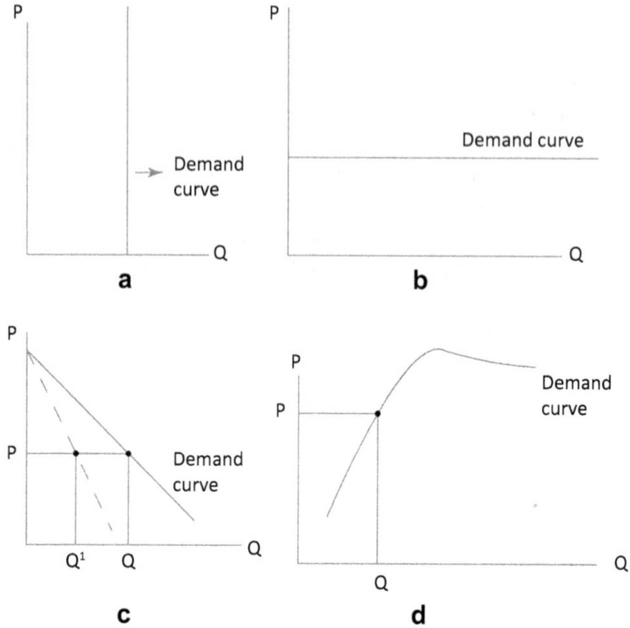

Fig. 3 Relationship between long-run and short-run Cost Curves

of firms so that no one firm can influence the market and its price; (ii) homogeneous product, i.e., no product differentiation; (iii) free flow of information; (iv) no new entrants to the sector. Interestingly the first two conditions are also known to apply in the case of cartels where the product is homogeneous and demand relatively inelastic. In a cartel information flow is restricted to the members of the cartel as an exclusive club. CCI cartel investigations into the cement cartel was on indications of price parallelism combined with evidence of sharing of information among the major players (Case No. 29 0f 2010, 2016–2017). When firms collide or form a cartel then as a monopolist, the joint demand curve is downward sloping in determining a uniform price and quantity as shown in Fig. 4. If $P > \text{MC}$ then cartel members have an incentive to cheat. In the next chapter on horizontal agreements, I discuss possible policy measures the Commission can advise the government to incentivize members of a cartel

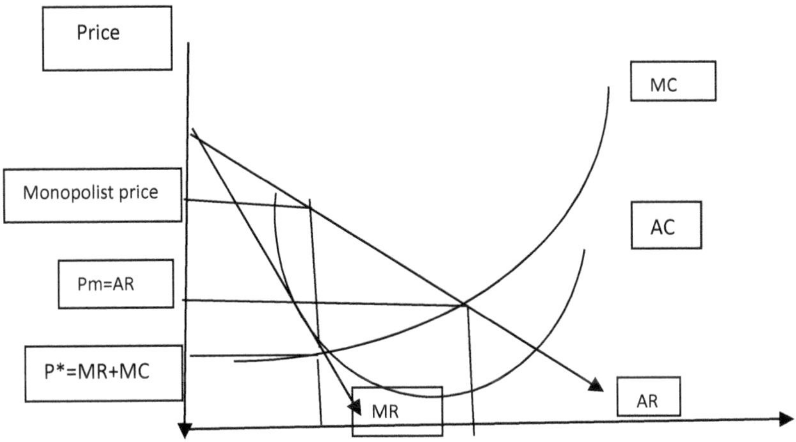

Fig. 4 Cartel monopolist

to cheat and break the cartel. This is over and above the whistle-blower incentive that competition authorities give.

Cartels are a form of collective dominance. The European Commission has made reference to collective dominance. In India, the Act does not have a separate reference to collective dominance.

Buyers cartels also exist and have been widely discussed and drawn the attention of competition authorities.[8] They are not a mirror image of sellers cartels or of monopoly and monopsony. Recent investigations are on small buyers getting together for a common price which questions the perfectly competitive market illustration of vegetable markets that I use. Buyers cartels easily include more participants and often resort to tacit collision. In the US, reference is to the labor market where it is most pervasive but in India the example will not hold. A distinction would require to be drawn between organized sector and unorganized sectors of the economy as there are several distinctions in labor markets in different sectors. A buyer cartel prevalent in groceries or vegetable markets is not sustainable in the long run as all buyers have to sell. Inventory costs are a deterrence. The onion market discussed in the next chapter is a buyers cartel in their purchase of onions from small farmers occurs and conformity in the auction bid price among themselves.

A diametrically opposite demand curve is a straight line upward sloping. Quantity demand is fixed whatever the price level represents a single seller or a monopolist. Under pure monopoly there is no need for a supply curve as the monopolist can set a price at any level. Upward-sloping demand curves would normally be associated with essential goods and services known in antitrust literature as 'essential facilities'. This distinction within monopoly market structures as noted earlier in the section on costs 'natural monopoly' is a special category where high fixed costs permit only a single firm to operate viably. Standard examples cited of natural monopoly include transmission lines, telegraph lines, and railway tracks. In India prior to economic liberalization in 1991, these essential facilities were in the public sector and referred to as public utilities. Post-liberalization and unbundling of public utilities separate sector regulators were established. As discussed in the previous chapter on regulation and competition, sectoral regulation was in the natural monopoly segment where prices or tariffs are fixed by a regulator to minimize the possibility of monopolistic control of their respective activity by the natural monopoly firm.

Two developments have caused a rethink on natural monopolies. Firstly, technological developments have reduced the number of natural monopolies and the emergence of new services such as bandwidth spectrum allocated to internet service providers also classified as 'essential facilities' are not natural monopolies in the conventional sense. The scope for competition among service providers has lead to a debate in India on the agency for regulation especially in the telecom sector pertaining to pricing of bandwidth of internet service providers (ISP) as between the sector regulator (Telecom Regulatory Authority of India) TRAI or CCI. Legally, the Acts that established the sector regulator preceded the Competition Act and TRAI claims jurisdictional precedence. Secondly, competition can be ensured through 'competition for the market' as against 'competition in the market' (Demsetz).[9] Pricing mechanisms of bidding and auctions are well-known instruments for ensuring competition 'for the market'.

A downward-sloping demand curves is of concern to competition authorities if the relevant market consists of few sellers. These markets are of monopolistic competition or oligopolistic. Among the sellers one firm is either dominant or aspires to be dominant through mergers. In the case of the former competition assessment pertains to 'abuse of dominance' or 'monopolization' of the market by the dominant firm. The analysis is ex-post. In the latter case, dominance is an outcome subsequent to merger of firms or acquisition of one firm by another resulting in a dominant firm. The ex-ante analysis by competition authorities is to anticipate the possibility of monopolization of market leading to subsequent abuse of the acquired dominance. Under both market conditions elasticity of demand curve is the appropriate indicator of restrictions to competition. In cases of oligopoly, a kinked demand is used to illustrate a demand constraint on the two players. A relatively inelastic but downward-sloping curve indicates larger scope for an enterprise to exercise market power in terms of fixing price and quantity than in highly elastic demand curve.

(iii) *Price elasticity and its derivation*

Price elasticity of demand both own-price elasticity and cross-price elasticity, therefore, play an important role in antitrust analysis. Elasticity is a pure number which makes it valuable as a concept easy to understand. It has the felicity of a number that can be used as a measure for drawing the boundaries of the antitrust market. For the same reasons, it can be used to measure the scope for market control or concentration of power of a dominant firm.

Firstly, elasticities measure the response of a change in price of a product to demand by consumers in defining the relevant market as stated in Sec 2(t) of the Act. As per this section, the boundaries of the relevant antitrust product market are demarcated by the extent of interchangeability or substitutability for the good or service that a consumer is willing-to-pay. Elasticity of demand for a good or service measures the extent of substitutability. The commonly used criterion the SSNIP test (small but significant non-transitory increase in prices) shows the extent of shift in demand to other products if prices of a product or services are increased by a small amount (5%). The consequent shift in demand to another product on account of the price demonstrates interchangeability (or substitutability) of products to consumers in a given price range. SSNIP is then the criteria for demarcating boundaries of the relevant market. It is a measure applied in cases of merger and acquisitions as the first step in measuring market share of the merged firm. This measure is consistent with the use of '*substitutability*' in defining the relevant market in the Act. Sec. 2(t):

> 'relevant product market' means a market comprising all those products or services which are regarded as interchangeable or substitutable by the consumer, by reason of characteristics of the products or services, their prices and intended use

The proposed modification to the Act looks at substitutability from the production or supply side but with refuted reference to elasticity of demand. Substitutability is defined in terms of switching production between such products and services without incurring additional costs.

Price elasticity of demand is given

$$\epsilon = \frac{\frac{\Delta y}{y}}{\frac{\Delta x}{x}} = \frac{\Delta y}{\Delta x}.\frac{x}{y} = \frac{\partial y(x)}{\partial x}.\frac{x}{y}$$

(ii) *Market Concentration*

There are two steps to defining market concentration. First is drawing the boundaries of the relevant markets and second the market share of the enterprise as derived using elasticities of demand. Demand as we saw earlier is the determining factor whether an enterprise designated as a hypothetical monopolist can exert market power by increasing prices. The simple measures of concentration are

(a) *SSNIP Test and Critical Loss Estimation*

The test which is used for defining the relevant market for a product is to include all substitutes that fall into the market. In simple terms, if there is a small but significant rise in prices the shift in consumers of a hypothetical monopolist to other firms the boundaries of the relevant market get drawn. But for the monopolist it is the loss in profit on account of losing on sales and consumers on account of the price rise.[10] A price increase is profitable only if

$$(p + dp - c)(q - dq) > (p - c)q \tag{1}$$

where p, c and q are the initial price, cost and quantity before the price rise while d denote the change in price and quantity. If price and quantity are more than the initial stage than the proposition is profitable which with manipulation comes to:

$$\frac{t}{m+t} > \frac{\Delta q}{q} \tag{2}$$

where t is dp/p, i.e., the proportionate price rise; and m is the $(p - c)/p$. The equation only shows the profitability of a price rise.[11] Elasticity also comes into prominence in exerting market power in the Lerner Index.

(b) *Market Power and Lerner Index*

Similarly, price elasticity of demand indicates the extent of market hold that dominant firm is able to assert. The Lerner Index is given by:

$$\text{Index} = P - \text{MC}/P$$

The index only indicates the price-marginal cost margin. The extent of price rise from the marginal costs depends on its own-price elasticity of demand. The Lerner Index in terms of elasticity would be: $-1/\in$ where $\in = \frac{d(PQ)}{d(Q)} \text{MR} = P + Q\frac{\partial P}{\partial Q} = P(1 + \frac{QdP}{PdQ}) = P(1 + 1/\in)$

Under competitive conditions MR = MC. So $P\text{-MC}/P = -1/\in$ (Bishop and Walker, 2010).[12]

The Lerner Index states the obvious. Market power of a firm is defined by the firm's ability to raise price. Pricing schemes are also weighted by the inverse of price elasticity of demand. A welfare maximization pricing scheme is that of Baumol and Bradford who have used the inverse of price elasticity of demand in pricing schemes for consumer welfare maximization (see Box I) 0.15.

I has not used the SSNIP test for identifying the relevant market or the Lerner Index. The HHI Index was more commonly used in the case of mergers and acquisition. Several consultancy services do estimate consumer demand. Estimating elasticity of demand is a process of collecting and collating consumption expenditure of the defined consumer using random sample surveys. Consumer expenditure data from the National Sample Survey have been used by some economists to arrive at demand elasticity (Ghosh, 2017). Elasticity so derived is for very broad categories and has limited applicability in arriving at the market boundaries.

(c) *Pricing for Consumer Welfare*

The intent of competition is to increase consumer welfare. Accordingly the objective of the competition, authority is maximization of consumer welfare. What is consumer welfare and how it is measured is not of significance. It is a concept, a welfare standard that needs to be understood. Economists define welfare in terms of total welfare, i.e., producer surplus and consumer surplus. Surplus to the producer is increase in quantity sold at a given price. Consumer surplus is the increase in quantities consumed with a decrease in price. Diagrammatically, it is shown as the area between the demand curve and the price charged. In Fig. 4, the competitive price is where the marginal cost curve cuts the marginal revenue curve. The MR curve shows the extra amount of revenue the producer earns with every additional unit of sale. Since MR is lower than the AR curve the sale of every additional unit will be at a lower prices. A dominant producer fixes quantity at the point where MR = MC but prices the product higher say where the AC curve is tangential to the AR curve. In welfare terms, the gain in producer surplus is the area bounded by the demand curve and the marginal cost-marginal revenue intersection. On account of higher prices, there is a decrease in amount demanded or consumed. Lower prices would result in more consumption. Consumer surplus is given by the hatched portion between the new price and the demand curve where MC cut the demand curve. If, on the other hand, output and price are fixed at the point where the marginal cost curve cuts the demand curve consumers gain from a decrease in the price and increased output. There is a perceptible increase in quantity consumed. A dominant firm pricing at a higher price and fixing output at lesser amount is a social welfare loss. This can be seen in Fig. 4 which shows a high price gives more producer surplus as compared to a low price.

The importance of welfare analysis comes to the forefront in terms of defining the objective of competition policy and in implementing the law. Economists refer to welfare in terms of producer and consumer welfare. The deadweight social welfare loss in the case of monopolist pricing ($P > MR = MC$) represents a loss to society on account of lower output at higher prices. The approach raises a fundamental issue regarding the objective of competition law.

In emergent markets of platforms, data markets and market for ideas where there is a greater tendency toward concentration on account of network effects emphasis on outcomes and benefits to consumers are the guiding factor for competition authorities. Is competition about harm to competitors or about harm to competition is the central issue that competition authorities need to address (Gouri and Salinger, 2018). The EU Merger Guidelines and of FTC and DoJ refer to 'effective competition' where the emphasis is on outcomes and specifically on benefits to consumers. The objective of competition law is to maximization of consumer surplus, and in economics, the reference is to total welfare or maximization of producer and consumer surplus. In merger analysis, CCI adopts a soft 'effective competition' approach by defining thresholds for clearance.

Some economists have argued that emphasis on consumer welfare is a short-term measure of competition (Lina, 2007).[13] Rather the emphasis should be on the market power that globally large firms are able to assert. The EU decision on Google internet search and on Google Android were prompted by this consideration. The argument is that consumers prefer to stay with a search engine or service rather than shift to other services and search engines creating entry barriers. Behavioral economics of consumers was brought to play rather than assess the loss to consumers from a search engine that provided multiple products and services.

1.1 Objective of Competition Policy

A major debate within CCI was regarding objective of competition policy. How does one define social welfare for a competition authority? Is it defined in terms of consumer welfare or it includes producer's welfare. Is it the objective of the Commission to increase the number of producers or is to benefit consumers be it competitive prices and quality.

In India the welfare objective for CCI is multiple. The Preamble of the Act states:

> An Act to provide, keeping in view the economic development of the country, for the establishment of a Commission to prevent practices having adverse effect on competition, to promote and sustain competition in markets, to protect the interests of consumers and to ensure freedom of

trade carried on by other participants in markets, in India, and for matters connected therewith or incidental thereto.[14]

The preamble provides for the flexibility of transition from a controlled and licensed industrial to a market-oriented economy. The framers of the Competition Act in replacing the extant and structuralist MRTP may have thought it appropriate for a transition clause, a clause that raised several debates in the Commission. Referring to the dilemma raised earlier posed before CCI as between encouraging competition or of looking at consumer gains is on how welfare is understood. In Fig. 4, hatched area below *P* is the loss to the consumer for prices being set at P'. Is welfare to be defined in terms of consumer welfare or a combination of consumer welfare and social welfare which is the combination of both producer and consumer surplus. In the Act as mentioned earlier producers are included as consumers in Section 2(f) where consumer definition could refer to the informant filing a case with CCI.[15] Several decisions raise doubts whether protecting competitors is protecting competition.

Ability to raise prices and exert market power is restricted for a firm when the demand curve is elastic. Raising prices may attract other firms to enter, while lowering of prices without the scope for controlling output suggests the presence of competitive constraints even when there is a single or dominant firm operating in the market. The existence of a single firm is defined by the cost curves and the scope afforded to benefit from economies of scale including network economies. Pricing policies in the presence of economies of scale are difficult to predict. In industries or sectors, where networks are involved often see low prices in the market as the firm expands his business to gain from economies. The presence of backward-sloping demand curve in network industries permits the monopolist to charge higher prices if consumers gain from the presence of deep markets of a single firm. The shape of cost curves in the new emerging business paradigms restricts the scope for generalizations on the market power of dominant firms.

The essence of pricing schemes in competition analysis is to evaluate the benefits of the schemes to consumers. While the above explanation is of understanding consumer surplus a glimpse of pricing strategies or differential pricing resorted to by firms to meet their revenue requirements has implications for consumer welfare. Differential pricing arises in the case of joint costs of production as in petroleum products. They are also applied if consumers can be differentiated in terms of their consumption patterns and utility maximization preferences. Difference in consumer utilities permit different pricing schemes for the same good or service thereby increasing consumer welfare of different groups. Depending upon knowing exactly the utility maximizing function of different consumer groups pricing schemes can be designed. Most notable examples are train ticket or airplane tickets where the firms are able to maximize profits through the process of cross-subsidization without reducing consumer welfare. Price elasticities of demand are used for weighting the price per good or service per consumer category. Governments for achieving diverse welfare considerations usually weight the products more on considerations of which consumer group they wish to subsidize. Implications of this subsidy scheme are political and not economic (Gouri, 1998).[16]

Pricing for Welfare
Price elasticity is used by firms in fixing the final price in relation to the demand for the product. Evaluating pricing strategies resorted to by firms is by weighting the price with the inverse of price elasticity.

Weighting of price by the inverse elasticity of demand would mean that products which have high elasticity of demand should be priced less. In terms of consumer utility maximization, a lower price would increase consumer welfare. Baumol and Bradford have shown the simple welfare implications of price weighting. Governments may, however, prefer a pricing structure where the interest is more in revenue maximization than welfare maximization. See Geeta Gouri, Pricing for Welfare, Petroleum Products in India, Oxford & IBH.

1.2 Monopolistic Competition/Duopoly

In the real world commercial decisions of firms on how much to produce, whether to expand capacity and what should be the sale price are shaped by information of rivals on similar matters. Models of oligopoly and monopolistic competition in incorporating interaction between rivals acknowledge the importance of business information. Strategies that firms adopt to meet competition have been honed continuously since Cournot the French mathematician (mid-nineteenth century) and Bertrand modeled plausible strategies of interaction between two firms. Advances in game theory have added sophistication to these models of monopolistic competition and the scope for collaboration among firms known as Nash equilibrium. The early models of duopoly Cournot and Bertrand are used to assess the presence of cartels or whether it is a Nash equilibrium as in later variants of monopolistic competition the 'dominant monopolist' model; 'leader-follower' model; and the Stackelberg model of imperfect competition. These models of monopolistic competition used the concept of residual demand curves to distinguish between the main firm and the smaller firms. An important outcome of the Nash equilibrium is that it cautions against premature intervention by the competition authority which I define as '*market activism*' (Gouri, 2017).

(i) *Cournot Model*

In the Cournot model, each firm competes by setting its profit maximizing output in response to the output of the other firm. Firm A's output maximizing output is a reaction to output produced by firm B. Perhaps it is simpler to refer to capacity rather than output as capacity is usually public knowledge. A reaction curve can be drawn for firm A and one for firm B. Price is determined by the demand for the product. To start with since there are only two firms in the market (duopoly) the capacity of each firm to meet demand determines the market price. The equilibrium profit maximizing output of both firms is given at the point where the two reaction curves meet. The resultant price is higher than of perfect competition but less than under monopoly. If the number of firms increases prices would fall as quantity increases. The model, however, provides no clue to the appropriate or viable number of firms. To the competition authority the possibility of enhancing competition and welfare hinges on increasing the number of firms and breaking the duopoly. It may, however, be a futile effort. Competition authorities normally investigate the possibility of entry barriers that restrain new firms from entering. The main restraint emphasized by the Cournot model is of high fixed investment costs. Prices have to be set higher than marginal costs for recovery of the fixed costs.

(ii) *Bertrand Model*

In the Bertrand model, the underlying assumption is of price fixing and not of output fixing. The Bertrand model is on homogeneous products and responses of each firm is to the price fixed by the other firm. Price responses of each firm to the other firms eventually lead to competitive pricing but as in the case of the Cournot model the two rivals arrive at price where marginal cost is higher than of perfect competition (Bishop and Walker, 2010).

In the cement cartel case, my younger colleagues did suggest that price parallelism noted in cement prices could be a Bertrand outcome. It requires investigation and will be explored in the later chapter.[17] A crucial assumption in the Bertrand model is that each firm produces output to meet the demand it faces provided they are not capacity constrained. Capacity constraint limits the output a firm can produce before indulging in price competition. A cartel with unutilized capacity always provides incentives for cheating as long as P > MC and demand curve is downward sloping.[18]

(iii) *Nash Equilibrium*

Game theory illustrates the Cournot and Bertrand equilibrium succinctly. The point where the two reaction curves meet is the Nash non-cooperative equilibrium. Under Nash equilibrium given the behavior of the rival firm profits will always be much lower than under monopoly but higher than under perfect competition. In a 2 × 2 box diagram, the lower corner box which shows that profits of both firms will be 5,5 which is much lower than the higher right-hand corner box 0f 10,10. The top most corner box shows high profits for both firms but is not a sustainable equilibrium. If firm A intends to double its profits by charging a lower price, then firm B makes no profits. Response of firm B is to lower prices. The undercutting of prices eventually leads to the left hand corner box. This equilibrium is reached non-cooperatively and is the Nash equilibrium. Using the Prisoner's Dilemma game Nash effectively proved how a non-cooperative market equilibrium of prices are arrived at without intervention by antitrust authorities.

Nash Equilibrium

		Firm A: High	Firm A: Low
Firm B	High	10,10	0,20
	Low	20,0	5,5

Prisoner's Dilemma is a fascinating game whose usage is extensive and in unexpected areas.[19] Its application to economics of monopolistic/oligopolistic competition and the non-cooperative Nash equilibrium have grown in importance for antitrust analysis and falls into the basic tools for economic analysis. The Prisoner's dilemma is of two prisoners having committed a crime kept in separate cells and questioned separately. The choice open to each of them is either to confess to the crime or to deny involvement. Since neither of them is privy to the decision of the other the expected response of either of the prisoner is the other will cheat and thus escape levy of penalty. If both cheat the full penalty is awarded to both of them. If both confess both get a lower penalty. Non-cooperation between the two prisoners is the Nash equilibrium. The dilemma is between individual rationality and group choice. The Nash non-cooperative equilibrium is the mutually beneficial exchange between the two firms in the Cournot and Bertrand models of oligopoly.

Responses of firms to market information dispel the assumption that the two firms in the two models will collude to form a cartel. The Nash non-cooperative equilibrium exemplifies it. Cartels are mimics of monopolistic competition and the suspicion of doubt that lingers with competition authorities is what prevents the two firms from colluding. In the Cournot model or the Bertrand model, a firm fixes its profit maximizing output as a reaction to the output (capacity) or price of the rival. For each amount of unique output of firm A on the reaction curve firm B fixes its profit maximizing output. Since these are movements along the reaction curve price and output are determinate. Price and quantity are fixed at the point where the two reaction curves of the firms meet. In the case of cartels, the price and output can fall anywhere within the boundaries of the reaction curve. Prices and quantities are indeterminate purely on account of the fact that cartels are not stable relationships. Based on loose agreements between parties, there is no guarantee that one member may not be tempted to lower prices and gain a strategic advantage. The determinacy of the industry output and profits is at the core of non-cooperative Nash equilibrium.

Recent models of monopolistic competition are based on product differentiation as against the assumption of product homogeneity. Under product differentiation each firm has a monopoly over its product as compared to its close rival. Should antitrust authorities treat each firm separately as a monopolist or define the market to include the competitor as should be under the SSNIP test.

Each firm has a monopoly over its product subject to the competitive constraint of rival firm(s) producing substitutes. Reactions between rivals, between incumbent firms and new entrants have spawned several strategic models in antitrust literature including 'Follow-the-leader' or the 'Stackelberg model'. The Stackelberg model brought to prominence the kinked demand curve. The dominant firm in terms of larger share of the market demand curve faces not the market demand curve but the demand curve net of the amount supplied by firms at the fringe. It is also referred to as the 'residual demand curve' the dominant firm faces and is able to service larger portions of the market at a higher price till the point where it has exhausted full capacity. The smaller firms take the residual part of the market demand curve but at the price fixed by the dominant firm. As the demand curve of the dominant leader whether the firm first sets the price or the output as in the case of Stackelberg the price never goes down to where MR = MC. Every monopolist firm will attempt to continue to produce till AC is tangential to the AR curve (Fig. 4) is useful to illustrate the tangency. The strategy is to capture the market for her product even though the tangency point is zero profit. Rivals attracted by the higher prices and scope for profits attempt to entice consumers at lower prices. Product development and innovation come to the forefront where large investments in R&D are required. The rival firms are also large firms to be able to invest in R&D leading to an entirely different genre of antitrust analysis that is not within the framework of product market analyses. Returning to the basic monopolistic competition of product market analysis several pricing options are available to the monopolist discussed earlier giving rise to a group of abuses categorized in the Act as 'exploitative abuses'. Having captured the market the monopolist can exclude competitors through price-related exclusionary barriers.

References to the shape of the cost curves, the demand curves are basic tools to assess the presence of effective competition in a market. Consumer welfare analysis underlines the importance of intervention by the competition authority provided the market is not self-corrective. Monopolistic competition is at the core of antitrust analysis for ex-post 'abuse of dominance' which are Section 4 cases of the Act. Or ex-ante in clearing mergers and acquisitions which fall under Sections 5 & 6 of the Act. Oligopolistic models provide an understanding of cartels or horizontal agreements under Sections 3(3) of the Act. In assessing the scope for anti-competitive outcome under Section 3(4) of the Act vertical restraints on competition weigh the pros of efficiencies of a single firm with its dealers/contractors as against consumer harm.

2 Economics of Antitrust Abuses Listed in the Competition Act

Abuses in the Competition Act as in any competition law are classified into exploitative and exclusionary abuses. Exploitative abuses refer to price and quantity abuses and can easily be discerned from the price-cost relationships discussed. Exclusionary abuses have an underlying price-quantity nexus but include other factors which create entry barriers. In establishing the abuse, it is important to define and limit the relevant market of antitrust concern.

2.1 Section 3 Abuses—Abuse of Agreements

Section 3 pertains to 3(3) horizontal agreements and 3(4) vertical agreements. There is a safe harbor provision in Section 3(3)(5) for Intellectual Property Rights (IPRs), trademarks, etc. and agreements pertaining to exports. Agreements as per the Act are of concern only if they "*cause or likely to cause an appreciable adverse effect on competition*". The presumption places greater weightage on economic analysis for two reasons: (i) the lower threshold of proof for cartels; and (ii) appreciable adverse affect on competition as defined in Sec 19(3) that combines both favorable and adverse affects of agreements both horizontal and vertical. Under MRTP the Supreme Court had directed that the presence of a cartel is acceptable in legal terms if there is an agreement in writing. This has been watered down under CA02 Section 2(b) where evidence of agreements could be an arrangement or an understanding. The idea of meeting of minds rests on the oft-quoted presumption that '*competitors meet not to discuss weather*'. Section 2(b), therefore, reference to an agreement

> includes any arrangement , understanding or action is formal or in writing; ....is intended to be enforceable by legal proceedings.

If there has been an understanding formal or informal, the importance of economic analysis comes to the forefront reference to Section 19(3). Cartel decisions of CCI are more quasi 'per *se*'. Recently, the NCLAT have reverted a decision of the Commission (Lead Battery case) as not meeting the requirement of evidence of a written agreement.

With respect to vertical agreements presumption of AAEC has to be established. The market is defined in terms of complements. Vertical arrangements between enterprises or persons at different levels of production can enhance efficiency which benefit consumers. They could also be perceived as a threat to new entrants in which case they are restraints to competition.

Price abuses listed under Section 3(3) are: directly or indirectly determines (a) purchase price or sale price and (b) bid rigging or collusive bidding. Both price abuses are in the framework of the Bertrand Model. Abuses associated with the Cournot model refer to agreements which (a) limit or control production, supply, markets, technical development, investment or provisions of services and (b) shares the market or source of production or provision of services by way of allocation of geographical area of markets, or type of goods or services, or number of customers in the market or any other similar way. Listing the abuses is to focus on the types of collusive agreements possible between firms discernible from the different models of monopolistic competition outlined above.

Price parallelism is the first indicator noted by competition authorities on the possibility of cartel operation. Homogeneous products with relatively inelastic demand are prime ground for cartel formation. In the Bertrand model, rivalry between firms leads to price parallelism between the two firms and of non-cooperative Nash equilibrium. Proof of a cartel in India still rests entirely on the availability of evidence. Since cartels are civil cases the extent of required proof is much weaker than if they had been classified as criminal cases.

Bidding rigging or collusive bidding the other abuse listed under horizontal agreements is also a policy instrument for introducing competition 'for the market'. As noted earlier in the case of natural monopoly where on account of high investment costs the market is able to sustain only a single firm bid rigging by a group of firms is a strategy used for selecting a firm with the understanding the market and product are divided among the firms in a pre-bid ranking arrangement. Bid rigging in India has largely been noted in public procurement of goods and services by large public sector enterprises as part of government policy for encouraging purchases from enterprises categorized as medium, small and micro enterprises (MSME) based on bids at the time of tender. This led to bid rigging by cartels formed by units whose authenticity as MSME is questionable defeating the very purpose of encouraging industrial development through MSMEs. Special preference or price preference given to medium and small-scale enterprises in supply of equipment and material to public sector enterprise may have encouraged the trend.[20]

Under the Act bid rigging is considered as anti-competitive with the potential for creating entry barriers. Cases of bid rigging under public procurement are referred to the government under Section 21(A) 'Reference by Commission' as advisory from CCI. Bid rigging in CA02 refers to agreements among people in the same trade colluding on the bid price. Modifications to the Act suggested by the Competition Law Review Committee is to widen the scope of bid rigging to include parties that could influence the trade with the addition to proviso in Section 3(3).

> Provided further that an enterprise or association of enterprises or person or association of persons though not engaged in identical or similar trade shall be presumed to be part of the Agreement under this sub-section if it is actively participating in the furtherance of this Agreement.

Bidding at auctions that bidders in a cartel resort to are diverse signaling mechanisms. There was also an investigation initiated Suo moto into auctions at the farm gate or primary mandis for onions. Bid collusion was noticed in auctions for farm products like onions at the primary mandis (market) among traders in the onion market. In a study done for CCI by the Institute of Social and Economic Change (ISEC) on traders in the onion auction market, the ability and modality of traders to manipulate the auction bid price were documented (Onion Cartel Study by ISEC). The auctioneer a government official was either an accomplice or a silent spectator to the rigging. Collaboration among traders was extensive starting from the primary mandis in Uttar Pradesh to the large onion markets at Yelhanka (Karnataka State) and then to transport services all over the country. Members of the cartel could not be established by the study only presence of cartels with broad reference to 15 families. Want evidence with reference to bills and receipts CCI closed the case.

A more subtle form of bid collusion is by way of sharing the market either geographical or sequentially. The way to establish the presence of cartels in these bids is to observe patterns in the bids using econometric analysis of large data. Bidding collusion patterns have been studied and documented in studies on stock markets where trader collusions within a group follow a pattern in the bids. In oil drilling fields, firms have bid in a pattern indicating market sharing by a cartel of firms engaged in exploratory activities. Bid collusion is an overlap of exclusionary and exploitative abuse. In the case of Section 3(3) abuses pertaining to horizontal agreements all abuses listed from 3(a) to 3(d) are exploitative. Exclusionary abuse does not arise as cartels themselves are exclusionary arrangements.

An emergent area for cartels is the scope for algorithm collusion an area that competition authorities are exploring with the growth of digital markets. Algorithmic price collusion is the new antitrust concern which has emerged. Artificial Intelligence and machine learning have led to algorithms of e-commerce that explore the internet leading to price parallelism but without human intervention.[21] It is phenomena of big data accessed by platforms. The jury is still not out on whether they can be classified as an antitrust abuse.

In Section 3(4) pertaining to vertical agreements the restraints listed as abuses are largely exclusionary. Section 3(4) abuses cover: (i) tie-in arrangement; (ii) exclusive supply agreement; (iii) exclusive distribution agreement; (iv) refusal to deal; and (v) resale price maintenance. Section 3(4)(e) 'resale price maintenance' could be both an exclusionary and exploitative abuse. The concept of 'hub and spoke' is included in the proposed modifications to the Act.

A vertical agreement is between the producer and dealers (wholesalers and retailers), sub-contractors. These agreements have the sanctity of a contract, but as a constitutional authority CCI can review the contract if it results in a restraint on competition. From a consumer perspective, a vertical agreement is efficiency enhancing as it avoids the problem of double marginalization. Transaction costs are minimized. The cost a consumer pays for a good or service includes all the required transaction for making available a final product. Transaction costs are minimized when car manufacturer access spare parts from designated sub-contractors or insists on a uniform price across India among all dealers (Gouri, Business Standard). To establish anti-competitive outcomes under Section 3(4) economic analysis or 'effects-based' analysis comes to the forefront. The dilemma of consumer gains from efficiency to possible consumer harm from limited competition referred to earlier as the divergence between maximization of consumer surplus versus total welfare that economists prefer would need resolution. In emergent markets, consumer gains where maximization of consumer welfare (surplus) may be a more appropriate guiding principle for assessing vertical restraints.

Contract design where large monopolistic firms are involved as in public utilities such as transmission networks or shipping contracts and of spectrum has brought to the forefront the application of auction theory. 'Competition for the market rather than competition in the market' was assessed in the contracts of Coal India and the power generating companies. It is a vast subject focused on the modalities of bidding.

2.2 *Sections 4 and 5& 6—Unilateral and Coordinated Effects*

In the case of Section 4 and Sections 5 & 6 exploitative abuses of price and quantity manipulation are restricted to Section 4(2)(a) (i) (ii) with a slight spill over to Section 4(2) (b) (i). The rest of the abuses Sections 4(b)(ii) to 4 (c) to 4 (e) are on exclusionary abuses. The difference between Section 4 and Section 5&6 is of ex-post versus ex-ante analysis of abuse of dominance.

The basic business model for competition analysis of the product market is to strategize moves of a dominant player or a cartel within the parameters of price movements and of quantity restrictions. Accordingly, any intervention on prices or quantities is construed as attempts to control the market. In platform markets, where network effects dominate or in the market for ideas, the price-cost exploitative abuses do not hold indicate a shift in the nature of antitrust abuses reflects complexities of modern business making the task of establishing abuse by the Commission more technical in terms of technological developments and their incorporation in economic tools of analysis.

Suppose, the dominant player's strategy is to lower prices maybe to prevent entry, consumers gain from lower price and the producer does not lose as long as his costs are covered. Would this constitute an abuse? The extreme situation is predatory pricing which refers to pricing below the marginal costs. Consumers gain, but the gain is discounted. As per the classical economics approach, these gains are ephemeral. The argument is that firms cannot continue to price below marginal cost indefinitely. Mounting losses refrain the dominant firm from continuing with the strategy of low pricing to deter entry. The argument postulated in antitrust literature is that consumers will have to pay higher prices in the future to compensate the loss of revenue. The argument remains unsubstantiated.

Under monopolistic competition, the demand curve or average revenue curve is sloping downwards suggesting scope for new entrants (Fig. 3). Should the Commission intervene or let market forces operating on the basis of profit constraint break the entry barrier? The lure of higher profits attract new entrants who have to come up with alternate pricing strategy or introduction of new technology and innovation. This is the crux of innovation and a major issue in high-tech markets and in neural markets. The decision requires two factors: (i) a good understanding of technology frontiers and (ii) faith in the market and profit constraint that sustain consumer surplus.

2.3 *Limitations of the Product Market*

The economic tools of price, cost and demand were explained in the context of the product market. There are limitations of competition analysis in this market. Under CA02 reference to the 'relevant market' is to the *relevant product market* and the *relevant geographic market*, which define the boundaries of the relevant market for antitrust intervention.[22] Section r(t) "*relevant product market" means a market comprising all those products or services which are regarded as interchangeable or substitutable by the consumer, by reason of characteristics of the products or services, their prices and intended use.*" The reference is to all substitutes among products/services a consumer *(or a supplier)*[23] considers as an alternative to the desired good, product or service. The parameter for finding substitutability as discussed is with reference to price assuming that other features and characteristics are met. Most commonly used tool for fixing relevant boundaries market is the SSNIP test. Market share is with the help of the (Herfindahl- Hirschman) HHI index. The Lerner Index is a measure of dominance again with reference to price elasticity.

Defining the relevant market of antitrust allegations is difficult in case of platform markets and market of ideas. The answer to the question 'Which is the relevant market' is not a simple process. In a 2-sided or multi-sided platform market which market is the reference of antitrust abuse in terms of substitutes defies clarity. Similarly, in the market for ideas the emergence of portfolio of patents involves complements forming a mesh of contracts draw attention to firms as fiduciaries of patents for digital markets. Whether defining the relevant market is necessary to understand the possibility of market power has also been raised in the literature on antitrust (Hovenkamp, 2019).

The relevant geographic market demarcates the boundaries of the market in terms of homogeneity of conditions defined by transport and transaction costs within the territorial jurisdiction of the Act. Section 2(s) "relevant geographic market" means a market comprising the area in which the conditions of competition for supply of goods or provision of services or demand of goods or services are distinctly homogenous and can be distinguished from the conditions prevailing in the neighbouring areas." The definition is clearly not applicable to digital markets whose reach is not defined by geographical boundaries or political boundaries. At present, the Act is applicable to only the respective country. In the case of mergers where the merging firms operate in several countries clearance has to be given by all competition authorities for the merger to be sanctified.

3 Conclusion

The product market analysis provides the basic tools laying the foundation for understanding of anti-competitive behavior of firms to the required cues for further investigation in business models and strategies adopted by firms. The Act framed in the conventional product market economic analysis of anti-competitiveness has its limitations. The limitations of Product Market for competition analysis are important to comprehend in implementing competition law. Price parameters the primary tool of antitrust analysis are itself under questioning with platform markets. The aspect of consumer welfare and maximization of consumer welfare have been posited against the growing tendency of monopolistic structure of platforms. Currently, the debate is on the structure of markets and of competition. These structures in defying the conventional tools of price–cost have drawn attention to the (in)ability to assess anti-competitiveness of platforms '*unequipped to capture the architecture of market power*' (Lina Khan, 2003).

Platform markets, data markets and market for ideas are markets that tend toward monopolistic competition largely on account of network effects. The numbers of firms in these markets are small and their ability to exert market power is limited. Antitrust abuses alleged against these markets are still under exploration of competition authorities. The European Commission has been more aggressive, especially with respect to platform markets. Nuances of these markets and diversity in consumer behavior suggest that unlike product market these markets do require a country-specific approach to assessing anti-competitive outcomes.

Notes

1. Discussions on demarcation of markets and the essential economic criteria in the distinction were with Shubhashis Gangopadhya when we were working on FRAND and Royalties, India Development Foundation.
2. Geeta Gouri, Convergence of Competition Policy, Competition Law and Public Interest in India, *Russian Journal of Economics* 6 (2020) 277–293. https://doi.org/10.32609/j.ruje.6.51303 Publication date: 25 September 2020; Geeta Gouri and Kalyani Pandiya, Decoding Digital Platforms: An Indian Competition Law Perspective. *Indian Law Review*.
3. It has been pointed that Article 39 which refers to the Directive Principle of State Policy is not in tune with the welfare dimensions of competition policy.
4. Geeta Gouri, Convergence of Competition Policy, Competition Law and Public Interest, *Russian Journal of Economics*, Vol 6, Number 3, September 2020, Special issue on Antitrust in BRICS: Agenda and achievements in comparative perspective, edited by Andrey E. Shashtiko.
5. Simon Bishop and M. Walker, The Economics of EC law: Concepts, Application and Measurement, Sweet and Maxwell, 2010.
6. Economists presume that gainers will compensate the losers. It is, therefore, not necessary to define the consumer group.
7. Geeta Gouri and Salinger, M, Protecting Competition Versus Protecting Competitors: Assessing the Antitrust.

   Complaints Against Google, The Criterion Journal on Innovation, Vol 2, 2017.

8. Peter Carstensen, Buyer Cartels: Defining Appropriate Competition Policy, Competition Policy International, June 29, 2021.
9. Demsetz, H., Why regulate Utilities., Journal of Law and Economics, 1968.
10. Simon Bishop and M. Walker, The Economics of EC law: Concepts, Application and Measurement, Sweet and Maxwell, 2010.
11. Ibid., I find Bishop and Walker use the required formulae at a simple and concise level.
12. Ibid.
13. Lina Khan., Amazon's Antitrust Paradox, The Yale Law Journal, pp. 710–805.
14. Competition Act.
15. Ibid.
16. Weighting of price by the inverse elasticity of demand would mean that products which have high elasticity of demand should be priced less. In terms of consumer utility maximization, a lower price would increase consumer welfare. Baumol and Bradford have shown the simple welfare implications of price weighting. Governments may however prefer a pricing structure where the interest is more in revenue maximization than welfare maximization. See Geeta Gouri, Pricing for Welfare, Petroleum Products in India, Oxford & IBH.
17. My economic advisor Payal Mallik was the first to raise the possibility of a Bertrand model in the cement cartel.
18. Economic Analysis of Collusion, presentation to Competition Commission of India, by Dr. Shubhasis Gangopadhya and Alisha Madaan, 6 February 2013.
19. I must thank my daughter Navika Harshe for exposing me to the innumerable usages of Prisoners Dilemma. Fresh from Harris School, University of Chicago and fully into game theory she opened to me the novelty and expanse of Prisoners Dilemma where even in Hindi (Bollywood) films used it extensively. Her favorite dialogue was Amitabh Bacchan's dialogue with Dona a rough translation reads when surrounded by the police as armed or unarmed "*I know, you know but they don't know*".
20. Prof Rosen, Industrial Change in India, 1958.
21. The Netflix docudrama *The Social Dilemma* is on algorithms, as also on human bias that make decisions go wrong.
22. op. cit.
23. Ibid.

References

Baumol and Bradford, Optimal Departures from Marginal Cost Pricing, American Economic Review, 1970, vol. 60, issue 3, pp. 265–283.

Peter Carstensen, Buyer Cartels: Defining Appropriate Competition Policy, Competition Policy International, June 29, 2021.

Policy Briefs of India Development Foundation.

Simon Bishop and M. Walker, The Economics of EC law: Concepts, Application and Measurement, Sweet and Maxwell, 2010.

CHAPTER 3

Economics of Emergent Markets Platform Markets, Data Markets and Market for Ideas

It is important to understand why a separate chapter on economics of platform markets, data markets and market for ideas is required. Introduction to these different markets was made in Chapter 1. In the previous chapter, the basic tools of economic analysis consisting of price, cost and quantity used by competition authorities in their assessment of anti-competitive activities were previewed in the framework of the product market. In this chapter, I show how price, cost and quantity in platform markets, data markets and markets for ideas suggest a new perspective on competition. The economics of each of these markets make it imperative for competition authorities to appreciate their distinct features while assessing for anti-competitive behavior. These three markets are interrelated and yet retain their own characteristics. Platform markets of online and of AI, algorithms and Robo-selling brought in their wake the other two markets and with it a vibrant debate on antitrust approaches raising the question whither competition. Algorithmic collusion, personalized pricing, zero pricing considered anti-competitive in traditional market economics represent dynamics of online markets where emphasis is on consumers gains. Institutions associated with data market and market for ideas have in my opinion till recently received minimal attention in competition literature. Growing e-commerce of the popular spread of shopping online through apps on smartphones is phenomenal in India.

G. Gouri, *A Commissioner's Primer to Economics of Competition Law in India*, https://doi.org/10.1007/978-981-19-9476-0_3

Growing e-commerce with allegations from offline traders of discriminatory pricing, discounts, biased contracts are current debates of antitrust abuses in these three markets. This chapter raises these currents debates.

1 Platform Markets

Platforms are spaces created for interaction between two or multiple sides of a market(s) without being direct sellers of products. To facilitate interaction with the two sides of a market platforms provide the required intermediation processes and facilities adding value to the interaction.[1] The defining feature of platforms is network effects and all actions and outcomes of platform markets have to be judged on this criterion.

Platforms negotiate their equation with markets from the perspective of consumers. To marketing strategists this may seem a trivial distinction. For competition authorities, the phrase "*to protect the interests of consumers*" in the Preamble takes precedence in platforms markets unlike product markets where the agenda includes "*freedom of trade carried on by other participants in the market*" (CA02). In terms of economic analysis, reference of platform markets is to maximizing consumer surplus (welfare)and on the theory of consumer harm as against maximizing total welfare in terms of producer surplus accepted in product markets. Further complications arise from artificial intelligence (AI) and machine selling. Learning algorithms mimicking human intelligence have brought to the forefront algorithmic abuses of Robo-selling that are independent of human intervention (Mehra, 2015). The paradox is that antitrust abuses associated with product markets may just be fallouts of the economics of platform functioning leaving competition authorities in a quandary first, on whether they can be categorized as abuses and second, on the appropriate action to be initiated constrained as they are by a law framed in the product market context. The interplay of network effects and of disruptive technology poses the issue on how to distinguish between market forces and machine reactions to the concern voiced "*How will antitrust law work when decisions are no longer made by humans but by machines*" (S. Mehra, 2015; Erazhi and Stuckle, 2019; CLRC, 2019).

CCI did a market study on e-commerce in India (CCI, 2020). The objective of the study was to engage with industry on market development and impediments to competition in e-commerce platforms. The narrative, however, was from the perspective of sellers on the e-commerce platforms. The perspective of consumers was not taken into account. The objective of the study was to engage with industry on market development and impediments to competition in e-commerce platforms in the context of prevailing CA02 restricted to.

> insights into conceptual and analytical questions such as delineation of relevant market, assessment of market power, business rationale for certain conduct etc. **relevant for the purpose of enforcement of the Act (emphasis added).**[2]

The study, however, provides insight into the allegations of sellers in their negotiations with platforms using the route producers frequently resort of 'firing from the shoulders of CCI' (Gouri, 2017).[3] We still await the decisions of CCI on Amazon and Flipkart.

Online commerce or e-commerce is a growing business in India expanding to Tier II and Tier III cities and rural areas indicative of the growing popularity of smart phones and network expansions. In 2019, there were 4575 startups largely in mobiles and electrical/electronic goods; lifestyle; travel and hotel booking; and food and restaurants. The study indicates a vibrant e-commerce market place platforms contesting either for displacing global platform markets or for negotiating a better deal.[4]

In this section, the focus is on the economics of platforms and alleged antitrust abuses of platform markets.

1.1 Platform Economics

The defining features of a platform market are network effects which sets them apart from product markets. In simple terms, network effects are about forces which create depth to a market making it attractive for users (both buyer and sellers) to the platform. In a market it clearly refers to the mechanisms of attracting consumers. They could be price related, quality related, convenience, peer relations, facilities of exchange or return, assured delivery, etc. The effect is contagious as more users stream to these markets. In the MCX-SX v NSE (Case No 13 of 2009) depth of stock markets facilitate diversity in instruments of transaction attracting more transactions. Furthermore in markets when there are large number of traders and buyers as in the stock exchange risk of default is minimized hedged by different trades. Interestingly, platform markets internalize network externalities and not the digital markets which explain the efforts at realizing these externalities. Offline markets can also generate networks and are attempting to do so. Their ability and scope are limited lacking the mechanism of Artificial Intelligence and machine learning to generate network effects.

There are two types of network effects—direct and indirect network effects. Direct network effects are on account of economies of scale and scope associated with L-shaped cost curves on account of high capex (capital expenditure) and low opex (operating expenditure). L-shaped curves are typical to natural monopolies as discussed in the previous section. Recovery of the high investment costs weighs in favor of a single firm servicing the market. Public utilities such as transmission lines, fixed telephone line are natural monopolies designated as "essential facility". Essential facilities when they are natural monopolies fall outside the purview of competition law. Platform markets do not qualify for this status of "essential facility" despite high capex costs. Heavy investments on account of digitalization followed by recurring investment in technology upgradation and innovation in algorithms keep capex costs high in platform markets.[5] Technology obsolescence's has seen major platforms such as Bing, Yahoo and You've Got Mail displaced by Google.[6] Platform markets require heavy investments and continuous flow of funds. Search for sources of revenue in platforms is circular as is the compulsion of growth. To stay in business platforms need to generate network effects and in turn investments in both hardware and software that facilitate design of algorithms that generate network effects. The main sources of revenue are from pricing schemes and advertisements, given the overriding criteria for platform markets of network effects and of harnessing them.

Indirect network effects define the success or failure of platforms markets. Toward generating network economies several strategies are followed to attract consumers. A few of the strategies are listed.

Firstly, marginal or zero opex costs permit platforms to charge zero transaction cost to consumers who pay no charges for surfing the web site of platform markets. As consumers are not charged a price extortionary abuses of predatory or excessive pricing as under Sect. 4(2)(a) of the Act loses relevance.[7]

Secondly, multi-homing the facility for consumers to connect to another network is a restriction that some platforms markets could indulge denying consumers the benefit of maximizing on the network effects of several platforms the benefit of multi-homing. Consumers do gain from multi-homing. Google as a search engine facilitates multi-homing for consumers. Single-homing restricts the roaming facility to one side most common in payment networks as brought out in United States v American Express, 2016. There can also be multi-homing on the one side and single homing on the other side.

Thirdly, network effects underlines the pricing mechanism as platforms court users on each side and accordingly design charges as noted by Rochet and Tirole to get the two sides of a market on board "*as markets in which one or several platforms enable interactions between end-users and try to get the two sides on board by appropriately charging each side*".[8] The two-part pricing schemes of charging a user fee and a membership fee is applied. A membership fee is for the capacity leased to a seller and a user fee is for running the show. As discussed in the previous section, pricing schemes for products and services price elasticity of demand remains the basic principle of price fixation. Platform markets for ensuring efficiency in resource allocation and of equitable distribution of cost burden weight the two charges with the Lerner Index of inverse elasticity of demand. The charges, of course, vary.

Lastly, the strength of platform market lies in Artificial Intelligence (AI) and machine learning. The fourth strategy for network economics is in the algorithms of platform market that translate into quick information flows for design of marketing strategies. Economics refer to them as 'feedback loops'. The software that goes into algorithms is programmed to mimic the market by taking into consideration prices prevailing in markets and related markets, seasonal variations, demand patterns of consumers et al. crunching data all the while. Consumers are confronted with dynamic pricing on real-time basis. Tools of price comparisons and ratings are additional features and part of the arsenal of well-known marketing techniques of attracting consumers.

Access to data of platform firms or aggregators strengthens their capacity to build profiles of consumers and use them to provide tools of search or for advertisers. Traditionally, data is always an important marketing strategy. In e-commerce, data collection is immediate permitting dynamic pricing. Referred to as the black-box algorithms capture consumer preference from a wide array of data that traditional data collection, analysts and marketing strategies are unable to match. The digital ecosystem powered by powerful technologies span across spectrum and internet connectivity locking consumers on to a platform market despite low switching costs and free surfing facilities.

In an article titled Antitrust and the Robo-Seller: Competition in the Time of Algorithms Mehra points to the fact that "*Traditional sales functions such as competitive intelligence gathering and pricing are being delegated to software 'robo-sellers'*."[9] Algorithms based on inferences based on data generate their own set of rules, reasoning. They mutate and changes structures, make decisions all independently of the platform for after all it is 'artificial intelligence'. These are algorithmic pricing that have minimal human intervention which may irk some of the sellers leading to allegations of abuse of dominance. It is important to understand what is learning algorithm, artificial intelligence and machine learning. The inability to comprehend the nuances and subtleties of usage in these terms has led to decisions by competition authorities that exhibit unwarranted aggressiveness rather than nuanced understanding of platform markets.

To provide clarity on terms used the Internet Society in a policy paper presented in simple language is reproduced: (i) Algorithm: a list of instructions used to perform a task. Learning algorithms generates a new set of rules, based on inferences and on data; (ii) Artificial Intelligence (AI) traditionally refers to an artificial creation of human-like intelligence that can learn, reason, plan, perceive or process natural language; (iii) Machine Learning: a particular approach to AI and the driving force behind recent developments. Instead of programming the computer every step of the way, machine learning makes use of learning algorithms that make inferences from data to learn new tasks. (AI and Machine Learning: Policy Paper–Internet Society, 2017).

Robo-selling unlike market prices set by humans can even cause supra-competitive pricing causing platform markets to lose out as customers drop out from the platform. The oft-quoted case is of Uber spike in prices on New Year's eve with algorithm inferring rising demand. The market response to the surge in pricing with an increase in supply of private cabs or share rides on New Year's Eve. This is a case of consumers gaming from experience. But not always is gaming possible. The market response to the spike surge is increase in the supply of cabs.

Search capabilities of algorithms see uniformity of pricing across a sector. A good example is a complaint lodged with CCI on collusion among airlines on airfares displaying splurges at the same time. Data presented to the Commission was innocuous. It only showed spikes in prices on account of demand surge of "Diwali". Algorithms of airline fares are built around given knowns of an understanding when demand shoots up as in the Diwali sale or when there is a slack in sale. Further learning algorithms gather larger amounts of data that profile demand scenarios which are used in pricing tickets. A good way of testing is to go on to several airline web site. Similar results emerge and these prices change dynamically simultaneously. People attempt to game it. Some succeed some don't. Conventionally, uniformity in prices is a signal of the presence of cartels. In the evidence presented before the Commission cartel prices collusion among airlines could not be established. The case was dropped as under Sect. 3 of the Act collusion has to be supported with an agreement or of informal understanding. In case of algorithmic pricing, there is no evidence of collusion. As independent collusion it cannot be classified as a cartel merely on the understanding that under Robo-selling algorithms set prices resulting in collusion. To break into the black box is treading on proprietary rights and could have repercussions on innovations and product development in the country. 'Algorithmic Abuses' or Robo-selling at the center of antitrust abuses of catching the '*eyeballs*' of users and getting competitors to agitate on abuse is again an attempt at using CCI for arguing against competition on merits.

Platform markets generally do not sell their own products but only offer the platform to markets on either side as '*conflict of interest*' restricts the growth of the platform. Platforms are perforce agnostic and platform neutrality considered an important factor of growth for e-commerce platforms (CCI Market Study in e-commerce in India). The CCI majority decision on Google proceeded on '*conflict of interest*' in ranking of web sites. The dissident decision did not find substantive evidence of ranking as basis to create entry barriers or to leverage into other markets. The argument of 'conflict of interest' works counter to network effects.

The suffix 'market' to platforms tends to restrict the section to e-commerce platforms. Lately there has been a diffusion in the segregation with search engines going for e-commerce and e-commerce also providing search facilities. Google was a search engine that sold space on its platform for digital markets to display their web sites. Now Google is competing with Amazon selling products directly. Amazon is a search engine for markets of consumption products with verticals of shopping sites. Defining a platform as purely commercial or as markets leading to distinctions between pure platforms and e-commerce platforms is just a click away. Search engines were classified as pure platforms in that the firm creating the platform is presumably not directly involved in e-commerce activity except for providing the requisite infrastructure for hosting of web sites of digital markets. Google, Bing, Yahoo and other search provided links to various web sites known as verticals (not to be equated with verticals in vertical arrangements) and many of them are shopping sites of sport goods, travel services. For a web site on Google is to get visibility for the respective business. Search engine platforms are mother boards for information commercial and non-commercial to consumers who surf the net. Digital markets bid for space and '*eye balls*' provoking a race for ranking on the listing of these markets. Separate boxes for consumer products and services are created by the platform to attract more users. Platforms involved in commercial activity e-commerce platforms, such as Amazon, Flipkart, Walmart, Fintech companies, such as Paytm follow similar tactics to court firms to sell their wares and for consumers to frequent their platform.

Lastly, a point which need to be pointed out is that Amazon, Flipkart, Netflix are known as 'over the top' (OTT) services offered on an internet or bandwidth. Google, Microsoft, Apple have developed the operating system providing access to platforms on smartphones and on a range of electronic devices. Then there are internet or telecom service provider (ISP/TSP) who lease spectrum space from the government paying a license fee. The TSP leases out spectrum space by building transmission towers which are passive platforms that host OTT platforms and services. In India the Jio platform houses RIL Telecom business under Reliance Jio Infocomm a mobile service network with nearly 400 m subscribers. The purchase of Future Group's retail chain Reliance Retail platform emerges as a major player shopping platform to Amazon faces little competition as of now but how the market responds has to be seen. Several international firms have invested in Reliance Retail Platform and include Facebook, Qualcomm, Intel and Google.[10] Amazon and Walmart (nee Flipkart) are also competing for a share of the growing e-commerce market. CCI is investigating into the business practices of Amazon and Flipkart. The US and EU are also investigating into the Big Five. The Indian scenario is of the Big Five four are investors in one of the largest industrial conglomerates (Reliance Industries) in the country, and there are several regulators apart from CCI from whom clearances are required.

1.2 Platforms and Shifting Terrains of Antitrust Abuse

The two effects network and economies of scale tilt in favor of platform markets large in size. Assertion of market power in using the conventional metric of market share loses its meaning as does the requirement of defining the market.[11] Antitrust concerns in India started with the argument of dominance and the abuse of market power and continue to prevail in the decisions of CCI firms. The Competition Act and the recent modifications proceed on abuses framed in the conventional product market framework. In the proposed modifications to the Act, there is a chapter on digital platforms with suggestions and modifications to Sect. 3(3) in introducing the concept of 'hub and spoke' and of MFN clauses in Sect. 3(4). Thresholds used in defining mergers and acquisition could consider 'value of deal' with an eye of future dominance by taking prescient action toward acquisitions of small innovative companies even in the CLRC. The overriding approach is, however, on dominance and the exertion of market power. The dominance dimension spills over to Sect. 3 on horizontal agreements (cartels), vertical agreements and on Intellectual Property Rights (IPRs) with considerations of including a provision in Sect. 4 to the abuse of dominance as expressed in a note to OECD by India (CLRC, 2019).

The dominance factor was clearly the primary focus in the cases cited. As noted zero transaction and abuses pertaining to predatory or excess pricing had no relevance with zero marginal costs as observed in the dissent order of MCX-SX v NSE. The case was adjudged on Sec. 4(2)(c) and 4(2)(e) creation of entry barriers and leveraging. Similarly, in the airline ticketing of algorithmic collusions, there was discussion on introducing the concept of group dominance as in the EU. The first Google case was filed pertaining to entry barriers and leveraging in the ranking of matrimonial web sites and travel sites. The allegation was that some sites were favored as their ranking was placed high on the list by the search engine. The Commission following the EU Commission arguments on shopping sites accepted the argument that ranking of sites was an abuse by Google a dominant search engine without evidence of travel sites having benefitted from the ranking. The argument that the number of clicks on a site is a measure of popularity benefitting the higher ranked site was not borne out by evidence in terms of earnings. The CCI study on e-commerce markets estimated that conversion rate of clicks in terms of purchasing the product or service is only 10 percent. The possibility of artificial intelligence and of algorithms that automatically ordered the ranking of sites with no human involvement are an aspect that will need to be examined. [12] Arguments of morality and moral responsibility of large firms in the European tradition of Ordo-liberal approach advanced in the majority decision need further proof of firm behavior and in my opinion makes for a weak case in terms of economic analysis. The importance of big data and its misuse in a combination of dominance and algorithms suggests lack of sufficient appreciation of the economics of platform markets.

AI and machine learning the centrality of algorithmic abuses are again grounded in arguments of dominance and the logic of platform markets. Several issues present themselves: How do we slice the abuse to distinguish between size and dominance which are on account of network effects and machine selling techniques ingrained in AI and algorithms. The e-commerce market study has skirted the issue of machine selling and learning algorithms concentrating instead on complaints of exclusive agreements forced by the platform market on sellers and of demands of discounts from wholesalers. The CLRC has preferred a cautious approach of wait and see. The challenge is to slice the abuses as assertion of market power from the dynamics of independent algorithms. Algorithmic antitrust abuses as "as decisions no longer made by humans but by machines into three groups" (Mehra, 2015):

- Algorithmic Collusion—the example cited is of airlines pricing and independent collusion as a cartel; but as we shall in the market for ideas interoperability and compatibility in standard essential patents is part of algorithmic collusion; collusion on account of mass crunching of data
- Algorithmic Personalized Pricing—pricing segregation on the base of age (senior citizens); volume discounts; or just the ability of the algorithm to dissect on willingness-to-pay. The welfare maximization of algorithmic pricing independent of human intervention is an integral part of the three degree of welfare maximization associated with discriminatory pricing policies. There could also be other forms of price discrimination that learning algorithms unearth.
- Algorithmic Prioritization—the case of Google and the ranking of web sites.

The ultimate test for platform markets is consumer sustainability. The term consumer sustainability is a wide concept broadly understood as the power of a platform market to sustain itself. Emergent literature on algorithmic tacit collusion has examined the sustainability of such cartels and the scope for markets readjusting (Ezrachi and Stucke, 2018; OECD,

2016).[13] What has been observed so far is that tacit collusion even under AI occurs in industries which have conditions that facilitate collusion namely, of product homogeneity, constant demand, etc. If there are only few players in the last section, the possibility of price parallelism as in the framework of oligopoly models of Bertrand appears inevitable. The evidence on algorithmic abuses is still awaited.

1.3 Whither Competition

Remedies to tackle anti-competitive abuses of platform markets have devolved on their large size and the fear of restricting competition using artificial intelligence and algorithms that crunch big data to give an edge to platform markets. The remedies suggested focus on restricting the privileged access to data and its multifarious uses and include: data portability; product interoperability; data sharing; and open standards/source. Several suggestions have been made on mergers and acquisitions to preempt large platforms emerging. Market forces attract new entrants as the CCI study clearly demonstrates. The e-commerce platforms and online trading are vibrant, and there is every possibility of new winners emerging. Intervention by competition authorities can lead to false positives with consumers losing out from the benefits of platform markets. In a sci-fi angle, artificial intelligence can be replaced only by more sophisticated AI.

Platform markets and disruptive technologies point to the two new Cs of competition assessment. They are *competitive constraints* and *consumer sustainability*. The term new is used as the reference earlier to the two C's flanking CCI were CVC (Central Vigilance Commission) and CBI (Central Bureau of Investigation) where the emphasis was not on competitive markets but on honesty of regulators.

The CCI study on e-commerce marketplace confirms the first 'C' with evidence of the presence of competitive constraints for platform markets in India. Platforms negotiate their equations with markets to get them online. Several markets or manufacturing firms sell both online and offline and accordingly strategize. The second 'C' of consumer sustainability acknowledged only in dissent Orders (MCX-SX v NSE, Google) is to attract consumers to the platform. Markets negotiate with platforms as do platforms to sell more online as compared to selling offline or on their digital web sites. Reference to unfair contracts platforms force on markets or of exclusive agreements with some sellers of forcing higher discounts perceived in the context of asserting dominance by platforms needs greater examination with an understanding of the requirement of network effects benefitting both platforms and markets on the platform. It brings to focus the need for studying contracts not just on platforms but offline between buyers and sellers. In a zero-sum game, there would be no other markets except those on platforms. The presence of e-commerce marketplaces as in the CCI study confirms the negotiating space between the two 'C's of competitive constraint and consumer sustainability. The peril of the two 'C's is that they need not operate conjointly. Consumer choices shift and if algorithms result in collusion independently of human intelligence as in the example of uniform air ticket pricing among all travel agents competition authorities have a tough task ahead. Similarly, personalized pricing may not apply in all segments of e-commerce, especially those that are fashion designed.

Emergence of Big Data and of AI and machine selling have brought to focus algorithmic abuses stated above are of Sect. 3 abuses. They pertain to agreements (horizontal and vertical) than of 'abuse of dominance' of Sect. 4. Conflation of Sect. 4 and Sect. 3 applied to algorithmic abuses as in the automotive parts case could be contradictory.

There are several questions that need to be explored as we await decisions of CCI on the Confederation of All India Traders v Reliance Jio. There are several unanswered questions which arise such as: How do markets on platforms react to algorithmic pricing? As independent pricing outcomes on which platforms exert little control markets may prefer a different pricing option. Are contracts of markets with platforms renegotiable?

CLRC took a cautious approach "the Committee felt that the absence of credible evidence demonstrating the anti-competitive concerns associated with such collusion and in line with approach taken by other jurisdictions, it may be premature to warrant a legislative intervention"

Under conditions of disruptive technology and changing market structures, there may be no single definitive approach to antirust abuses. Growing importance of data personal and non-personal has seen the emergence of data markets the subject of discussion in the next section.

2 Data Markets

Quick flows of information and of data on the internet have spawned data markets spurred by several factors that see merit in data market places. A perceptible change in the attitude about data is in its emergence as an asset that can be bought and sold.[14] Rather than create and assemble data renting data has emerged as a valuable alternative laying the foundations for monetizing data. Antitrust interventions of data portability, data sharing, platform neutrality addressing the market power of platforms markets and access to data have also contributed to the emergence of data markets. Big Data as the source of market power and the price consumers pay in surfing these platforms have also raised concerns on privacy and consumer data rights prompting legislation on personal data protection and non-personal data protection. Both bills are awaiting parliamentary approval. Currently, the thinking of the government is more on Data Trusts, Data Commons, Open Source in the wake of the Information Technology Act, 2009.[15]

Incipient data markets such as the Centre for Monitoring Indian Economy (CMIE) and Prime Data Base have been in existence for a long-time referring to themselves as business Information Company, which is what a data market place is about. CMIE combines data in the public domain such as balance sheets and (limited) access to national surveys, however, used extensively by research scholars. Large private corporate sector firms also collect required data for their business strategies.

As offshoots of antitrust allegation of platform markets data markets have structures that merit a separate section.

2.1 Data Markets

Data markets are aggregator markets. Firms or vendors aggregate data engaged in buying and selling of data. It is, therefore, not a platform market offering a platform for markets on either side. Nor is it a product market with manufacturers or sellers on the one side and buyers on the other side. The structure, therefore, of data markets is distinct from platform markets and product markets. The common feature of data markets and platform markets is the importance of network economies that weigh in favor of large firms.

There are two important characteristics of data markets. Firstly as aggregator of data there are several processes and protocols to be fulfilled on raw data before they are available for access and usage. These processes can be grouped under four headings. They are: i) sourcing of data; ii) data architecture; iii) governance of data; and iv) data consumption (Mckinsey 2020).

1. Sourcing of data—public domain on the internet; procuring it from customers; carry out customer surveys; purchase from platform markets algorithmic data
2. Data architecture—formatting of data which includes technology in formats that are easy to access amenable to requirements of customers
3. Data governance—maintaining data quality and updating data, search for new sources of data, data artifacts, such as dictionary/thesaurus, confirming with data protection rules of privacy
4. Data consumption—data analytics, generation of reports.

A data market aggregator unlike in platform markets collect, format and sell data whereas in platform markets the platform is created for interaction between markets on either side, providing value in terms of a payment mechanism.

Typical data marketplaces offer a variety of data for different types of transactions. Vendors normally specialize in one set of data specific to a sector. For instance, National Sample Survey data of district level income and population distribution are used by FMCG marketing strategy could be combined with other data available in the public domain but related to strategic factors that influence demand. For convenience of analysis, the data is offered in formats such as panel data in time series. With several functions and process heavy investment is involved in the development of data markets. Mckinsey estimates that the average spend is over $ 229 million in 2019–2020. In Financial Services, it is $ 323 million and in packaged goods at $192 million (Mckinsey, July 2020).

Secondly, data is a quasi-public good. It is non-rival but exclusive. Non-rival in that if one person consumes the good it does not reduce the amount available to others. Exclusive as data can be monetized. Users pay for access and use of the data. Data market firms rent out data. They cater to varied clientele whose requirements are not standardized and hence pricing schemes can range from zero price to the amount of value added as they create and assemble valuable data. The added advantage is that cost of maintenance of data is avoided if you don't own the data.

I am not including proprietary data in this section. Proprietary data are those safeguarded by Patents, trademarks, copyright, etc. which are private goods with the exception of Standard Essential Patents where a private good becomes a public good. This will be examined in the next section on Market for Ideas. The Personal Data Protection Act envisages data of consumers proprietary whose rights have to be protected until the data is anonymized.

2.2 *Pricing of a Quasi-Public Good*

Monetizing or selling of data removes the non-exclusive feature of data drawing attention to pricing schemes for recovery of investment and for controlled access and use of data. Data is a saleable asset whose value is best discovered by the market. The Free Rider problem where people have access to data without paying is also a possibility as in the approach on 'Data Commons' when data is treated as a public good.

Data markets unlike platform markets have high Capex and high Opex. Both technology and data have to be upgraded continuously. The L-shaped cost curve discussed earlier does not apply to data markets setting it apart from natural monopolies and from platform markets where network effects are important. Pricing schemes for data markets have to address high investment costs, high running costs and the characteristics of a quasi-public good.

The criticality of data for diverse usage ranging from academic research to commercial innovation and business strategies pricing strategies tends to be individualized referred to in economic theory as discriminatory pricing structured into three degrees—personalized pricing, menu pricing and group pricing. The main risk is that discriminatory pricing can come under the scrutiny of CCI. The basic scheme is two-part pricing schemes that would consist of a membership fee and a user fee. Varying models of data monetization can be applied depending on the sophistication of the data market. Capex is covered under membership fee while Opex is related to metered usage in terms of number of days.

A mix of free and open source data when combined could have security implications. The user fee is a license for usage on which other conditionality's and terms of conditions such as reselling of data can be loaded.

A rough idea can be gleaned from the Table 1.

As an emergent market structure, there is a lot of economic analysis that have still not been well blended with competition law. In the case of data markets, antitrust abuses come under vertical restraints Sect. 3(4) where the analysis is on "effects-based" and not "per se". On the other hand, the two-part pricing scheme is a contract between a user and the vendor.

Table 1 Data markets compared

	Azure	*Data market*	*Factual*	*Infochimps*
Data sources	Broad range	Range, with a focus on country and industry stats	Geo-specialized, some other datasets	Range, with a focus on geo, social and web sources
Free data	Yes	Yes	–	Yes
Free trials of paid data	Yes	–	Yes, limited free use of APIs	–
Delivery	OData API	API, downloads	API, downloads for heavy users	API, downloads
Application hosting	Windows Azure	–	–	Infochimps Platform
Previewing	Service Explorer	Interactive visualization	Interactive search	–
Tool integration	Excel, PowerPivot, Tableau and other OData consumers	–	Developer tool integrations	–
Data publishing	Via database connection or web service	Upload or web/database connection	Via upload or web service	Upload
Data reselling	Yes, 20% Commission on non-free datasets	Yes, Fees and commissions vary. Ability to create branded data market	–	Yes, 30% Commission on non-free datasets
Launched	2010	2010	2007	2009

Source Edd Dumbill

3 Market for Ideas—Intellectual Property Rights[16]

In the previous section, we had looked at data markets both personal and non-personal data that have crossed the threshold of being proprietary data. In this section, we shall briefly look at data markets for proprietary data, i.e., patents and Intellectual Property Rights. These rights are outside the purview of competition law and in the legalese of competition law they are referred to as the 'Safe Harbor' clauses Sect. 3(5), unless there has been an exercise of dominance by the licensor or holder of patents in contracts with the licensee. [17]Cases filed with CCI have been on the issue of dominance of patent holders and their abuse in the contracts pertaining to royalty ad related conditions. It has been viewed as the conflation between the two sections between Sect. 3 and Sect. 4 in allegations pertaining to IPR rights. The modification to the Act suggested by CLRC of extending rights of patent holders to Sect. 4 is acceptance of conflation.[18] Distinction is further drawn between individual patent rights which are private goods and portfolio of patents namely Standard Essential Patents (SEPs) which are private goods converted to public goods on account of meeting standards. An important and critical feature of SEPs is that they should meet international standards of interoperability and compatibility set by Standard Setting Organizations (SSOs). In meeting standards, SEPs get converted from a private portfolio to a portfolio of public goods, non-rival and non-exclusive.

SEPs are a special category in the family of patents clubbed and licensed as a portfolio of patents. The licensor firm is both a buyer and licensor of patents. The firm buys patents from other entities and individuals and also contributes its own intellectual property rights by investing in research and development which places it in a different category of data aggregators.

This section on data market for IPRs to borrow an old phrase 'Market for Ideas' is focused on SEPs. As portfolio of patents with characteristics of public good essential for production of mobiles, smartphones and accessories SEPs are directly linked to consumption of end consumers. It raises a fundamental issue for competition authorities on assessing allegations of antitrust abuse in consumer markets that get created and sustained in a regime of licensed proprietary data. The two Cs, competitive constraints and consumer sustainability, discussed in platform markets remain the guiding principles for antitrust assessment by competition authorities in this market also.

3.1 Institutional Structure of SEPs

The mobile telephony industry is representative of the expansive technological advancements that have taken place in the last two decades and their myriad application in several sectors. In fact, mobile technology has been the single source of innovative growth with largest amount of investment in R&D as compared to other sectors. Clearly, observable the industry has grown from simple voice connection of handsets to multiple usages of data accessible on smart phones from messaging to streaming of music, films, to banking. Heavy investment in R&D which has permitted multiplicity of operations over and above the core function on interoperability between networks and instruments is reflected in the emergence of Standard Essential Patents (SEPs).

Technological advancements saw the number of contributions of essential patent that constitute a standard in cellular technology increase from 8882 patents to about 571,366 in 3G and much more in 5G. Simultaneously, the number of SEP firms or patent owners has been decreasing. Some estimates place it at 13 firms while others place it at 15 firms.[19]

This decrease in the number of firms contributing to standards has led antitrust authorities to examine whether the potential market power embedded within the structure of an SEP can lead to raising prices (royalty) in a monopolistic market. Surprisingly, although the market structure in terms of normal concept of number of firms is monopolistic, the market is highly competitive in terms of consumer benefit. In a study of the SEP market operating in vertically differentiated handset market the methodology of royalty payment should be linked to the end-price of the handset (Policy Briefs IPR/2018, IDF).[20] This pricing scheme benefits consumers and SEP firms.

The mobile industry is among the most R&D intensive as compared to other industries except perhaps bio-technology. Since wireless communication functions on scarce spectrum allocation heavy investment in R&D is toward optimizing the available spectrum space making possible transmitting of voice and data in new products. Each application and related product development grew from simple analog voice transmission of 1G, to simple data transmission and digital voice of 2G; to global internet connections and broadband usage with growing application of apps on smart phones with streaming media, music and films on 4G. A complete paradigm shift is expected to occur with 5G where applications consist of devices such as smart homes, smart cities, smart cars and use of Artificial Intelligence in devices grouped as the 'Internet of Things' (IoT). The move from 3 to 4G and to 5G is best associated with billions of small devices wired together. As mentioned earlier 3G itself consists of 571,366 patents in a SEP. India is still with 3G and 4G but 5G is on the anvil as the pace of digitalization picks up momentum.

3.2 Royalty Rates and Market Creation

The SEP License covers all patents in the portfolio and have assumed a significant role in the application of Artificial Intelligence extending beyond International Communication Technology (ICT) to Internet of Things. Digital equipment which include mobile telephony, smartphones are produced to meet conditions of interoperability and compatibility necessitating the use SEPs or chipsets embedded with SEPs in their products.

The licensing of proprietary data is separate from data market analysis of the previous section. License or right to use is by way of royalty payments that is usually recurring linked to sales of every product using the proprietary data.[21]Cases filed with CCI by phone manufacturers against Standard Essential Patent firms (SEP firms) were also based on allegations of abuse of dominant position (Sect. 4) in the technology of GSM, 2G, 3G,4G and now 5G in imposing exorbitant and discriminatory royalty rates violating FRAND commitments. Phone manufacturers were required to sign Non-Disclosure Agreement (NDA) considered as violating conditions of openness that is part of FRAND commitments. The abuses were classified into two groups "patent hold-up" and 'royalty stacking' that undermines the competitive process of choosing among technologies and of transparency.

The salient features of SEPs that create markets firstly, can be observed in the move from 2 to 4G and then 5G is a move to portfolio of patents that are complimentary. Clearly demand for a patent is related to its market value. In the case of SEPs value is dependent on its success in the telephony market. SEPs generate revenue from licensing possible on a large scale where the portfolio of complimentary patents paid by licensee permits flexibility of production of differentiated products both horizontally and vertically. Technology of mobile telephony industry and requirements of compatibility between products required pooling of patents for consumers to get all their basic needs inside one product. The lack of compatibility between products creates inefficiencies for manufacturers more so if technological products do not follow consistent protocols. Secondly, in order to mitigate inefficiency issues and create a cohesive structure, the need to standardize technological products came into play, especially with regard to technology. The legal definition of a standard is "any set of technical specifications that either provides or is intended to provide a common design for a product or a process" (Lemley, 2002).[22] Since standards established consistent protocols that were universally accepted and adopted, it formed the fundamental building block for product development (IEEE). The creation of 3GPP (Third Generation Partnership Program) was created with the agenda to develop a common wireless cellular system out of 489 members of 3GPP about 85% did not declare any SEP for a given standard which indicates that only 130 firms declare patents essential to standards within which ten firms own between 72 and 84% of the essential patents with about twenty firms owning more than 90% of the essential patents (Llobet and Padilla, 2016).[23]

Telecommunication witnessed fast rates of technological process from 1G having a non-interoperable system and analogous communication to 4G which enabled wireless internet access, enhanced voice, streaming of media at a high rate and faster rates of internet connection. This technological progress required the usage of sophisticated standards such as GSM, UMTS, Bluetooth, LTE. All of these standards required numerous complementary innovative components to work cohesively together, for example the 4G standard required several SEP (Standard Essential Patents) to work together simultaneously. Due to this, standards in the ICT sector started being viewed as a "portfolio of patents". Since standards are essentially a portfolio of patents, the technology sponsors of SEPs started frequently holding and licensing SEPs as a bundle. It was also observed that there was an increase in trading between complementary standard essential patents. Some of the most prominent cases was the acquisition of Norton's portfolio of patents by Rockstar (a consortium of companies which included Apple, EMC, Ericsson, Microsoft, Research in Motion and Sony) and the acquisition of Motorola's mobility (over 17,000 granted patents and approximately 7,500 pending patent applications) by Google.[24] The merging and acquiring of *complementary* standard essential patents has led to number of contributions to essential patent that constitute a standard in cellular technology to increase but the number of SEP firms contributing to decrease.

Thirdly, decrease in the number of firms contributing to standards raised anti-competitive concerns prominent among them being abuse of dominance. In a perfectly competitive market, which consists of large numbers of buyers and sellers, homogeneity of products, and free entry and exit of firms no business or company in theory, should have the liberty to exercise control over the market especially when it comes to price determination. An enterprise once it enjoys a position of strength which enables it to profitably increase prices independently of competitors/suppliers/consumers is deemed as having a dominant position. In the case of SEP as it protects the required essential technology any manufacturer of phone sets is required to obtain a license for the SEP bestowing a position of strength to the licensor qua the freedom of a SEP owner to increase prices independently of competitors. It is in this framework the institutional structure of Standard Essential Patents (SEPs) markets endows a significant dominant market power on their owners. However, having a dominant position in the market does not necessarily lead to abuse of dominance. Lastly, an SEP holder can abuse its dominance through two mechanisms, the first is by excluding competitors. Competitors in this context would be the manufacturers who are in need of the Standard Essential Patent, the SEP holder can exclude competitors and second by a) charging excessively high royalty rates or cross-licensing fees; b) bundling patents together leading to excessive pricing since the portfolio of patents held by the SEP holder is essential for the manufacturing of the product. Hence, a portfolio of patents held by a single SEP holder might lead to implementers to license more than they desire on the argument made in their filing to CCI that royalty should be only for the required patent and not the portfolio. The obverse argument is that patents held by a single firm reduce transaction cost or double marginalization with the advantage that licensing a portfolio of patents allows for flexibility in the range of products that are open to the licensee to manufacture.

Thus standard essential patents being sold as a portfolio of patents led to a very pertinent question as to whether the size of a patent portfolio determined an owner's ability to charge royalty rates.

Pohlmann et al. (2014)[25] find that there is a significant increase in market power on SEP holders who own the portfolio of patents related to the standard. They find that SEP owners with a large portfolio size are more dominant than the SEP owners with a smaller portfolio size. This according to them is due to an enforcement margin, an SEP owner with a large portfolio size can demand more royalties since the means to collect royalties ultimately depends on the owner's ability to enforce it in court. The enforcement margin occurs due to the high transactional costs required for litigation. If the portfolio of patents is strong, the SEP owner collects more revenue and hence the trade-off for fighting in courts becomes more profitable. Hence, a large portfolio of patents ends up giving market to an SEP owner since it can negotiate licensing terms in court. However, the scope for a SEP owner with a large portfolio of patents to abuse its dominance by charging exorbitant royalties is constricted by a demand bound margin on prices. As the royalty rate increases for the SEPs, manufacturers in the downstream firm would reduce production and this would in turn lead to a decrease in demand. Thus they conclude by stating that trading between firms for SEP is most economically efficient and profitable when SEP owners with a large portfolio sell their patents to medium-strength licensors. This is because medium-strength licensors are not bound by the demand margin, and hence can benefit from an increase in demand without raising their royalties.

However, trading patents and increasing the size of the portfolio of patents is not desirable for consumers and manufacturers since it results in higher cumulative royalties which then leads to a negative double-margin externality. Double marginalization is when there are different firms in the same industry that have market power but at different vertical levels in the supply chain. This allows them to apply their own mark-up price. The mark-up price is the "added price over the total cost of the good or service that provides the seller with a *profit*." Due to two different companies exercising their own mark-up prices, a deadweight loss is incurred, and since it's two companies instead of one, the deadweight loss is incurred twice, this is referred to as a double marginalization which hinders output. Pohlmann et al. (2014) thus conclude by stating that the only way to mitigate double marginalization is to merge portfolios together since a merger results in removing one licensor. Due to complementary patents being sold as a portfolio in the downstream market rather than individually it encourages innovation upstream, since more companies have access to all the complementary patents, and don't have to go to different companies to obtain them.

The scope for the prevalence of the classical Cournot model is debatable. Licensing of complementary technologies often generates the classical Cournot-complement models problem. The classical Cournot model stipulates that "each firm chooses a royalty without internalizing the effect of the higher price on the profits of other firms". It is thus argued that this effect creates a "royalty stack" "Royalty stacking is where licensee pays royalties to multiple parties in order to commercialize a product". [26] In terms of economic logic, royalty stacking impacts on the profits of downstream producers which is self-defeating for SEP firms. Evidence of unprecedented rate of growth in which demand has not fallen and prices of mobile phones have not risen despite strong evidence of royalty stacking rules out the Cournot effect.

3.3 *Standard Setting Organizations (SSO)*

The institutional structure of Standard Essential Patents (SEPs) endows a significant dominant market power on their owners. Dominance has often been measured through evaluating market share. However, unlike other jurisdictions there is no clear definition what consists of market share. The CCI looks into a variety of anti-competitive behavior such as vertical integration and market structure and size of the market to evaluate if the given enterprise can influence prices independently of their competitors.

Most of the cases refer to abuse of dominance (which falls under the first category), however, very few cases in India as undertaken by the Competition Commission of India evaluate the effects of dominance on furthering innovation. Bundling of SEPs together with Non-SEP has been a cause of concern for furthering innovation, since it creates a barrier of entry to the producer of the substitutable Non-SEP, since it comes free with the SEP which is required.

Damien Geradin argues that anti-competitive behavior such as excessive pricing is becoming a rare occurrence in high-technology due to the fact that standards essential patents are getting bundled and hence cross-licensing between producers is becoming increasingly more common.

The prima facie Order on Ericsson and Micromax (3 others) left me with sense of unease—how does one assess anti-competitive behavior of patents which are natural monopolies as an abuse of dominance. Is our understanding of markets restrictive ? Is the CA02 restrictive having stayed in the conventional product framework on competition. Attempts to escape saw several discussions and intellectual discussion papers now evident in the Competition Law Review Committee Review(CLRC) report. Modifications have been included but in a cautious manner. A clause pertaining to SEPs is to be inserted into Sect. 4 and in expanding the merger framework. Antitrust analysis needs a rethink on the economic analysis of the market for ideas and how they impact on consumer welfare. If innovation and technological development are an important aspect of economic welfare, the competition law must take a more public interest orientation (Gouri, 2020).[27]

The institution of SSOs (Standard Setting Organization) brings to the forefront the competitive constraint of one institute over another—SEP firms are restricted by SSOs who on grant of standards commit firms to a) FRAND; b) agree to license to all; c) all license agreements to be freely negotiated. SSOs are market created standard organization and consist of:

a. SEP firms
b. Implementers—only in India the implementers are not members of SSO (TDSI)
c. Scientific community and general public

Standards, once set, can be used by any producer (non-exclusivity) and the use of a particular standard by one producer does not preclude other producers from using the same standard (non-rival). The antitrust approach to SEPs is not of dominance of SEP firms but of being involved in the SSO process. Nagging question that has arisen is in the exercise of power in the selection of standards and the inclusion of select patents into the accepted pool of patents.

4 Conclusions

The economics of emergent markets widens the door of competition assessment and the acceptance that static competition law CA02 would have to be more vibrant. It raises a crucial question—should competition authorities intervene and when?

Notes

1. Well-known examples are credit cards or UPI payment where the platform is a facility for processing payments on the net. Or of videogames where platforms are the video consoles to attract players and persuade game developers develop new games. The two examples are single activity platforms standalone or linked to multi-activity platforms such as Amazon that most of us are familiar.

2. I find that the CLRC also did not take the perspective of consumers.
3. This is a view I have held consistently reflected in my dissent Orders.
4. A recent stay given by the German Federal Court on the decision of Bundeskartellamt on Facebook of using its dominance for furthering monopoly is under review. The emphasis of Bundeskartellamt was on larger concepts of privacy and ordoliberal values of responsibility of large business than on competition issues(Witt, 2020). A dangerous trend that has been noted in competition assessment where platform markets are concerned is a perceptible shift to 'form-based' rather than 'effects based' which is dangerous trends (Jameel, 2020).
5. A good insight can be gleaned from the recent investments into Jio platforms amounting to Rs.1,52,056 crores from financial and strategic investors. RIL the parent company raise Rs.2,12,809 crs through rights issue.

   The scope for funding through which venture capital fro start-ups also tend to be limited. Venture capital funds are reluctant to fund business that compete directly with digital platforms and are termed as "kill zones" Stigler Report, 2019), (Raghuram Rajan, 2019).
6. Geeta Gouri co-authored with M. Salinger, "Protecting Competition v/s Protecting Competitor: Assessing the Antitrust Complaints against Google", *The Criterion Journal of Innovation*, Vol. 2, 2017, pp. 531–558, also at http://ssrn.com/abstract=2787343
7. An aspect not considered by CLRC. If data is the new price then Sect. 4(2)(a,b,c) would require modifications.
8. Jean-Charles Rochet, Jean Tirole, Platform Competition in Two-Sided Markets, *Journal of the European Economic Association*, Vol. 1, Issue 4, 1 June 2003, pp. 990–1029, https://doi.org/10.1162/154247603322493212, Published: 1 June 2003.
9. S. Mehra., Antitrust and the Robo-Seller: Competition in the Time of Algorithms, *Minnesota Law Review*, Vol. 100, Temple University Legal Studies Research Paper No. 2015–15, 60 Pages.
10. Subhomoy Bhatattacharjee insight into the battle royale an interesting twist of Amazon and Flipkart investigations by competition authorities world over is a major investor in Reliance, a huge industrial conglomerate venturing into retail business with all the global five investing in the e-commerce business. Business Standard, June 30, 2021. Apart from CCI, SEBi is investigating an then there is the NCLT and as a young scholar speculates on the possibility of Forum Shopping.
11. Kemal, Mehmet, in Social Media Platforms' Rush on Personal Data and Competition Law: Facebook Decision of German Federal Cartel Office, Competition and Innovation Institute suggests a different measure of market.

12. "In general, any type of behavior that constitutes an abuse in an offline industry is also likely to constitute an abuse online" was the accepted understanding. The Evolution of Competition Law in Digital Markets in India.

    By Augustine Peter, Neha Singh, Competition Policy International, October 8, 2019.
13. Ariel Ezrachi and Maurice E.Stucke, Sustainable and Unchallenged Algorithmic Tacit Collusion, downloaded from the internet.
14. The draft report on Non-personal Data Protection discusses the importance of data as an asset whose value is best determined by the market. The Bill discusses in detail the creation of data markets but tends to mix up data markets with platform markets.
15. Information Technology Act, 2009, emphasizes the organization of data in 'trusts'. It was the first attempt to look at security concerns of data and to ensure that no breaches occur. Standards for security were the overriding concern. Outsourcing was considered once security considerations are well defined with protocols of breaches laid out. The old distrust for private participation was clearly visible in data outsourcing. The Economic Survey of 2018 treats data as a public good. Public goods can also be priced.
16. The work in this section is part of the on-going research project Intellectual Property Rights, Standard Essential Patents and Digital India at India Development Foundation (IDF). The team apart from myself included, Shubhasish Gangopadhyay, Ishan Banerjee, and Satyaki Chakravarty. This section is based on discussions I had with Shubhasish and his team at IDF which I was associated for over a year.
17. Proprietary Data categorized as Intellectual Property Rights (IPR) under Sect. 3(5) covers: Copyright Act (1957); Patents Act (1970); Trade and Merchandise Act(1958) or the Trade Marks (1999); Geographical Indication of Goods (1958); Designs Act (2000); Semi-Conductor integrated Circuits Layout-Design Act (2000); and the right to export goods from India exclusively to the production, supply, distribution or control of goods for such export.
18. CLRC has proposed a new Sect. 4(A) extending the safe harbor protection to IPRs.
19. Kirti Gupta and Mark Synder, Smart Phone Litigationan Standard Essential Patents, Hoover Institution Working Group on Intellectual Property, Innovation and Prosperty, Stanford University, 2014.
20. Policy Brief IPR/201/01, Should Frand Royalties be based on SSPPU or downstream prices? An analytical framework. Policy Brief IPR/2018/02, An Exploration int Royalty Stacking and Price Posting, India Development Foundation, Gurugram, Harayana, India.

21. Shubhashis Gangopadhyay, Primer on Intellectual Property Rights prepared for Competition Commission of India, 2010.
22. Lemley,Intellectual Property Rights and Standard Setting Organisations, 90 (6), *California Law Review*, 1889–1980 (2002).

    See Pohlman Pohlman, Tim, Peter Neuhausler and Knut Blind (2016), "Standard Essential Patents to Boost Financial Returns", *R&D Management*, 46(May), 612-30.and Quint, Daniel (2014), "Pooling with Essential and Nonessential Patents", *American Economic Journal: Microeconomics*, Vol. 6 Issue 1, pp. 23–57.
23. LLobet and Padilla., The Inverse Cournot Effect in Royalty Negotiations with Complementary Patents, accessed from the internet, April 2020. Llobet, Gerard and Jorge Padilla, "The Optimal Scope of the Royalty Base in Patent Licensing," *Journal of Law and Economics*, Vol. 59, No. 1, 2016, pp. 45–73.
24. Op.cit.
25. Op.cit.
26. Policy Brief IPR/2018/02, An Exploration into Royalty Stacking and Price Posting, prepared by Satyaki Chakravarty, Shubhashis Gangopadhyay and Geeta Gouri, India Development Foundation.
27. Op.cit. 1.

References

Ariel Ezrachi and Maurice E.Stucke, Sustainable and Unchallenged Algorithmic Tacit Collusion, downloaded from the internet.

CCI Market Study in E-Commerce in India.

Competition Law Review Committee Report, Ministry of Commerce, Government of India, 2019.

Damien Geradin, Patent assertion entities and EU competition law, Tilburg University.

Intellectual Property Rights, Standard Essential Patents and Digital India at India Development Foundation (IDF).

Information Technology Act, 2009.

Stigler Committee on Digital Platforms, 2019, Booth School Chicago Stigler Centre for the study of the Economy and the State.

The Platform Law Blog Mckinsey Report, July, 2020.

CHAPTER 4

Economic Analysis of Horizontal Agreements and Vertical Agreements (Section 3)

Business run on agreements and contracts. They can be written or tacit. Competition law is concerned only if agreements restrict competition which binds on competition authority to identify anti-competitive agreements. The first layer of distinction is between horizontal agreements and vertical agreements. In the Act, the distinction is between Sections 3(3) and 3(4). The former Section 3(3) is on agreements between enterprises, persons or association of enterprises or persons ring bells for the authority usually associated with cartels with a caveat that joint ventures do not fall in this category. Agreements among enterprises or persons at different stages or levels of production which constitute the distribution chain from production to reaching the consumer fall in the category of Section 3(4). There can be situations of abuse where both 3(3) and 3(4) occur as in the case of Drugs and Chemists Association. In analyzing vertical agreements, it is important to guard against two common mistakes. Firstly, on conflation between Section 3(4) and Section (4) most cases filed with CCI on allegations pertaining to Section 3(4) indulge in conflation. The Commission has to respond to allegations related to both sections the likelihood of distorted decisions on market functioning which cannot be ruled out. Exploration is therefore warranted as the underlying economics of the two sections vary as do the criteria listed in the Act. Secondly, the legality of *de hors* in the enforcement of Sections 3(1) to 3(4) could have outward manifestations in the organizational structure or it could be

G. Gouri, *A Commissioner's Primer to Economics of Competition Law in India*, https://doi.org/10.1007/978-981-19-9476-0_4

inherent with nuanced distinctions. Directions from the Supreme Court in Competition Commission of India v. Steel Authority of India & Ors., Civil Appeal No. 7779 of 2010 have frowned on conflation pointing to the requirement of *de* hors.[1] Agreements that do not fit into the strict categorization of horizontal or vertical has been flagged by the Review Committee of Competition Law (2019)[2] given the practice in EU and US of not distinguishing between the two types of agreements but primacy to anti-competitive outcomes of consumer harm.

1 Section I: Cartels, Collusion and Horizontal Agreements

Cartels have the mystique of underworld activity and glamor that tinsel town brings to the potent threat of illegal activity. The excitement spills over to investigations by antitrust authorities with all the ingredients of 'mafia culture'. Once considered as the most pernicious of market structures, cartel breaking ranked high on priority for competition authorities. It still does. But caveats have emerged from rethinking over the decisions of CCI which I explore in this chapter with reference to cartels in different sectors posing two questions: whether the factors identified warranted intervention by the Commission and whether the suggested remedies including penalties are deterrents to cartelization.

The basic assumption of a cartel is that enterprises, firms or persons come together to fix prices, quantity and share the market among themselves.[3] The attempt is to restrict competition earning the rubric of 'pernicious' by antitrust authorities. To denigrate cartels as the most pernicious of anti-competitive activities is however treading on slippery grounds of false positives merely on grounds of price parallelism. They can also be outcomes of aggressive competition among enterprises engaged in vigorous price wars. Distinguishing cartels from competitive markets is not simple. Comparable outcomes of cartels and competitive markets raise value judgments on welfare gains and losses posing a dilemma to competition authorities whether to intervene or wait as competitors join the fray tempted by higher earnings. The present pandemic times have seen a new category of cartels labeled as 'crisis cartels' with the issue of the new Green Regulations issued by CCI. Related to modus of clearances of acquisitions, the crisis cartel will be dealt in the next chapter.

The incentive to cheat by one of the members is always a strong possibility resulting in the cartel breaking. As cartels are often of short duration, the competition authorities have to take a call on letting the market readjust or to intervene with the appropriate grim trigger that breaks cartels. In analyzing CCI cartel decisions, it is tempting to pose the question "*Did we get it right*" the answer to which lies in gaming responses of competitors. Incentive mechanism that sustain the cartel and the design of appropriate trigger points is attempted in each of the case studies. There is no uniform approach breaking of cartels. Cartels among merchants with strong social and caste equations represent an entirely different genre of cartels. The work on Maghribi traders of the tenth and eleventh centuries (Grief, 1998)[4] is one such study on social networks as is Ostrom's (Elinor Ostrom, 1990)[5] analysis on commons action with an alternative perspective on design of control mechanism.[6]

1.1 Setting Standards for Cartels

Changing contours of cartels provoke resetting standards. This is difficult. The case studies selected was based on whether standards set out in the Act have been met, are they sufficient and what are the prevailing limitation of standard as laid out in the Competition Act, 2003. The Competition Act distinguishes between horizontal agreements or arrangements and vertical agreements. Horizontal agreements look at anti-competitive outcomes of firms in the same line or product and result in AAEC of which cartels constitute the main abuse. The proof of cartel is premised on the basis of an agreement among enterprises, persons, association of enterprises or association of persons. The agreement can be formal or tacit as an arrangement. The proposed modification to Section 3(3) is to expand the cartel association to include enterprises, persons "*though not engaged in identical or similar trade shall be presumed to be part of the agreement if it actively participates in furtherance of the agreement*".[7]

Supporting evidence for cartel is controls on pricing, quantity manipulation, market sharing and bid rigging listed in Section 3(3) (a, b, c, d) as Agreements *that "cause or likely to cause an appreciable adverse effect on competition (AAEC)"* (Act, 2002). Interestingly, procedures for enquiry into Agreements Section 19(3) was considered as applicable to only vertical arrangements. In my opinion, it is a biased perception stemming from the understanding that cartels are pernicious per se and need no reasoning of possible benefits to consumers. Agreements whether horizontal or vertical can result in AAEC by hindering competitive market functioning. The contra that agreements could benefit consumers in terms of efficiency and enhanced productivity needs consideration. Of the six factors listed in Section 19(3), three clauses emphasize hindrance to competitive market functioning and three clauses the possible benefits to consumers of agreements.[8]

Discussion on cartels in the initial years of CCI revolved on the standards required for proof of cartels. The 1993 judgment of the Supreme Court (Union of India v Hindustan Development Corp, 1993, SCC) had weighed in favor of written agreements as the required substantive proof of presence of cartel and incorporated in the Monopolies and Restrictive Trade Practices (MRTP) Act (Bhatacharjee, 2003).[9] Competition Act,2002 under Section 2(b) adopted a softer approach as proof of cartels whereby an "*agreement includes any arrangement or understanding or action in concert .... whether or not such arrangement, understanding or action is formal or in writing; or .....is intended to be enforceable by legal proceedings*". The Act in providing a wider and softer criteria of proof of cartels was necessary in the context of economic liberalization policies initiated in 1991. Competition and market orientation required breaking of licensed cartels that were fallouts of the licensing regime pre-1991.[10]

In the early phases of industrial growth, all large and medium industries and services permitted to the private sector required a license to set up their units. Trading in licenses combined with concentration of licenses in a few industrial houses lead to concentration of economic and market power quite opposite to the intent of diversified ownership of industrial planning (Gouri, 1995)[11] The first intervention in regulation was the Monopolies and Restrictive Trade Practices Act (MRTP) which saw the establishment of the MRTP Commission. The focus of the Commission was on prevention of concentration of economic power rather than competition in markets. Cartels were not perceived as market hindrance to competitive markets and as expected the number of cartel cases were limited (Bhatacharjee and De, 2005).[12] Continuation of the MRTP regulatory framework ten years post economic liberalization revealed the limitation of an extant market regulator. The requirements of a modern competition law became imminent with cartels viewed as pernicious horizontal agreements and their impact on AAEC.

The softer conditions (Section 2(b)) for defining a cartel saw CCI inclined to a quasi per se approach than the pure per se approach permissible under the law. The approach was rebuttable as the phrase "*shall be presumed to have an appreciable adverse effect on competition*" connotes.

Reference to determining whether any agreement results in AAEC is listed in Section 19(3). Section 19(3) lists 3 indicators of benefits which include: (i) accrual of benefits to consumers; (ii) improvements in production or production in distribution of goods and (iii) promotion of technical, scientific and economic developments of means of production.[13] Consumer harm is not defined. The presumption is that the negative conditions lead to consumer harm. They are (i) creation of barriers to new (sic emphasis added) entrants in the market; (ii) driving existing competitors out of the market; and (iii) foreclosure of competition by hindering entry into the market.[14] Section 19(3) made the approach to assessing cartels, on the basis of effects or a quasi per se approach. Inclusion of the condition 'benefits to consumers' was seen as a contradiction to the concept that all cartels are pernicious was discussed in the Commission. Some of the officers argued that Section 19(3) was applicable only to vertical arrangements. The view was not endorsed by the Commission. COVID-19 advisories issued by CCI in the case of mergers and acquisitions and clearances does send signals of a wider perspective on cartels (Gouri, 2020).[15]

Amendments proposed to the Competition Act have suggested at looking at cartels from the buyers side and not restrict to sellers alone. Monopsony or oligopsony of cartels are as pernicious as monopolistic or oligopolistic structures.

1.1.1 Criterion for Defining Cartel

The first criteria under the Competition Act and perhaps the only criteria under the law for establishing a cartel is in finding proof of an arrangement in terms of sharing sensitive information on pricing, quantity produced and sold, market sharing, bid pricing and bid rigging. In a recent decision, the NCLAT (National Council Law Appellate Tribunal) reversed the tradition of going by unwritten or informal agreements and ruled that agreements have to be written as proof of cartels.[16] The decision is thought provoking. In highly competitive conditions, relying on circumstantial evidence or stimulation of adopted business strategies have an element of doubt. Whether monopolistic structures are created by cartels or veer toward monopolistic structures as in platform markets, the determinant of cartelization is a written agreement. Other arrangements are flexible business arrangement to meet competition in which case the defining criteria shifts to 'consumer harm'.

Investigations to unearth the required circumstantial evidence are a painstaking job that CCI's investigation wing undertakes. Data on price changes, quantity and capacity utilization are collected as the supporting evidence. The second criteria relates to the robustness of evidence as proof of cartel presence in market operations. As is to be expected, robustness of data is the refrain often used by the opposite parties. In antitrust analysis, while appropriate data is important and essential an overload of data can be a worry. I place greater weightage on counterfactuals. Parameters of cartel formation, for example of price parallelism, could be reflective of conditions of competitive markets in fact, super competitive markets. It is here counterfactuals are important. The rapid pace in which prices of consumer goods (FMCG) of competitors respond in tandem is a call for the CCI to make to associate cartels with price parallelism especially when there are no visible entry barriers. Management experts refer to 'myopia' in markets when competitors follow the dominant player.

The third criteria that is gaining importance is the need to define the relevant market of cartel operation. Based on the recommendations of the Raghavan Committee Report, defining the relevant market was not considered necessary. In the European Commission, since no distinction was made between horizontal and vertical agreements definition of a relevant market was not considered important. In the US under Section 1 of the Sherman Act, the per se approach to cartels does not require defining the market.[17] Sieving a cartel to a specific product market "*comprising all products or services which are regarded as interchangeable or substitutable by the consumer by reason of characteristics of the product or service, their prices and intended use*" is debatable. In the judgment on underground sea cables, the European Court of Justice pronounced that the Commission has to prove the presence or existence of a cartel with respect to a particular product.[18] Some manufacturers produce a range of products while others may restrict to single or dual product base. Should cartel be of the enterprises and persons acting in cohesion or in the market of the cartelized product are debates which as we shall see later affects the penalty to be levied related as it is to turnover of the product.

CCI did a study for ICN on the use and efficacy of screens for identifying potential cases for further investigation on the presence of cartels. There can be several types of screens economic, statistical or behavioral "*in order to identify the existence of any anti-competitive behaviour to be established. Using data points such as prices, production details, bids, market shares etc., screens serve to identify patterns.*" The Office of Fair Trading

(OFT) UK uses screens. Screens are academic and useful in econometric studies for predicting cartel formation. CCI had come out with a study on screen tests that cover both structural and demand data. The intent is to come out with data-based screen tests using AI as have several competition authorities.[19] As scanners, the Commissions' deployment in markets traditionally prone to cartels as in standardized products with relatively inelastic demand such as cement, or in acquisition of small firms with new patents by large firms (Gouri, 2020).

Screen tests would require a complete redesign for establishing cartels under algorithmic pricing. In digital markets where price responses for competing products are instantaneous referred to algorithmic price collusion, these prices are without human intervention earning the rubric Robo-selling (Mehra, 2009) and are without written agreements.[20] CCI has been examining contracts of sellers on a dominant platform market as unfair practices of dominance and not of the presence of cartels. Algorithmic collusion that was referred to in Chapter 1 awaits CCI's understanding of cartels on platforms. Encrypted messages on WhatsApp are perceived by CCI as another challenge for busting cartels.

The Commission is also confronted in defining *appreciable* in assessing the AAEC of a cartel presence. The identified abuses of market power listed in Section 3(3) refer to outcomes resulting in price parallelism; controls; production; distribution; technical development; market sharing in terms of source of production or geographically; and bid rigging on the touchstone of AAEC. Appreciable remains undefined.

1.1.2 Information, Penalties and Cartels

Competition authorities rely heavily on insider information for tracking cartels. Knowledge of the presence of cartels and its operations in a sector depend on insider information. Measures adopted by competition authorities are: (i) leniency measures and (ii) private antitrust action. Leniency measures lower the penalty applicable to a firm in case of insider information.

Penalties the deterrence mechanisms of antitrust are harsh in the Indian competition law. Section 27 has both monetary and non-monetary components. The penalty can rise up to 10 ten percent of the average turnover for the last three preceding financial years. Alternatively, in the case of any agreement entered into by a cartel *the Commission can impose upon each producer, seller, distributor, trader or serve provider included in that cartel, a penalty of up to three times of its profits for each year of the continuance of such agreement.* The amount to be levied as penalty is the decision of the Commission based on the damage caused to competition and consumers. Turnover initially was defined as the firms' total turnover later modified to the turnover of the relevant product in which a cartel was known to operate. This would therefore be restricting cartels to a specific product and not to the entire enterprise would require defining the relevant market.

Penalties are also levied on individual directors and chief executive of companies held responsible for contravention of the Act in keeping with the responsibilities of Directors on the Board of Companies under the Companies Act. The Act under Section 32 empowers the Commission to take action against foreign cartels provided '*Acts taking place outside India but having an effect on competition in India*' (Gouri and Kalyani, 2020).[21]

i. *Lesser Penalty*

'The Competition Commission of India (Lesser Penalty) Regulations, 2009' was introduced to incentivize insider information. An amendment was issued on 22 August 2017 to the Leniency Regulations which supplements Section 46 of the Act[22] The amendments set out the statutory provision for grant of leniency in matters involving cartels and enables parties to 'blow the whistle' on cartel arrangements and avail up to 100% reduction in penalties. The costs of cheating on a employer by an employee can be very high and could lead to loss of job. The modified regulations to Leniency by CCI have been expansive as compared to the earlier regulation.[23] The modifications to provide benefit to individuals from leniency have removed the limitation on number of markers. A marker is a ranking given by CCI to those who can claim leniency in terms of lesser penalty. The ranking or markers were initially limited to 2. Confidentiality of information in the leniency application would be maintained or what CCI has named as the 'Confidentiality Ring'[24] The information considered for leniency is to be limited to India. The new confidentiality regulations in the offing have suggested developing a Confidentiality Ring

Leniency is however no assurance that CCI will not examine the presence of anti-competitive practices. In the case of Schaeffler, National Engineering Industries and Tata Steel while granting leniency the Commission noted that during the period 2009–2011 these companies had engaged in discussions on pricing strategies in the supply of automobile parts to Maruti and Bajaj automobile firms. It was a clear sign of cartelization. The case was discussed and decided that cartelization must be noted and reprimanded. The investigation was initiated by the CCI based on the leniency application filed by Schaeffler disclosing the existence of the cartel. No penalty was imposed. Modifications to the leniency regulations was post this case.

In India, the large presence of government departments and public sector undertakings (PSU) bid rigging and collusive bidding in the procurement of public goods and services and those related to purchases by state owned enterprises (SOEs) cases were initiated by CCI on information provided by senior management in these enterprises. A whistle blower from a PSU poses less risk to career options and can help mitigate the scrutiny from Central Vigilance Commission (CVC) or the Central Bureau of Investigation (CBI). There is really no case of bravado for whistle blowing in the public sector unlike in the private sector and the issue of lesser penalty does not arise. It is not surprising that in the case of bidding and auctions of private sector procurement, the cases were adjudged by CCI on the basis of abuse of dominance.

ii. *Private Antitrust Action*

Several countries have also permitted private antitrust action by which private parties can sue suppliers. Private action has been a major deterrent to cartels in advanced countries and are yet to make an entry in India. Referred to actions taken by purchasers on suppliers, private antitrust action was introduced in the US as a supplementary measure. Under this legislation, treble damages can be claimed in a court.[25] Most scholars are skeptical of private antitrust action. It is difficult to imagine a David purchaser pursuing cartel action against a Goliath seller by investing in detecting. The gains have to be substantial as the work is heavily data based..[26]

An important aspect of the softer approach to agreements as arrangements or understanding is in the assessment of information provided by 'whistle blowers' and on business strategies. Questions that need to be examined is on the value of information that is accessed and on circumstantial evidence to comprehend the business strategies of monopolistic structures that cartels create. How relevant is the information that is shared by competitors? Can firms in an industry ignore a pricing strategy followed by a large player whether the action is of price cutting or raising of prices? Should it be judged as cartel or as business strategy? Are consumers harmed? These are difficult questions to answer but they need to be posed. In the cases selected, I shall look at the decision with regard to (a) nature of agreement; (b) nature of circumstantial evidence available from DG's investigation, "whistle blower" and other sources; (c) possible business models; and (d) consumer harm. There has been criticism on the lack of consistency and predictability of CCI in assessment of information on cartelization. In the next section, a few high-profile cartel cases will be examined by posing the question whether competitive conditions were mistaken for cartelization and of resetting standards.

Economics of cartels have come a long way from endorsing agreements and arrangements to modern business networks and information flows.[27] In India, we still go by tracking cartels on the basis of cases filed defined as 'complaint procedure or leniency program' (Bos, 2009).[28] Merger clearances have emphasized 'non-compete' clauses but from the perspective of unilateral conduct and not on the possibility of cartel structures. Recent regulations on Mergers (Green Regulation) do have the potential to create cartels during COVID-19 enthusiasm. A proactive mechanism for detecting cartels was suggested such as tracking prices, and changes in quantities in products that display tendencies for cartel formation. The advice was again reiterated in a recent article on mergers in the pharmaceutical sector and health (COVID-19)-related equipment (Gouri, 2020).[29]

1.2 Case Analysis-Ex Post

The following cases have been selected:

Cement Cartel—The Classic textbook example;
Cartels in Association—Drugs and Trade Association;
Cartel Unacknowledged—The Maghribi Traders of the Onion Market;
Cartel Dilemma in Public procurement

Several approaches have been adopted by CCI for finding cartels: on the basis of cases submitted under leniency approach, by concerned public authorities; suo moto on the basis of newspaper reports and earlier cases of MRTP. The strength of evidence varies among the cases even in leniency cases. DG Investigation vested with the powers under Sections. 240 and 240-A of the Companies Act applicable to the Commission vide Section 41 of the Act is critical. Data is also sought from the parties themselves on specific issues and sometimes reference is made to consultancy firms specializing in economic data analysis. Studies are assigned to research firms and consultancy firms to build the data archives. All cases analyzed in this section refer to ex-post cases where reference is to Section 3(3).

(i) Cement Cartel–the Classic textbook example[30]

Cartels are expected in cement sector and refer to it as the textbook example of competition economics on account of three features. They are (i) homogenous nature of the product; (ii) relatively inelastic demand; and (iii) relatively small number of firms i.e., oligopolistic market structures. It raises the pertinent question how is cheating to be prevented in a relatively homogenous product market. Some players can benefit by raising or lowering their prices and booking profits. This depends on the demand curve and capacity constraints. If the demand curve facing a firm is horizontal and there are no capacity constraints, no firm has the market power to raise or lower capacity and prices to book more profits. To recollect from Chapter 2, the demand curve each firm faces will be horizontal P = AR = MR. Raising prices (P > MC), profits do not get maximized for the unsold quantity. If, however, the firms decide to form a cartel, the firms jointly will face a downward-sloping demand curve like a monopolist and choose their combined output where combined marginal revenue equals marginal cost as given in Fig. 1 (IICA Module 4). The Figure 1 illustrates a scenario when firms join to form a cartel.
The market was defined as oligopolistic (CCI, Case 29 0f 2012) facilitating cartelization. Allegations of limiting and restricting the production of cement and of price fixation by the top 11 companies was filed by the Builders Association of India (BAI). Reference was to two major groups: the Holcim group and the Jaiprakash group, suggesting cartelization in the cement market despite the number of cement firms were 49. The

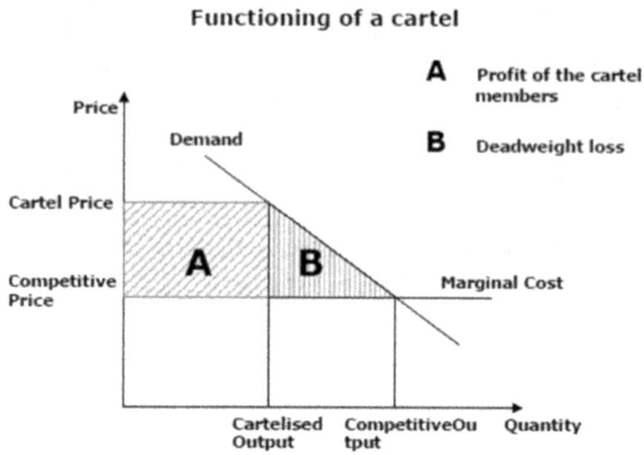

Fig. 1 Basic Pricing of Oligopolist

period of the cartel (2009–2011) saw rise in prices of cement unlike the pre-2009 period. Simultaneously, there was expansion in capacity but with capacity unutilized. The build-up in capacity observed during this period suggests a business strategy of raising prices and then ramping up capacity and needed exploring. An unusual feature of the case was the platform of Cement Manufacturing Association of India (CMA) for cement firms to meet on a regular basis.

The cement cartel case attracted the highest penalty (Rs.6316.593 crs). The penalty was for the 11 cement companies that formed the cartel. The penalty was taken as 0.5% of the net profits for the years 2009–2010 and 2010–2011. As per the Act, the Commission can either take net profits or turnover as adumbrated earlier. The decision to levy 0.5% critics points to the amount as not sufficiently strong in the face of large amounts of profits earned by the cartel. The Commission held the view that a high penalty can be self-defeating in the face of the criticality of the construction industry for an expanding economy. CMA was however fined 10% of total receipts (gross turnover) for the two years which was Rs. 0.73 crs.

The verdict was disputed at the Tribunal on grounds that CCI had not followed due procedures in terms of natural justice in examining all the evidence and data submitted.[31] The Tribunal remitted the case back to CCI. Reexamination of evidence confirmed the presence of a cartel among the cement manufacturers. The case at present is in the Supreme

Court. I shall refer where required to the Orders on the basis of the dates of the Order. The first Order was issued on 26.06.2012. The second Order was issued on 31.08.2017.

1.2.1 Analysis of the Decision

The key features of the case of significance to antitrust analysis are:

(a) Defining 'agreement'
(b) Large number of firms with multiple cement units
(c) CMA the platform for meeting and interactions
(d) Price parallelism, dispatch parallelism, supply restriction
(a) Defining "agreement"

As the first Order of cartelization, the Commission observes that the definition of the term 'agreement' "*is an inclusive definition in the Act. It inter-alia includes any arrangement, understanding or action in concert irrespective of whether it is written/ formal or otherwise or intended to be legally enforceable.*" As per the Act, the requirement of a written agreement is not explicitly stated. The Commission opined that it would be naive to expect cartels like mafias to enter into written agreements that can easily be used by rivals or informants. The phrase used was '*circumstantial evidence*' placing emphasis instead on plus factors of price parallelism and sales parallelism. (Order, 26.06.2012 Para. 6.5.3,p152). The second Order (31.08.2017) defines an agreement as existing when there is "*preponderance of probabilities*". The presence of cartel is on the basis of deduction of facts and outcomes. The Commission notes that "*In most cases, the existence of an anti-competitive practice or agreement must be inferred from a number of co-incidences and indicia which, taken together, may, in the absence of any other plausible explanation, constitute evidence of the existence of an anti-competitive agreement*". (para....) The law does not bar the use of circumstantial evidence.

Both definitions emphasize the soft approach inherent in the definition provided in the Act laying stress instead on the economic parameter of cartels that of price parallelism. Reference was drawn to the OECD paper on 'Prosecuting Cartels without Direct Evidence of Agreement' (February 2006) that the law does not make a distinction between written and verbal agreements as proof of cartel. This was consistent with the approach taken in earlier cases of cartelization by CCI in Neeraj Malhotra vs Deutsche Post Bank and others and Flat Glass manufacturers.

(b) Large number of firms with multiple cement units
The number of cement units and cement companies as mentioned are around 49. Cartels tend to arise in markets where there are few firms and each firm has a significant share of the market.[32] There were two major groups at the time of investigation. Holcim group (ACC, Ambuja, and Ultractech) then controlling 39 to 40% of the market and the other category of Jaiprakash Industries, India Cements, Shree Cements and Madras Cements and 18 other players took up 50% of the market with the rest consisting of medium and small cement firms. In the subsequent periods, cross-holdings among firms saw emergence of different groupings through mergers and acquisition. Expansion of several small units further modified the scenario. At the end of the investigation, several small units had expanded as demand for cement grew exponentially with the construction industry responding to higher growth rates of GDP.[33] By and large, the big players have been consistently large players. BAI had alleged both 'abuse of dominance' (Section 4) and cartelization (Section 3—3(1),(2) (3) and Section 19(3)). The cement market is divided into 5 zones, and the big players operate in all the zones. DG investigation showed that no firm has the individual capacity to control the market in any one zone. There is no concept of "collective dominance" or "joint dominance" in the Act. The market structure does not show any firm being dominant, and the application of Section 4 was ruled out.

(c) CMA—the platform
The role of the Cement Manufacturing Association of India (CMA) as a platform for the large players to meet, decide on prices, capacity and mechanism of collusion, provides a dimension of cartel facilitation hitherto not highlighted in antitrust literature. BAI in their allegation included CMA so the total number of opposite parties was 12. CMA regular meeting enabled members to meet frequently. A trade body corporate CMA was established to provide data to the government on cement prices to facilitate data inputs for the plans and industrial policies of the government. Under Section 3(1), CMA will not qualify as a partner in '*crime*' unless there are agreements or arrangements with the cement firms but as

an Association it was an 'umbrella' for all cement companies named in the complaint to CCI by BAI. Investigations revealed that CMA was the platform used by the cement companies to interact with each other. Meetings hosted by CMA in various cities attended by cement companies were followed by rise in prices. To the Commission, it was hardly a coincidence. To expect fellow competitors to meet regularly to discuss the weather has never found acceptance in antitrust analysis. The minutes of meetings of CMA collected by DG showed that prices and factors that affect cost including taxes and duties were discussed.[34]

The Commission notes that the CMA was not just a platform. It was an active participant by way of providing reports and analysis of price movements, capacity availability and utilization sent to the government with its members.[35] According to Section 3(3) "*any decision taken by any 'association of enterprises' engaged in identical or similar trade of goods or provision of services which are engaged in the specified activities described therein is presumed to have an appreciable adverse effect on competition within India*" (para 190, p. 101).

(d) Price Parallelism

Circumstantial evidence combined with discussions with dealers indicated that the major cement players in each zone set the price resulting in price parallelism. Price parallelism can also be indicative of coordinated pricing in oligopolistic market structures as argued by the cement companies. The Commissions analysis of price parallelism indicating of the presence of cartel was affirmed form the data collected at different time periods of the 11 cement companies in the five zones. Coefficient correlation was calculated of the prices for each of the States.[36] The matrix tables show a close positive association among the select cement companies. Price parallelism refers to the direction of change in prices and not the response in terms of absolute amounts that is calculated by using regression analysis. The results of the coefficient correlations put a number on the data and the relationship between companies. The same data when plotted on a graph provided a visual presentation of price parallelism.

The decision of CCI went on traditional lines. First, the presumption of an arrangement on the CMA platform. Second, evidence of price rise and capacity restrictions weighed in favor of the presence of cartelization. The Commission had sent out a warning by levying penalty. Cartels get broken and cartels keep re-forming.

1.2.2 Game Theoretic Model and Trigger Mechanisms[37]

Price parallelism which is used as the textbook indicator of cartel raises a fundamental question of business strategy pointed out by several of the parties. The contention that in an oligopolistic market structure the firms form cartels to make decisions on output and price, there always exists a trigger that breaks up a cartel. For the competition authorities, the issue is whether to let the trigger automatically set in or create conditions that releases the trigger.

A simple illustration is shown below to explain trigger forces. The model is of a oligopolistic market. Distinction is drawn when each firm is oligopolistic and when firms form a cartel to mimic a monopolist. In the former case as shown in Fig. 1, the demand curve is downward-sloping as it is a case of monopolistic or oligopolist competition and no firm individually has the ability to influence price by either raising or lowering capacity. The demand curve in the figure is a joint demand curve.

The primary question to be asked is what is the incentive for cartel members to cheat as P > MC. Some members of a cartel can charge a lower price but higher than MC and take a larger share of the market. In the Bertrand price competition model, each firm (assuming the cartel is a duopoly) can charge a lower price resulting in both firms charging a lower price.

Nash Equilibrium

		Firm A	
		High price	Low Price
Firm B	High Price	10,10	0,20
	Low Price	20,0	5,5

The illustrative 2 × 2 Nash model is shown above with reference to a simple single game. Firm A could choose to price low-earning profits of 20 leaving no option for earning profits for Firm B but to exit or alternatively Firm B charges a low-price making profits of 20 forcing Firm A to exit. If demand remains unmet, both firms could charge a higher price with profits of (10,10) which is possible if the two firms collude and form a cartel. Under competitive conditions, one of the firms prefers to low prices and earn more profits in all likelihood to be followed by the other firm in cutting prices and earning lower profits as shown in the lower right quadrant which typifies firms competing aggressively. The Nash equilibrium is a non-collusive equilibrium where P > MC and not of perfect competition where P = MC. Both the upper left quadrant and the lower right quadrant display price parallelism although cartel relates to the upper quadrant. In observing price parallelism, the authorities have to distinguish between the two quadrants.

The Nash equilibrium proceeds on the assumption that both firms are not capacity constrained. Lowering prices and meeting demand suggests that each firm is able to meet the demand with its given capacity. Cheating from the cartel frame occurs when there are capacity constraints. Who sets the price and who has unused capacity is illustrated with the two simple games played?

> Game 1: In a cartel, Firm A and Firm B agree to lower price in unison. If Firm A has reached full capacity and there is unmet demand and if Firm B has unutilized capacity, then Firm B can raise prices and make profits by breaking the cartel.
> Game 2: If Firm A lowers prices and restricts capacity, then Firm B has no option but to comply and is left holding larger stocks. Raising prices in this situation would lead to further additions to stocks and inventories, an expensive propositions.[38]

The trigger for the cartel to break is defined by the manufacturing capacity of each firm.

To sustain the cartel, a commonly used solution is for the firms to divide the market according to capacities of each firm proportional to their production capacity. This was documented by DG where the two major groups had shared the market among themselves. Further, expansion plans were either under implementation or on the anvil. The cement manufacturers argued before CCI that the industry was in an expansionary mode which is not so in a cartelized industry. Reference was made to mini cement plants expanding to grow into mid-size plants enhancing production capacity and of additional plants established by large firms again adding to capacity. The sector has seen several mergers and acquisitions and entry of foreign firms. These developments indicate there are no obvious barriers to entry. The formation of cartel among cement manufacturers and the sustainability of the cartels merely on the basis of prevailing price parallelism need to be considered. This was countered by the DG who mapped every increase in price with production levels and capacity utilization. He noted that in the period 2010–11, a period of high prices' average capacity utilization came down to 73 from 83% in the previous year. Dispatches showed similar trends. Exercises were carried out of price, production and capacity utilization with growth rate of GDP and specifically of the construction industry. Statements recorded of companies and dealers pointed toward coordinated pricing (para 271, p. 158).

Based on DG's investigation and pointers of price parallelism and capacity restrictions, CCI's conclusion was that the major cement manufacturers had formed a cartel. The clinching issue was the use of CMA as a meeting platform. Ever meeting was followed by a rise in cement prices.

Reverting to the Nash equilibrium, the non-collusive equilibrium or competitive equilibrium is with profits settling at 5:5 as against a cartel cooperating scenario with collusive pricing profits which are higher at 10:10; the criteria is to observe prices and profits of cement companies. Data over a longer period of time is required as cartels are unstable. They break and get formed again. For the competition authorities, the difficult decision of whether to break the cartel or let market forces operate does not arise this despite the Nash non-collusive equilibrium. Cartels restrict competition and need to be broken perhaps a bit myopic in advanced market economies but not so in young competition regimes such as India who are facilitating market dynamics. Intervention by the competition authority is important only to send a signal that cartels are anti-competitive. Shastitko (2020) aptly refers to selection of high-profile cases by enforcement authorities as 'reputation-maximizing' objective noticeable in BRICS.[39] Clearly, penalties do not distract a cartel from re-forming to emerge again. The penalty levied by CCI was a detractor and not the trigger. Fresh allegations of price co-ordination and collaborating levels of cement supply have seen CCI-conduct dawn raids on the offices of CMA and of top cement companies which include Ultra Tech Cement, Shree Cement, Ambuja Cement, ACC, Dalmia Cement and Rockstrong Cement (Indian Express, 11th Dec. 2020)[40] For the competition authority, the main issue is to design the appropriate trigger to break the cartel.

What could be the trigger? It could be a sudden growth in demand on account of mass housing schemes; a gap as new capacity has to still be ramped up while old plants function at lower capacity; or restrictions on inter-state movement of cement. These triggers are not part of competition policy but of larger government policy. However, in Section 21-A the Commission can make reference to the appropriate statutory Authority the Government (Gouri, 2019).[41] The advice based on its investigation and analysis of the evidence gathered the Commission can design an appropriate trigger policy for Government to consider and implement. What trigger should CCI advise in the case of cartel remains an unexplored area.

1.2.3 *Resetting Standards*

What standards need to be reset considering that the first cement decision was remitted back to the Commission and with second Order reiterating the first decision is being challenged in the Supreme Court.

The first standard that has to be reset is to find evidence of written agreements. The Act would require modification. Cartels keep forming, and as the game theoretic model indicates, the presence of unutilized capacity and scope for raising prices for higher level of profits persuade a break out. With alert competition authorities, the scope for cartels existence in terms of years gets shortened.[42]

The second standard is data monitoring of prices, quantities and capacity utilization. The Bertrand model shows that price parallelism is weak as evidence of cartels unless backed by a written agreement. The correlation employed by DG was as expected. It gave no indication of causation.

The third standard is to develop action points that set the trigger without direct intervention.

(ii) Association of Druggist and Chemists—Cartel or Vertical Arrangements

There have been several cases of trade associations and their violation of competitive conditions examined by CCI.[43] These include those in the entertainment industry, transport sector, road sector and pharma sector.

Trade unions were encouraged during the socialist phase of industrialization as an assertion of political and labor power. Their assertion of power on pricing, market restrictions and production curtailments were noticed in some of the sectors restricting the fair play of markets resulting in consumer harm. In fact, these anti-competitive activities formed part of the Memorandum of Understanding and Minutes of Associations agreed by members of the Association as noted in the Chemists and Druggists Association. Several cases filed with CCI raised concerns of the hold of the Druggist Association on vendors and chemists. The case study selected the Chemists and Druggists Association as unusual for several reasons.

The cartel is indeed peculiar. Spawned out of an ineffective drug regulator, the original objective of the Associations was to bring some order in the retail business of chemists with the intent to control the sale of spurious drugs. The Mashelkar Committee[44] tasked with the problem of controlling the increasing production and trade in spurious drugs had advocated setting up trade associations in the wholesale and retail trade of drugs. One of the recommendations of the Committee was for pharma Trade Associations to take up a proactive active role by mandating membership of the Association of all chemists and druggists. Sale of any drug only to be against a cash/credit memo was the other major suggestion of the Committee for reducing the sale of spurious drugs. The opposite parties in their defense of trade associations raised this point.[45] The strength of the Associations to a large extent arose from government support. Based on its recommendations, trade associations made an entry into the drug and pharmaceutical sector. Started as an institution to control trade in spurious drugs, trade association activities eventually lead to market distortions creating entry barriers leading to market distortions.

Government of India initiated the process of creating wholesale and retail trade association as appropriate quasi-regulatory institutions for ensuring what was perceived as a situation of 'information asymmetry' in the pharma industry. The Committee (Mahshelkar)had suggested trade associations as a way of streamlining the pharma sector in India from exploitative pricing policies of private enterprises. A well-intentioned, welfare-oriented public policy over the years turned the tide to a peculiar situation of '*market capture by the regulator*'.[46]

The Chemists and Druggists Association is an unusual cartel. Firstly, it was not a cartel to hoard drugs or to deal with sale of drugs in the black market. It was a cartel of Associations controlling entry and of price fixation falling within the ambit of CCI. The initial cases were filed under Section 3(3)(b) i.e.,

> directly or indirectly determines purchase or sale prices; limits or controls production, supply, markets ,technical development, investment or provision of services.

Resulting in AAEC in violation of Section 3(3)(a) in the category of horizontal agreements Section 3(1) viz. cartels. Later decisions of CCI on chemists and druggists associations considered the activities of Chemists and Druggists Associations as violating Section 3(4). Sharing of information on prices, stocks and other commercial information is a concerted manner in violation of Sections 3 (4) of the Act. The arrangements were classified as vertical arrangements and not as cartels.

Secondly, the drug and pharma sector is a web of trade associations. Apart from AIOCD drug manufacturers and their associations, there is the Organization of Pharmaceutical Producers of India ("OPPI") and the Indian Drugs Manufacturers' Association ("IDMA"). The All India Organization of Chemists and Druggist (AIOCD) is the *'Custodian'* to the wholesale and retail sale of drugs. It is the apex association with state-level associations. The Association was a hierarchical pyramid structure with the All India Organization of Chemists and Druggists (AIOCD) at the helm and branches of Chemist and Druggists Associations in each state.

Thirdly, all chemists and druggists are required to be members of the Association before permission is granted to them to sell drugs. AIOCD fixed trade margins at 20% for wholesale trade and 10% for retail trade. No discounts permitted. The sale price as per instructions of the AIOCD was to be at the Market Retail Price (MRP) inclusive of margins. New entrants to the pharma retail trade had to be members of the Chemists and Druggists Association hence forth Association in each state and agree to the rules set out by the association.

This hierarchical umbrella structure of local retail associations followed by state and then topped by the All India Wholesale Association in the drugs and pharma sector displayed a well-oiled retail trading mechanism that asserted control over entry of stockist and chemist on the grant of No objection Certificate 'NoC' from the respective associations. The NoC was for a consideration. There were no agreements between the entrants and the association. The retail chemists and druggists associations were also required to print Product Availability Information ('PAI') and Stock Availability Information ('SAI') which were then sold to small local distributors for the purpose of promotion of drugs.

Conceptualized as a regulatory mechanism surprisingly to regulate a competitive market structure, the associations created a hierarchic structure which caused the industry to degenerate to a monopolistic structure.

Fourthly, the number of firms manufacturing drugs in India is large ranging from small-scale to- large-scale firms. In terms of numbers, it is a very competitive market. The manufacturers predominantly manufacture generic drugs or under license produce patented drugs (generic drugs).[47] Generic drugs compete on basic active ingredients (API) that only differ in the company name. Branded generic drugs compete on the brand name and price their products on the brand name. These are patent-expired drugs but market on the brand name to charge monopolistic prices. The industry's diversity, the criticality of the industry combined with ignorance of public on drug pricing, drug availability and drug efficacy saw emergence of horizontal and vertical agreements that strengthened monopolistic pricing. Some of them as mentioned are members of OPPI and IDMA with links to AIOCD. The government regulates prices and quality but clearly the AIOCD called the strings.[48]

Against the background of the poor public health systems in India, control over drug prices, over discounts and control of entry by the druggists and chemists associations carry ethical overtones.[49] The orderly sale of drugs raises the basic contradiction whether consumers are harmed by the cartel approach of uniform drug prices with no discounts as against the gains to consumers from freeing wholesale and retail trade to competitive forces with free entry and exit. Control over trade in spurious drugs is of the drug regulator the drug controller. The jurisdictional boundaries of the competition regulator and the drug regulator were mixed.

Section 3 (1)(2) and (3) permits a 'per se' decision rebuttable by the parties. On the other hand, Section 3(4) points to the importance of economic analysis for balancing the positive and negative effects on consumers of vertical arrangements or agreements. Different mechanisms of deterrence were effected by CCI in penalizing and constraining the anti-competitive practices of trade associations. The interventions of CCI ranged from the traditional fines, to public notices and to imposing behavioral remedy of self-realization by conducting advocacy courses.

Office bearers of the Association were also penalized and at higher rates of 10% compared to 7% on the associations.[50] Drug manufacturers' associations OPPI and IDMA were not part of the investigations of CCI, and no penalty was levied on then.

1.2.4 History of CCI and the Association(s)

The first set of cases are Peevear Medical and Chemists v Kerala Drug Association et al. in 2011; Sandhya Drugs and Chemists and Assam Drug Dealers Association et al. in 2011; Arora Medical Hall and Ferozepur Druggists Association et al. in 2012 Varca Chemists and Ors. Vs. Chemists and Druggists Association, Goa with several cases in subsequent years. Prior to CCI, several cases of unfair trade practices were filed with MRTP. In fact, one case of Vedanta Bio Science was disposed recently in 2019. Allegations point to the contravention of Section 3(1)(2)(3) by associations relating to instructions on trade margins, pricing and discounts. Later charges extend to include Section 3(4).

CCIs experience with Chemists and Druggists Association of more than 20 cases (there has been clubbing of cases) extended to the healthcare sector are over 52 cases prompting CCI to come out with a policy note on the healthcare sector (CCI, Policy Note 2018). Further the CCI's Compliance Manual underscores the need to be alert to Trade Associations forming cartels and in creating entry barriers.[51]

These cartel cases were adjudged entirely on circumstantial evidence. The anti-competitive arrangements between trade associations, retails, wholesaler and naturally the manufacturers were culled from the letters and interviews conducted by DG which were used as evidence of the prevalence, and the Commission decisions were 'per se' as the evidence was direct and the need for economics analysis was not considered as required.[52]

In the last Order, the Commission notes that Bengal Chemists and Druggists did not fully heed the warning given by the first Order of the Commission in 2013. The Order instead preferred to adopt the approach of changing perceptions in highlighting to Bengal Chemists and Druggists the importance of competition relegating to trade associations to undertake advocacy. Advocacy and persuasion rather than the earlier approach of fines was preferred. CCI has adopted the approach of advocacy as a better mechanism to making markets work.

An interesting inclusion can be seen in the later Orders by bringing into the fold of anti-competitive activities Section 3(4) where cartels created by trade associations extend in a vertical chain from manufacturers to wholesale to retail trade and chemists. The assumption is that trade associations operate on the same level and the agreements pertained to horizontal agreements. Agreements along the vertical chain are equally responsible for restricting competition by supplying stocks to only those permitted by the association and to their members. Section 3(4) is not a per se clause that needs to be rebutted and will be only in contravention of sub-Section (1) "*if such agreement causes or is likely to cause an AAEC on competition*". That was not spelt out in the Order. Restrictions and control on the downstream retail trade can have different outcomes that are debatable. Firstly and most important, it can strengthen the monopolistic structure upstream. Secondly, territories of operation get marked and again impact on competition. The assumption is that trade associations operate on the same level and the agreements pertained to horizontal agreements. Lastly, consumers may benefit from streamlining the distribution trade.

Each retail chemist is required by law to have a qualified pharmacist. And in any case, the NOC requirement limited the number of wholesalers, not retailers. The usual arguments in favor of restrictions on downstream competition are therefore inapplicable to drug distribution. On the other hand, reducing intra-brand competition by limiting the number of distributors in a territory can soften inter-brand competition and increase both upstream and downstream profits at the cost of consumers and social welfare.[53] And maintaining downstream prices can facilitate upstream collusion: transparency and stability of retail margins ensure that changes in retail costs are not automatically transmitted into prices, which could otherwise be misinterpreted by other upstream firms as a deviation from a collusive arrangement, thereby triggering a price war. The CCI did not go into any of these issues.

A workshop was organized on *Making Markets Work for Affordable Healthcare*' (CCI, policy note 2018) of all stakeholders. The policy note laid emphasis on 'information asymmetry' as the basis of anti-competitive practices resulting in:

1. "*Unreasonably high trade margins*" due to drug companies and trade associations.
2. 'Conventional generic-induced price competition limited and restricted by a market dominated by branded generics' in turn defining quality perception

3. ***Vertical arrangements in healthcare services*** with incentive-based referral system tends to effect consumer choice.
4. Multiplicity of standards/regulators governing the pharmaceutical sector at the center and state level leading to inequality in implementation.

There is no finality to cartel cases. In a recent case, stockists of CIPLA attempted to gain an edge by complaining on non-availability of stocks, higher prices, etc. by the Bengal Chemists and Druggists Association. The complaint was dismissed. It was a commercial dispute and not a competition issue. CCI has to be on the alert more so in these COVID times where CCI has taken a bold step in introducing the Green Channel for clearances of mergers and acquisitions. The April 19 advisory has relaxed the presumption of appreciable adverse effect on competition ("AAEC") of concerted action in joint ventures in supply chains of health and essential commodities (Gouri, 2020).[54] There are caveats in the Ordinance to the possible emergence of vertical and horizontal linkages. The CCI is however upbeat on concerted actions to address the disruption caused "in supply chains including those of critical healthcare products and other essential commodities and services." It would do well to remember the chemists and druggists cartels.

An area of concern outside CCI's control regimen but remains under its gaze is vertical arrangements in referral-based systems that affect consumer choice. Branded generic drug companies market their product through private clinics and doctors. The consumer or patient is dependent on doctor's prescription and the choice of the doctor and not the consumers. The health system function is a trade-off between public health service, private provision of health facilities and insurance. As CCI policy note points out, the attempt is to the removal of information asymmetry. The Commission has made interesting attempts with public notices, fining of trade associations.

Trade associations are strong and to prove their anti-competitive structures require strong structural screens. The presence of strong trade associations spills over into bidding agreements where public procurement is concerned. The peculiarity of public procurement is a fall out of the large public sector enterprises in all major industries and sectors.

(iii) Cartel Unacknowledged–Maghribi Traders of the Onion Market;

Some trades have traditional filial links akin to the Maghribi traders whose networks are historically well known for coalition and collusion.[55] The mystique of cartels among merchants in how they occur and break has been the subject matter of economic historians, sociologists and organizational behavior apart from economics of competition. Grief in his study on Maghribi traders of the tenth and eleventh centuries (Grief, 1998)[56] provides insights into the smooth flow in trade on account of informal communication systems of social networks among merchants. Grief highlights punishment for defaulters in the network referred to as the grim trigger in the language of game theory. Fascinated by the study, I have titled the cartel of onion markets as Maghribi Traders of the Onion market. Trade traditionally in India has been caste-associated Marwaris, Baniyas who have knitted themselves as one class/caste. They have their own grim triggers that ostracize internal defection. Similarly from an unlikely study on cartels (Elinor Ostrom, 1990),[57] Ostrom's analysis on commons the enforcement of rules and regulation through collective action provides an alternative perspective on design of control mechanism. With the failure of the state-designed enforcer Agricultural Price Monitoring Commission (APMC) as a grim trigger in the cartel of traders in Ostrom's framework, local panchayats may have a greater stake in enforcing rules.

Merchant traders are prolific in specific commodities, usually a single commodity like spices, gold, onions and potatoes. They have their own code of honor, deal largely in cash with no bills of exchange. Information flows of market price and quantity desired within the network are not open to outsiders even the Authority. This description fits in with the merchant caste/class in India. In a caste-structured society like India, most of the traders belong to the same caste/class. Their equation with their clients often extend to lending activities too. One such case of cartel among traders we explore is of the onion market.[58] Trade in vegetables are transacted in formal market structures set up by the government under the Agricultural Produce Markets. In the local language, vegetable markets are known as mandis. The suffix 'formal' is sometimes attached to the APMC market as to distinguish from traditional markets or mandis.[59]

December 2010 saw an unusual rise in prices of onions peaking at Rs. 70/kg in the Delhi markets and of Rs.40/kg in other markets persisting for over two weeks. The possibility of speculative activity was suggested by several economists including the then chief economic advisor Kaushik Basu, (Economic Times, 06.01.2011)[60] prompting the Commission to constitute a suo moto enquiry in the onion market.

1.2.5 Structure of Onion Market

Price rises in vegetable markets are of short durations depending on the store life of the vegetable. In the case of onions, transactions are also of short duration with a storage life of three months. The crop is usually grown twice a year. the kharif and rabi seasons and sometimes in between the two seasons. Onion is basic to Indian food and consumed throughout the year. The operation of vegetable markets where markets get cleared in short time periods depends on the storage life of the vegetable. In the case of onion, it is usually about 2 months combined with the fact that different parts of India like different varieties of onion. Information flows of quantity and price remain within the strict boundaries of trader communities. There have been studies on onion prices and marketing of onions (Kulkarni, A.P. and Prema Basargekar [1997])[61] on the possibility of cartels or at least speculative activity.

On the basis of investigation, the Commission arrived at the conclusion that data examined revealed no unusual patterns in price and quantity movements for the period under review. The decline in supply of onions was preceded by unseasonal rains. Data used in investigation was from the Agriculture Produce Market Centres (APMC) web site, the official record of transactions in agricultural markets. Correlations were run on arrivals in the Azad Mandi (Delhi) and prevailing market prices. The correlations showed positive relationship between price increases and market arrivals of onions at the Azad mandi in Delhi moving in tandem with decreasing supplies. The presence of cartel among onion merchants remained unacknowledged.

With no material evidence of meetings or agreements between traders, the requirement of Section 3(3) of the Competition Act was not met (*Majority Order*, *Suo-moto Case No.01/2011*) and the case dismissed. Records at the auction platforms at Lasalgaon and Pimpalgaon the main onion markets of India and the books of traders or Arathiyas were examined. The extensive exercise revealed no discernible spike in prices or of speculative hoarding during the period under investigation. The DG on deputation from the Indian Revenue Service looked at income tax records to ascertain whether the income tax department in their tax investigations had come across any evidence of hoarding onions to control supplies and prices. Income tax records did not reveal hoarding of onion stock by traders. Given the preponderance of evidence pointing to normalcy the Commission closed the case.[62]

Cartels in the onion market that operate in short spikes is well known but unacknowledged as under the law a cartel without any agreement, formal or informal, and does not stand scrutiny as responsible for AAEC: "*No enterprise or association of enterprises or person association of persons shall enter into any agreement ..... that causes AAEC*" was the conclusion of the Majority Order.

The Economics Division came out with a separate order (*Minority Order, Suo-moto Case No.01/11*) stemming from discomfort of ignoring peculiar features of agricultural markets important for cartel analysis in these markets. The intent of the minority Order was to develop a framework for understanding the control of merchant traders in vegetable markets missing in the main Order.

1.2.6 Onion Markets

These markets display characteristics of competition in terms of large number of players and as asserted by the DG indicate presence of competitive markets. The limited information provided in DG's investigation, however, reveals that market share of traders tends to be concentrated with few trading families. For example, share of Sri Saibaba Trader in Lasalgaon market trades varied between 12 and 26% indicating domination by a few traders. Licensing of traders limits the number of traders with no significant new entrants. As with licensing in other sectors, there is cornering of licenses within families.

Doubts on the authenticity of APMC data was another concern raised in the minority order as all APMC data is fed by the traders themselves. As primary data for onion markets cartel investigation depends on field studies for reliable data, the Order points to data distortions of data provided by vested parties viz. traders and commission agents. The APMC data also gives no indication of transactions pre-auction between farmers and traders. Indebtedness of farmers to traders for loans is well documented.[63] Loans are given by traders against the collateral of the standing crop. Records of these loans are not maintained. Traders are in a position to exert downward pressure on the price of the crop prior to harvesting and definitely before the produce reaches the auction platform. The entire produce may not reach the auction market at all. The floor price at the auction may already be fixed.

The different scenarios of the onion market suggest a distorted market, but proof of cartel operation and of collusion between the traders based on social bonds of caste equations needs further field-level study of the markets. In this case, it was not lack of evidence but to expand the investigation and in acknowledging the possibility of cartelization in trades with filial links. To look for evidence in channels of information on cartels that are caste based modern forms of communication such as emails are inappropriate. Alternatively scrutiny of tax returns on trades that run on cash with no bills of exchange is also a futile exercise. These are efforts to meet requirements of establishing a cartel vide the legal requirement of '*evidence*' remains devoid of economic reasoning and analysis.

1.2.7 Auctions and Cartels in Onion Markets

Theoretically, auctioning is the least biased mechanism of arriving at the appropriate price to buyers and sellers provided there is no collusion among the buyers. The APMCs were established by governments to provide a level playing field for sellers the farmers and buyers the traders, with the auctioneer as the government agent. The process of bid rigging is not on the basis of tenders floated but of bidding for the produce brought to the market by the farmers. To suggest collusion of APMC and onion merchants in an open auction process where farmers are involved and aware of prices is not a foregone conclusion. It is at the most about the blunt instrument of government intervention and the APMC auction Collusion of auctioneer with the arthiyas ceases then to be a pure competition issue and more of corruption. The possibility of collusion among merchant traders is difficult to prove compelling me to keep returning to the decision of CCI. In a seminal paper by Meenakshi and Banerjee (2005) on bidding process in APMC, mandis paddy (parimal) in Harayana show that the win bid price depends on competition among the bidders viz the millers.[64] Their analysis based on field studies showed that as the number of bidders increased the win bid price was lower than when the bidders colluded. Meenakshi and Banerjee conclude that competition among bidders reduces the win price. Their findings affirm the well-accepted adverse effect of cartel operations on the bidding process. The onion cartel case is more complex. The assumption is that traders are linked to each other across the entire country as onions are consumed all over suggests that all mandis are linked. The APMC for onion sale is, however, only in a few places predominantly Lasalgaon and Pimpalgoan and then Hebbal.

Auctioning is the well-established mechanism of arriving at competitive prices provided, the auction is free. Cartels at auctions are discerned by observing patterns in bids of which the commonly used technique is of bid rotation among members of the group. It suggests looking at data patterns over a long period.[65] The assumption of free auctions where sellers and buyers meet as independent agents and auction prices are competitively arrived lacks credibility if information flows are controlled. Correlations have to be done carefully. The negative correlation posited by DG was not in conformity with arrivals in the Delhi wholesale market (Azadpur mandi) during the period of sharp spikes in prices. In fact, when cartels operate price spikes and arrivals are positively correlated. Discomfort was expressed on the negative correlations.

The Institute of Economic and Social Change (ISEC) was commissioned to do a study on the onion market.[66] Based on field data, the report pointed to the small holdings of onion cultivators; concentration of traders on account of holding multiple licenses; close association of traders with APMC officials; and creation of wide social networks through truckers and traders. Price information flows through the social network in other markets not accessible to farmers contributed to the consolidation of trader networks. Seasonal indices of arrivals and prices from 2002 to2011 showed that months with higher prices also showed higher arrivals of onions. Response to higher prices by farmers does not arise on account of their small land holdings and no storage capacity. The assumption is also that farmers are in the know of higher prices in wholesale and retail markets. Correlation of daily market arrivals on modal prices showed no negative relationship with small exception in the case of Jaipur as can be seen in Table 1.

Coefficient of variation showed greater volatility of prices in wholesale as compared to retail prices.[67]

1.2.8 Qua Maghribi Traders

The analysis and data while indicative of interactions between the onion traders still need enough proof to suggest cartelization. While as a caste the merchants may present a united front but in terms of bidding can there be splinter groups.

Table 1 Nash Equilibrium

Market	*Data availability*	*Correlation of arrivals and modal price*
Kolkata	268	−0.085
Mumbai	264	−0.053
Delhi	284	−0.025
Bangalore	263	−0.07
Jaipur	204	−0.416

Taking the simple game theory used in the cement cartel, the question let us first look at the strategy that onion merchants when bidding for the onions at the APMC mandi auction. Every strategy is defined by the circumstances under which the bidding takes place. We already know that many of the farmers are in debt to the merchants. The full crop does not come to the auction. The two groups are farmers or panchayat council and the merchants in the APC. The APMC auctioneer is not relevant as he is only the umpire.

Nash Equilibrium

		Merchants: High price	Merchants: Low Price
Farmers/ Panchayat Council	High Price	10,10	0,20
	Low Price	20,0	5,5

The farmers would like a high price while the merchants prefer to buy at a lower price. Two games that can be played are taken among several others.

> Game1: Merchants in this mandi having already taken the crop as collateral for earlier loans prefer to pay a low price even if farmers would prefer the higher price. The high price is higher profitability for farmers. For the merchants, a lower purchase price will be higher profits in the resale mandi to which the farmers have no access. The Nash equilibrium would be 5:5 defined by history of credit between farmers and merchants.

> Game 2: The panchayat council puts up a united front and demands a higher procurement price for higher profits. The merchants with limited options may opt for the higher price as farmers' profitability in repayment of loans will compensate for the difference in procurement prices. Sale price at retail mandis will be high and as the elasticity of demand for onions is relatively inelastic there is never any shortage of demand. The Nash equilibrium would be 10:10.

In both games, merchants or traders as middle men only cover the risk of handling and transport logistics. The strength of bargaining for farmers comes from bidding as a group which is seen in the Nash equilibrium between Game1 and Game 2.

Neither of the games indicate how the merchant cartel can be broken. Game 2 shows, however, the strength of bargaining power if panchayat councils bid as against an individual farmer. It is also possible for panchayats to become monopolistic and perhaps be partners with the merchants working out a separate deal internally.

Meenakshi and Banerjee indicate in their paper that competition among the bidders lowers the win bid price which would be Game 1. The pattern observed by them is that when there is collusion among who are the buyers of rice, bid rotation has been the practice. Paddy markets are different from onion markets. In the case of paddy, the government is actively involved in purchase of paddy for distribution in the public distribution system. The levy price is what the government levies on the mill to secure milled rice for sale in the public distribution system (PDS). The paper does not indicate how the cartel can be broken.

There can be cartels but these are unacknowledged cartels and as suggested in the minority Order a revisit of the onion market is required. Government intervention in the APMC is to moderate the volatility of prices. It is not an instrument to introduce competition. The onion markets' procurement of onions at the base mandi auction by the kaccha arthiya on the basis of bids is a fair process of arriving at the appropriate sale price for farmers. Studies have highlighted the control of merchant traders (kacha and pucca arthiyas) over small farmers through the credit/loan route and most onion farmers are small farmers. Small farmers need loans without collateral. The failure of the co-operative movement to fill the gap between institutional banking system based on collateral and money lenders who demand usurious rate some of whom are merchant traders is a failure of rural credit system as pointed out in the minority order. The basic conditions for free and fair bidding were non-existent. Even if there are two groups or merchants splinter groups with scope for collusion that exists for the merchant trader, the farm gate purchase price is a pass through that can be recovered in other mandis on account of relatively inelastic demand for onions.

Two issues continue to bother me about the onion market cartel case. The fundamental issue is of the extent of harm that smooth functioning of mandi markets ensured by merchant traders can exert on consumers as onion is an essential item of food. As the merchant trader filial connection extends to wholesale mandis the Laslgaon to Hebbal, to Delhi route, possibility of speculative activity exists. The cartel of "filial merchants" disrupts the smooth functioning of mandis the issue then is what could be the possible grim trigger to break the cartel.

Resetting standards

The inclusion of merchant traders in the smooth functioning of markets to be treated as 'joint ventures' under proviso to Section 3(3) if such filial relationships "increases efficiency in.......supply, distribution, storage....provisions of goods".

(iv) Cartel Dilemma of Public Procurement—Bureaucrats Antitrust

Bid rigging in public procurement is a major concern for competition authorities in countries which have had a long history of Public Sector Undertakings (PSUs). I call it a Bureaucrat's Antitrust as bureaucrats head the PSU or manage procurement of equipment in the Ministry. They are comfortable with the tendering process of procedures and protocols, of issuing tenders and of vetting the bids aware of the different forms of bid rigging that suppliers are known to indulge in. Public procurement is a priority area for CCI[68] Section 3(3)(d) deals with bid rigging or collusive bidding presumed to result in AAEC. Section 3(3)(d) is a bureaucrat's clause. They relate to agreements amongst competing bidders in fixing the bid price. Two possibilities can be envisaged under Section 3(3)(d): (i) when the suppliers form a cartel to fulfils the order and (ii) when the PSU insists on a certain price and supplier falls in line.

Bidding process in public procurement is different from bidding in the earlier case of cartel among merchant traders in the onion market which is in response to tenders placed by PSUs or departmental enterprises, government hospitals, etc. It is mandatory for procurement of any material, equipment or spare parts where government finances are involved. The counter effort by the PSU to get a good price not necessarily the market price creates the dilemma of cartels in public procurement. Primarily, there is no market outside the PSU for many of the parts required and for which tenders are placed. Several cases filed with CCI relate to purchases of parts by Indian Railways (IR), the last bastion of PSU. Railways buy from vendors who have been long-time suppliers of the spare parts. Consequently, a symbiotic relationship develops between the supplier and the procurer. As there is no demand for many of the products outside of the railways, it is normal to expect arrangements between suppliers.

Two factors favor purchase of products from these enterprises. Firstly, these parts have already been cleared by the R&D division of IR and are in the category of classified vendors. This is important for safety in the running of trains, and time is saved between placing orders and getting RDSO clearances. Secondly, the railways are assured of long-term supply of spare parts important for the smooth running of the railways. Many of the spare parts' manufacturers are encouraged to set up manufacturing units as ancillary units to IR requirements. With no demand outside of railway requirements, these units are dependent entirely on orders from IR. Conceived as part of the policy of the government of India to encourage manufacturing activity among medium and small-scale enterprises (MSME), the issue therefore of supply cartels by eliminating competition was never considered. Intervention by the CCI saw the beginnings of a new perspective on public procurement and bid rigging as a serious anti-competitive activity which was taken for granted. Investigation is a simple process of looking at tenders and the vendor participants in these tenders to establish participation in a cartel arrangement. Most of the enterprises admitted to having collaborated on the price and on sharing the quantity among themselves. Some lie while some give evasive answers. Since the quotes are on paper and with no outside source of demand, the suppliers perhaps have limited option. They can either be honest upfront or be evasive. The suppliers can accept their cartelization and escape with a small fine or warning. Or they can be quiet and face a larger fine or even lose their license to supply the railways. In all cases, we shall see CCI has preferred the softer option as suppliers have confessed to bid rigging. The Prisoners Dilemma enacted as suppliers left with two choices–own up or face the consequences.

The DG's investigation of the tenders reveal similarity of language, of handwriting and often submission by one firm for the group. In fact of the hearings, the firms admitted that all just get someone to fill up the tender forms and deposit. Once the tenders are opened post negotiations, the price set by the procurer is accepted.

How to define these cartels they are open and in the knowledge of PSUs? Are these cartels to be broken without upsetting symbiotic relationships and disrupting existing supply chains? These units are open about their meetings and of quoting a single price. They are agreeable to a price fixed by the PSU (public sector unit). Consumers do not land up bearing the brunt of higher prices. The markets are competitive with several small units manufacturing. The interventions and decisions of the Commission reflect this dilemma. Nevertheless, cartels as the most pernicious form of anti-competitive activity have to be broken. Cases on public procurement just on procurement process of IR reveal variety in bid rigging.

1.2.9 Legal and Procedural Framework

Public procurement and competition law is part of the legal and procedural framework of public procurement drawn up by the government through Article 53 of the Constitution and The Government of India (Allocation of Business Rules, 1962 and The Transaction of Business Rules, 1961). The financial powers of government are vested in Ministry of Finance which are delegated to sub-ordinated authorities under the General Financial Rules (GFRs) and Delegation of Financial Powers Rules (DFPR). A new Bill was in the offing in Parliament on Public Procurement (2012) to bring transparency and efficiency. The Bill also covered the aspect of promoting competitiveness.[69]

(i) Case Histories

The cases in this section will refer to supplier side cartels to IR. Competition concerns that when they arise from the procurer side they come under abuse of dominance. Information is provided by railways but the cases are taken as suo moto to avoid in many cases disclosure of identity of the informant.. The railways are huge in India and are among the largest network in the world. Aware of the competition law, six cases as on date have been filed with CCI.[70]

The first cartel case of public procurement transferred to CCI from MRTP was Case No. C-145/2008/DGIR and date of decision 06.04.2011. The Railway Board, Ministry of Railways had observed that suppliers of RMG Polyvinyl sheets cleared by RDSO four of them had formed a cartel in their bids and raised prices by 80%. The signs of cartel observed by DG in this case were: (i) same handwriting and similar language; (ii) same price quotations which were immediately reduced on start of investigation. There is no Agreement as required by Section 3, and the firms are not dependent on procurement orders from the railways. The case was not maintainable, and it related to a period prior to the establishment of CCI and adoption of the Competition Act.

The second case was of rigging the bids and sharing the market. Identical rates were quoted for other divisions of the railways. Simultaneously quantities supplied were reduced at less than 50% of the total tender quantity. The tenders related to procurement of feed valves. Reference Case No. 05 of 2011 filed under Section 19(1)(b) of the Competition Act, 2002 by Shri B P Khare, Principal Chief Engineer, South Eastern Railway, for procurement of Anti-Theft Elastic Rail Clips with Circlips from RDSO approved firms. In response thereto, 29 approved firms submitted offers. The rate quoted by most of the firms was @66.50 (all inclusive). The quantity quoted by each of the firms was far less than 50% of the total tender quantity.

The third case was of bid rotation. Suo Moto Case No. 03 of 2012 Re: Alleged cartelization in the matter of supply of spares to Diesel Loco Modernization Works, Indian Railways, Patiala, Punjab v M/s Stone India Limited;. M/s Faiveley Transport Rail Technologies India Limited; M/s Escorts Limited. It was a case of quoting identical rates although all three were located in different cities. The strategy adopted in filing defective bids is well documented in antitrust literature. Not Complementary/cover bids are filed to give the illusion of a large number of bidders and to prevent the stalling of the auction. In this case, no such attempt was made to cover for the lack of sufficient vendors. The Tendering Committee preferred to let CCI undertake the investigation of bid rigging. Despite filing the case with CCI the railways placed orders with the same vendors.

The Commission noticed a pattern of rotation in the bidding process. Out of three companies two tenders were invariably invalid. Escorts Limited one of the enterprises pointed to the practice insisted by IR on matching the lowest quote, the 'fall clause' as they describe it. CCI also made the distinction between "first-time contraventions" and the "first-time established contraventions". Penalty of 2% was levied on each of the parties.

The fourth case on bid rigging was a case that had all the features of Prisoners Dilemma. Suo Moto Case No. 03 of 2014 v M/s Pyramid Electronics; M/s R. Kanwar Electricals; M/s Western Electric and Trading Company fans referred to CCI by CBI during an investigation into the alleged misconduct of one of the officers. This was with regard to cartelization in respect of tenders issued by the railways and Bharat Earth Moving Equipment Private Ltd (BEML) of procuring brushless DC Fans and other electrical items. Bid rigging was established on the basis of emails and telephone conversations among the three companies on as regards quoting the same rates. The final rates quoted were more or less similar.

The case makes interesting reading on the application of Prisoners Dilemma. One of the parties sought waiver under Section 46 of Lesser Penalty by agreeing to be an approver. The other two parties preferred to deny cartelization in bid rigging. Penalties were accordingly levied, a lesser penalty for the first party and higher penalties for the other two. The Prisoners Dilemma is whether you confess to a crime and your accomplices fail or to confess then you go free. If you fail to confess but your accomplice confesses, then you will be convicted with the maximum jail sentences. If both confess, the sentence will be less than the maximum sentence. If neither confess the charge will be framed on tax evasion charges.[71] The regulations on lesser penalty permit the benefit of reduction in penalty up to or equal to one hundred percent, if the informer is the first applicant and the disclosure is vital.

The fifth case Reference Case No. 06 of 2018 *In Re:* Chief Materials Manager/Sales, Informant Eastern Railway And M/s Laxven Systems and M/s Medha Servo Drives Pvt. Ltd. The case relates to tender for procurement of Microprocessor Control and Fault Diagnostics System ("**System/Item**") for Electric Locos as per Research Designs and Standard Organization ("**RDSO**"). Out of the two vendors, only one quoted and a very high price.

The last set of cases on account of clubbing refer to Reference Case No. 03,05 of 2016; Case No. 01 of 2018; Case No.04 of 2018; and Case No.6 of 2018 all relating to variants of Composite Brake Blocks by Hindustan Composites Limited vs Industrial Laminates (India) BIC Auto Private Limited (now Masu Brake Pads Private Limited) et al. total of 12 reported by South Eastern and Eastern Railways. No evidence of sharing information or of cartelization was found with regard to the last two suppliers, so the cartelisation was among 10 vendors. The first case was on identical rates.

The approach of CCI is in adopting a behavioral remedy rather than that of levying penalty which has been influenced considerably by the procurement policies of PSUs toward medium and small enterprises. They have noted in the Order (Para 50).

"*to cease and desist in future from indulging in practices which have been found in the present order to be in contravention of the provisions of Section 3 of the Act*", In Para the Commission on the issue of penalty noted that "*the concerned parties have not only cooperated but have even admitted their respective role/conduct in the said tenders*" As most of the parties are micro, small and medium enterprises with low annual turnovers, penalty was not considered appropriate.

Private Procurement

Price cartelization in the case of Ball bearings among four suppliers of steel a similar approach was adopted by CCI in Suo Motu Case No. 05 of 2017 In Re: Cartelisation in Industrial and Automotive Bearings Against: (1) ABC Bearings Limited (now amalgamated with Timken India Limited) (2) National Engineering Industries Ltd. (3) Schaeffler India Ltd. (previously known as FAG Bearings India Ltd.) (4) SKF India Ltd. (5) Tata Steel Ltd., Bearing Division.

Para 33 *The Commission, in terms of Section 27 (a) of the Act, directs the Opposite Parties NEI, Schaeffler, SKF and Tata Bearing and their respective officials who have been held liable in terms of the provisions of Section 48 of the Act, to cease and desist in future from indulging in practices which have been found in the present order to be in contravention of the provisions of Section 3 of the Act, as detailed in the earlier part of the present order.*

Para 34 *Regarding penalty, it is observed that in light of the peculiar facts and circumstances of the present case as detailed in this order, ends of justice would be met if the parties cease such cartel behaviour and desist from indulging in it in future, as directed earlier. The parties are however, cautioned to ensure that their future conduct is strictly in accord with the provisions of the Act, failing which any such future behaviour would be vied seriously with attendant consequences.*

Resetting Standards

- Cases on public procurement just on the procurement process of IR reveal variety in bid rigging.

- The Vickrey rule for ensuring competition in bidding is to fix the second highest bid price.[72]

1.2.10 Conclusion

Price sharing data within an Association or mandatory sharing with the government were all efforts of bringing in transparency into the activities of firms. As part of the transparency move, public procurement also facilitated bid rigging. Cartels in the Drugs and Trade Association displayed the negative effects of Association. An interesting case of an undetected cartel relates to the onion market. The informal trade links cemented by family relationships is a classic example similar to trading merchants of perhaps sixteenth century where information flows remained well controlled. There will be a lot more of undetected cartels for which CCI has been proactive in terms of encouraging whistleblowers by way of lower penalty and with the new leniency in clearing mergers under the Green Channel COVID-19 Advisories (Gouri,2020).[73]

2 Section II: Vertical Agreements and Restraints for Enhancing Efficiency

Agreements under Section 3(4) are classified as vertical agreements and are between enterprises at different stages of production. Vertical arrangements are fundamentally competitive. Its inclusion in Section 3, the chapter in the Act on agreements leading to AAEC with several cases filed with the CCI has seen perverse assessment of competition. As mentioned earlier, two conditions need to be present for assessing antitrust abuses of vertical restraints. Firstly, the conflation of Section 3(4) with Section 4 in most of the filings made to CCI. A noticeable common error in this conflation is that while Section 3(4) is of dominance of the manufacturer Section 4 deals with 'abuse of dominance'. [74] There can be overlaps arising from similarity of language in the abuses listed in the two sections but the base of the abuses and their analytics differ. Conflation is what lawyers are comfortable as different sections of the Competition Act are combined in their arguments with no reference to the economics theory and analysis that underlies each section. The practice of lawyers of combining different section of an Act or jurisprudence in matters of civil or criminal arguments creates distortions and errors of judgment when applied to competition law. This conflation of two sections has diffused the central focus of Section 3(4) on vertical agreements as restraints on efficiency. The second related condition of *de hors* that of defining a complete vertical arrangement for applying Section 3(4). The decisions of CCI will be analyzed from these two conditions. I have titled this section as 'vertical agreements and restraints for enhancing efficiency'. Vertical agreements refer to arrangements between firms at different levels of production assembled to produce the final product and of distribution or final sale. Incomplete vertical arrangements of platform markets of Section 4 on account of conflation have been taken up to highlight the awkwardness of vertical restraints as a tool of anti-competitiveness. Vertical integration is now under investigation of DoJ and FTC in their Vertical Merger Guidelines (2020).[75]

2.1 Setting Standards in Vertical Agreements

Setting standards in vertical agreements depends entirely on understanding the vertical structure of arrangements. The automobile spare parts case is a classic example of complete vertical integration while Hiranandani is on incomplete vertical integration.

2.1.1 Defining the Vertical Relationship

Assessment of vertical agreements or arrangements is in understanding the economics of business and refers to linked chain of firms downstream. Linking different stages of production constitutes the main characteristics of vertical arrangements. The original producer referred to as OEM (original equipment manufacturer) is serviced by the OES (original equipment supplier). These relationship between the firms at the two levels are bound by contractual arrangements designed to improve efficiencies and minimize transaction costs. An agnostic attitude to accept that vertical agreements have resulted in AAEC require applying the 'rule of reason' in establishing anti-competitive behavior unlike the 'per se' approach of horizontal agreements.

Arrangements could be of activities within the same firm or enterprise or they can be organized into separate businesses in the identified stages sequence till the retailer end or the consumer point of sale. Vertical relationships are both upstream and downstream, between input firms and retailers. Vertical restraints are contracts to achieve the same efficiencies as producing and selling all under one roof. The question then arises why break up the process. When size and scale matter viability of vertical firms upstream and downstream come into focus. The arrangement between the manufacturer and the retailer to the consumer could be of hub and spoke or just a one-step arrangement.

Vertical markets are fundamentally competitive. The chain of vertical upstream firms and downstream firms consists of competitive markets as the downstream firm and the upstream firm are complimentary to each other. A simple way is to think of the downstream firm producing the inputs for the upstream firm in a relation of complementarity competition each firm would prefer to lower the price of its product expanding demand in the process for both levels of firms. The demand for a product rises as the price of the complimentary product falls. In a horizontal agreement, the products are substitutes. The demand for a product rises or falls with the increase or decrease of the substitute. If they are substitutes then each firm would prefer to have his competitor raise the price and soften competition. The argument is that the OEM the primary producer who has to take on other OEM producers will ensure that his price is competitive. No OES following the same line of reasoning will want to price the inputs higher as this would increase the final product price making it counterproductive. Competition among the OEMs keep prices low. The one link that has been of distraction in the vertical relationship is of the upstream relationship between the manufacturer-dealer relationship prominent in the automotive sector. A car dealer is the point of sale and the linking is upstream. The manufacturer could directly be the seller of his product or appoint firms (dealers)to distribute and sell the product, or prefer to have showrooms that is owned by a separate firm(s). The restraint of vertical resale price maintenance (RPM) and of limits to dealer discounts has been argued as anti-consumer. Is the vertical arrangement only up to the manufacturer or to the point of sale? With one OEM and multiple points of sale is RPM conducive to tacit cartel arrangements shifting anti-competitive abuse to horizontal practices if not agreements.

Section 3(4) of the Act on vertical agreements must be seen in conjunction with Section 19 (3). Section 3(4) refers to vertical restraints to competition of tie-in arrangement; exclusive supply agreement; exclusive distribution agreement; refusal to deal; and resale price maintenance. Section 19(3) lays down the conditions for determining AAEC and the list of 6 includes both positive and negative outcomes. The first three relate to softening of competition while the next three conditions describe the benefits/mitigating factors.[76] What emerges from the reading of Section 19(3) is the fact that for vertical agreement to be anti-competitive, cumulative negative impact of such an agreement would necessarily have to outweigh efficiency-enhancing/welfare-inducing effects emanating from the agreement.

Most Commissions are wary on assessing anti-competitive effects of vertical restraints. The EU has preferred to provide for Block Exemption from Article 101(1) with the *de minimis* condition of 30%. Even on crossing the threshold Commissions are averse to intervening unless the negative effects clearly and strongly outweigh the positive outcomes. The US has enacted the 'Right to Repair Act' to curb restrictive practices if any, by automobile manufacturers. Several conditions and market scenario listed out by both EU and DoJ in the Guidelines highlight the difficulty of proving anti-competitive effects of vertical restraints.

2.2 Analysis of Cases of Vertical Agreements

2.2.1 The Automotive Spare Parts

Section 3(4) case is largely of the automobile sector. The first set of cases (Case No. 3 of 2011dated 28/08/2014 and 27/07/2015) on Shamsher Kataria v Honda Siel subsequent to which there have been several cases including that of dealers discount of Maruti Suzuki (Suo Moto Case No.1of 2019). Recently, investigation has been taken up on Tata Motors and dealership agreements (Case No. 21 of 2019 and Case No. 16 of 2020).

The first case (Case No. 3 of 2011) which was on Honda Siel extended to include 14 car manufacturers centered around the requirement of parts for replacement and the need for servicing the vehicle by authorized dealers of the OEM. Parts manufactured by OES are under agreements as they incorporate designs and techniques specific to the requirement of the OEM. Similarly, the tools for servicing are also specially designed and manufactured under agreement with the OEM. The Agreements signed by the OEM with the OES can have restrictive clauses pertaining to price. Similarly, the number and location of authorized service centers is the decision of the OEM.

The exercise of market power of an equipment manufacturer as in the case of car spare parts and services on how to assess competition in the aftermarket if aftermarkets are proprietary and constrained by competition is the core argument I shall address. The allegation of the informant was on the lack of choice in servicing his vehicle in independent garages on the availability of spare part, tooling kits and requisite manuals on account of the dominance of car manufacturer in control and exercise of power in the secondary market of spares and services.

The informant has alleged violation of:

1. Section 3(4)(a) by indirectly determining purchase or sale prices of parts and servicing, maintenance and repair jobs;
2. Section 3(4)(b) by restricting and limiting the sale and supply of spare parts and technical information, diagnostic equipment and tools to independent automobile service providers or in the open market automotive aftermarket;
3. Section 3(4)(d) by refusing to deal, supply, distribute, sell or trade in the spare parts, diagnostic tools and technological information pertaining to the vehicle dealt with and manufactured by them with the independent repair workshops.

In a supplementary information, the informant further alleged that OEMs or car manufacturers are asserting dominance of the OEM or car manufacturer over their authorized dealers from taking up dealership of other cars manufacturers in violation of Section 4(2)(a), 4(2)(b) and 4(2)(c) of the Act. The requirement of conflation of two sections was never explained by the informant.

2.2.2 Background

The first case (Case No. 3 of 2011dated 28/08/2014 and 27/07/2015) was prompted by firms interested in developing new lines of business in the automotive sector that of sophisticated specialized garages (not the hammer and tongs garage I grew up with) for instance Carnations persuaded by the boom in demand for cars post-liberalization. The initial ventures for the emerging garage business were thwarted by attempts to get spare parts, technical knowhow and software to detect the fault codes essential for servicing. It was a case of emergent business and on hindsight the attempt was to further the business by "*firing from the shoulders of the Commission*". The emergence of an alternative to the existing dealers for servicing cars post the warranty period was growing as the number of car owners increased. The demand for independent garages often involving accident claims required by-passing the car insurance that authorized dealers preferred. The amount of insurance provided by car insurers is so small that it is often simpler to forgo the insurance to reduce insurable amount in the subsequent period. Modern servicing centers require modern equipment and access to digital software all of which were under contractual agreements between the OEM and OES including foreign suppliers.

Business models significantly affect the way car manufacturers segment their product, dealership network and availability of components and provide glimpses of the competitive constraints car manufacturers face. According to CII-Mckinsey Report,[77] the automotive aftermarket in 2010 was around Rs.1900crs to Rs. 24000crs excluding services which is estimated to be in the range of Rs. 8000crs–12000crs with an estimated growth rate of 11% per annum. At present, OEM-franchised dealers constitute 50% of the market, but that leaves 50% of the market outside the structure adopted by the Commission of OEM-OES linked structures. The market is still small in comparison to the global automotive market of US$ 540 m. Globally, emerging trends are of independent dealer networks where OES are selling through their networks and on contract to OEMs with both parties aiming at developing the generics product market. Competition among company dealers, sales depot and service garages also exist either in the market or for the market when the initial selection process is made. Simultaneously, online markets in spare parts have emerged.

A dominant feature of this industry is of outsourcing or subcontracting. Components or spare parts are manufactured outside the main car manufacturing center. It is important to note that over time, components have increasingly become modular manufactured off-site and available as knocked-down kits capable of being assembled on an assembly line where replacement is not part-by-part but modular. Simultaneously cars are shifting to use of digital components with involvement of high-tech algorithmic-based companies. Auto tooling, auto design has shifted from the mere mechanics of motor, door, etc. to the realm of intellectual property blurring distinct categories of generic and proprietary. These developments explains the interest of independent service centers Carnations a high-end servicing center who sought permission to present their case before the Commission.

There are 17 car manufacturers in India with a wide range of models from budget (mini) cars to to sophisticate premium high-end cars. As per DG reports, market share of the three major manufacturers include Maruti (44.94%); Hyundai (14.26%); and Tata Motors (13.97%). These three account for more than 73% of the total market.[78] The car market India was for a long time dominated by 2 makes Ambassador and Fiat and a small section of Standard Herald. Mid-eighties saw the entry of Maruti which saw the beginnings of choice for the emerging middle class. Even to this day, two-wheelers retain a large segment of private vehicular transportation. Post-liberalization, India emerged as a hub for car manufacturing as also for manufacture of spare parts.

The allegation of the informant was on the lack of choice in servicing his vehicle and on the availability of spare part, tooling kits and requisite manuals in the open market on account of the dominance of car manufacturer in control and exercise of power in the secondary market of spares and services. Over the counter, sales were essential for the rise of independent garages. In this framework, the prime issue is whether vertical restraints impact on competition denying consumers the choice of alternate service centers. A corollary question is whether independent service centers are required and whether these restraints influence consumer choices in purchase of cars.

2.2.3 The Market Defined

In vertical agreements, defining the relevant product market is important unlike in horizontal agreements and in conformity with the definition of the relevant market in Section 2(t):

> a market comprising all those products or services which are regarded as interchangeable or substitutable by the consumer, by reason of characteristics of the products or services, their prices and intended use;

The relevant product market is the end product manufactured by the OEM. There can be multiple manufacturers as in the case of cars but each car manufacturer (OEM) has its own vertical arrangements with OESs. Allegations pertain to the markets of the OES. Can they be defined independently of the OEM? In the automotive sector, allegations were on restrictions on the sale of spare parts, of diagnostic tools, etc. produced by OES but for OEM the car market. The informant avers the abuses cited in Section 3(4) that have the potential of causing or likely to cause an AAEC in the upstream and downstream competitive markets of vertical relationships. The relevant product market definition for OES in Section 2(t) is not applicable resulting in verbal gimmickry of defining the market in the Order.

The vertical agreements identified in Section 3(4) are:

a) Tie-in-arrangement: purchase of a good tied with some other good;
b) Exclusive supply agreement: restrictions on the purchaser in the course of trade from acquiring or dealing with any other good other than those of the dealer;
c) Exclusive distribution agreement: limits or restrict or withhold supply of good or allocate any area or market for the disposal or sale of the good;
d) Refusal to deal: restrict by any method the person or classes of person to whom goods are sold or bought;
e) Resale price maintenance includes any agreement to sell goods on the condition that the prices to be charged on the resale by the purchaser shall be stipulated by the seller unless otherwise clearly stated[79];

In the literature on antitrust and vertical restraints, reference is to after-markets a market that comes into focus post the sale of the primary products. Aftermarket refers to the market for spares, post-warranty services and other requirements that are required for replacement of broken parts, for repairs and for servicing post-purchase of the product. The aftermarket definition does not capture the allegations of the informants who are interested in starting a newline of business that of service centers parallel to the service centers of the OEMs. Antitrust cases involving aftermarkets since the US Supreme Court Judgment (1992) on Kodak[80] have traversed the entire gamut of antitrust from market power abuse in aftermarkets; to agreements and vertical restraints; and to intellectual property rights. CCI is traversing the same path.

The OEMs submitted that there is no separate relevant market for spare parts distinct from the primary market for sale of cars and that the relevant market in the instant case is that of an indivisible, unified 'systems market'. An important point to note emphasized by the OEMs is that since spares, tools, etc. are complementary to the primary product the secondary market of spares is part of the primary market which defines a unified systems market. The market for spares, tools and diagnostics are complements and not substitutes, and markets for complements prefer to keep prices low so as to remain competitive.

2.2.4 Investigation

Definition of the markets is particularly important in vertical restraints. The DG defined two markets: the primary market and the secondary market in all the cases while the Commission prefers to use the term 'cluster market' in the first case 03/2011.[81]

The DG's proceeding two markets was accepting conflation of Section 3(4) and Section 4. The two markets are.

1. The Primary Market: consisting of the manufacturing and the sale of the passenger vehicles.
2. The Secondary Market which is the "Aftermarket" comprises of spare parts, diagnostic tools, technical manuals and after sales repair and maintenance services that are required to be purchased after the purchase of primary product.

The definition put forward by the opposite party was of one indivisible 'systems market' consisting of a durable primary product and complimentary secondary products. In the opinion of the DG, a systems market is defined by two criterion. The first criteria is of interchangeability of parts among cars of different makes as per Section 2(t) which refers to interchangeability or substitutability as constituting a relevant market. The second criteria is scope for switching cars from one manufacturer to another to avoid high costs of spare parts. There was no scope for consumers to (i) switch parts of one OEM or car make to that of another and ii) or to easily switch to another car resulting in financial losses with a few exceptions of generic products such as tyres and batteries. The DG found no rationale in the definition of a systems market while economics finds no rationale in the DG's definition. Both conditions for defining the market in terms of two markets as against systems market missed the concept of vertical arrangements that consist of OEMs and OESs constituting one system.

The definition of the market by DG was defined by the need to establish anti-competitive abuses raised by the opposite party rather than that of analyzing whether vertical restraints are efficiency enhancing or whether they are dependent on competition from independent service garages. That the car manufacturer is dominant in the aftermarket of that car is axiomatic. As dominance is not the criteria for assessing the anti-competitive effects of vertical restraints, the definition of DG and subsequent analysis remained facile.

The Commission was also not inclined to accept the system approach based on whole life cycle costing. Their argument that in India the consumer although price sensitive: (i) is not in the know of the costs of spare parts to do a whole life costing; (ii) cars in India once bought are only sold after a minimum of 10 years; (iii) there are switching costs involved in changing of models; and (iv) preference for local service garages on account of logistics and servicing charges. They preferred to use the concept of 'cluster market' to overcome the presence of innumerable aftermarkets for each car influenced by the US Supreme Court decision in the case of Kodak where each spare part is part of a cluster. In a car, it is difficult to imagine that 25,000 parts need replacement especially when now the move is toward modular parts. A cluster market concept is similar to a package of complimentary product as a part requires appropriate tooling for replacement.

Defining the aftermarket as a separate market, the Commission concern was on "*competition issues in the aftersales market usually emerge in cases where the firm, the supplier, is also able to control the aftersales markets*". The question therefore is whether the dominant position of the OEM in the aftermarket can enable it to exercise its market power or whether the OEM is constrained by competition in the primary market.

2.2.5 Case Analysis

Several arguments mainly relating to systems market were examined by the Commission in this case. The economics of these arguments are briefly analyzed.

(i) *Installed Base Opportunism (IBO)*

The systems market approach is based on the concept of Installed Base Opportunism (IBO) where the scope for a monopolist car manufacturer to exploit his dominance in the aftermarket is restricted by the competitive constraints of the primary market. Arguments that Indian consumers are averse to changing models on account of switching costs or of high information costs may have been applicable when the Indian car market was a closed market with production of only 3 cars which makes all three basic models amenable to roadside mechanics and garages. The scenario is now very different with 17 car manufacturers in all ranges and design. The car market is a growing market with annual growth rate of 12–15% in the last decade. With the current proportion of cars to population and growing middle class, India is gradually emerging as a hub for car manufacturing. In this market do customers get locked into a car with no information about costs of spare parts or of servicing facilities. In attempting to take on competition especially at the entry information on servicing is highly publicized as also information on car prices, simultaneously there has been a growth of insurance with extended warranties. There is also the emerging trend of independent OES suppliers who have their own distribution network.

(ii) *Pricing-Unfair and discriminatory*

Management experts refer to higher aftermarket pricing as a marketing strategy giving examples of high-priced blades and under-priced razors or of building brand images. The objective function is to maximize the joint profit of the vertical and not the individual profit of a dealer. The use of profit margins as an approximation for control vide pricing of spare parts requires several caveats and assumptions which I consider necessary to discuss. Let us look at Table 2 given reproduced from the Order.

Based on the parameter of profit margins of OEMs and of OES the.

Commission concludes that pricing of spare parts is high in the aftermarket controlled by the OEM. Choice of profit margin as the appropriate parameter is justified as evidence of discriminatory and high pricing:

> that in all the cases the margin from spares business exceeds the margin from car business substantially. In fact several OEMs are incurring overall losses as well as that from the sale of cars, however profits have been generated from spares parts business.

First, a look at the argument of high-priced tools and spare parts and then look at the concept of joint pricing. Two important considerations both denied by the Commission emerge from the table. First, uniformity of

Table 2 Profit margins of OEM's

OEMs	*Margin (%) from automotive business*	*Margin (%) from spare parts business*	*Comments*
Maruti	4.4% (2008–09); 8.7% (2009–10) 4.7%(2010–11)	20–0% (2008–09); 21.0% (2009–10) 21.0% (2010–11)	Maruti's margins from vehicles are substantially lower than those derived from sale of spare parts
Volkswagen	(−)23.7% (2008–09) (−)17.15%(2009–10); 0.40% (2010–11)	49.3%	Volkswagen is making substantial losses from sale of cars and has made normal profit only in FY 2010–2011
BMW	21.78%(2008–09); 16.70%(2009–10); 22.36%(2010–11)	27.08% (2008–09); 31.18% (2009–10); 42.77% (2010–11)	BMW's margin from sale of spare parts are higher
Skoda	(−)3.19% (2008–09) (−)2.96% (2009–10) (−)0,35% (2010–11)		DG has observed that Skoda as a whole is incurring losses but is making significant profit margins from the sale of spare parts
Fiat	(−)88.35 (2008) (−)10.44% (2009) (−)6.62% (2010)	5.72% (2009–10) 9.30% (2010–11)	Honda is making negative margins from sale of cars, whereas it is selling spare at substantial profit
Honda	(−)8.12% (2008–09) (−)0.10% (2009–10) (−)2.02% (2010–11)	26.02% (2008–09) 22.70% (2009–10) 8.02% (2010–11)	

Source Order of the Commission on Case No 3 0f 2011; pp. 165–166

margins between the two markets among all firms emphasize the interlinkages between the primary and the secondary market confirmed by the quote from CII-Mckinsey report used in the Order: "*The aftermarket contributes a modest 24% revenues to OEMs however, a sizable 55% of profit is derived from the segment*". Second, consumers are aware of prices of spare parts even if the information is partial. The data on spare parts if linked to sales of cars negates the argument that consumers in India are ignorant of spare part prices unable to undertake whole life costing.

2.2.6 *Economics of Cross-Elasticities of Pricing*

As the allegation pertain to pricing abuse, let us cast the argument in terms of economic tools of pricing. Pricing of a product as noted in the chapter is determined by elasticity of demand. Higher the elasticity of demand, lower the price. The strategy for a car manufacturer is to keep car prices low as the elasticity of demand which is higher than for spare parts and rising on account of stiff competition. In the case of spares, elasticity of demand is relatively lower given the fact that replacement is not a regular feature as prices can be kept high. Reputation of a car is based on how often parts require replacing.

The framework of a standard 2×2 matrix will help to understand market power on profitability and pricing strategies in the two markets.[82] Table 3 sets out the possibility of different combination of prices in the manufacturing and in the aftermarket markets. Primary market prices are low while those of aftermarket are high.

Pricing strategies are more complex than shown above where broad elasticities have been assumed. As there are 25,000 spare parts, aggregation of parts combine low and high price elasticity. Parts that require frequent replacement maybe priced low or it is equally possible for generic products to emerge in these segments. Moreover, some of the parts may be under patents. Without layered data, no nuanced analysis of the spares market is possible.

Defining the relevant market as a separate independent market is an affirmation of the axiomatic dominance by an OEM in the aftermarket but not of abuse. Recourse as in this case, is to vertical restraints that fall in the domain of Section 3(4).

Table 3 Analysis of Market Power on Profitability

	Aftermarket Price High	Aftermarket Price Low
Primary market Price High ↑	Unlikely to happen	Unlikely to happen
Primary market Price Low ↓	Is the most representative case	Unlikely to happen

2.2.7 Access to Service Centers

The allegation that access centers are limited inconveniencing the consumers is also not a sustainable argument when the primary market is very competitive. These refer to servicing post-warranty. From the responses of various car manufactures, it is clear that the establishment of service centers is influenced by several factors primarily arising out of the spread of demand influenced by income, status and popularity of a model. A people's car like Maruti or Honda would have wider coverage in terms of setting up service centers than say a Lamborghini or a Mercedes Benz whose sales are limited as they fall in the high-end range. In a market where competitive pressures are high, every company is tuned to providing after sales services. The allegation is not with reference to the spread of service centers but the access to service centers which are not authorized by the OEM. Request of Carnation an emergent service center to depose before the Commission is to be seen in this light. It is more of an attempt to enter into the privileged class of authorized centers. My interest is not in this policy of the car manufacturers but in competition issues. An internal war of selection of car vendors or dealers does not help in understanding whether it is a competition issue or a corruption issue.

Two questions are posed: (i) does introducing independent garages and service centers increase consumer choice? (ii) do costs come down with the entry of independent garages? On both counts the answer is negative. With fierce competition, car manufacturers would be tuned to factors that reduce their sales prime among these factors which is the availability of service garages. Palio is an example of a car manufacturer failing to read the market signals and eventually left the Indian market. Moreover, consumers are concerned about safety and the need for using certified parts. Certification does not fall in the jurisdiction of competition commissions. It is also unlikely that with entry of independent garages, prices of spare parts will come down. The order provides no data that can confirm these two arguments.

The argument that provision of these services by authorized centers are expensive and restricted by OEMs needs more investigation in light of global trends where OES are combining or offering high-end service centers. Is it possible for OEMs to exercise their market power and deny spare parts and tooling kits to these service centers. This is a possibility as old business practices get threatened by new practices. Globally, the trend is toward OES combining services their own distribution and service centers in integrating diverse skills and capabilities along the value chain with the potential to create additional value (CII-Mckinsey Report 2010).[83] The report gives examples of such service centers Hella Logistics Center of Bosch Car Service and Stahlgruber with outlet such as Mesiterhaft and Autocheck.

These centers are looking at markets for servicing cars post-warranty, of second hand cars and vintage cars. The requirements of these centers are for original spare part, tooling kits and manuals as their clientele is for the high end. Capacity of OEMs in controlling and restricting the supply of spare parts to service centers ceases to be an issue of 'AoD' as the business model shifts from OEMs to OES. The addition of leveraging Section 4(2)(e) as an abuse by the Commission is not applicable in the automotive spare parts case. It is a case of mixing apples with oranges The view of the Commission is ambitious in an attempt to encourage the emergence of independent post-warranty service centers such as Carnations. In the Order it is opined that

> structurally modifying the competitive nature of the Indian automobile market will itself induce market self-correcting features, by enhancing consumer-choice and access of independent repairers to effectively compete in the Indian aftermarket.

Modern servicing centers have not fully made their entry in India. The arguments pertaining to software and technical codes and claims to Section 3(5)(i) covering both the Copyrights Act and the Patents Act with regard to OES overseas is a separate area for investigation on the global rules and practices on trademark registrations. The Commission noted in its Order that though registration of an IPR as pointed out by the DG exemption as per Section 5 is on the word 'necessary'. Mere selling of spare parts does not compromise the IPRs of OES. Critics refer to the reductionist approach of CCI on patents and IPRs.

2.2.8 Rethink

The aftermarket case points to the scope for Type 1 error. Dominance of OEMs is axiomatic but AoD in verticals need strong proof and evidence including examination of efficiency dimension. There is the perverse reality of vertical agreements be assessed for AAEC from the perspective of horizontal agreements of cartels among car manufacturers based on a uniform approach to open market sales of parts and access to software and technology. Section 3(3) on horizontal agreements refers to '*practice carried on*' without the requirement of a formal agreement.[84] Vertical arrangements to horizontal agreements is competition changing direction and substance will be examined in the case study on hospitals.

2.2.9 *Resale Price Maintenance*—the continuing story

The second set of cases in this segment shifts tack from downstream vertical arrangements to upstream arrangements between the manufacturer and the dealer. The suo moto case on Maruti Suzuki (MSIL) is of MSIL of denying consumers the benefits of dealer discounts by fixing the amount of permissible discount. The informant brought in the mystery man employed by MSIL to keep tbs on MSIL's discount. A similar case has just been filed on the dealership contracts of Tata Motors (Case No. 21 of 2019 and Case No. 16 of 2020). Since these are suo moto cases, the intent of CCI is to developing insights on the vexatious antitrust abuse of resale price maintenance (RPM).

CCI in this case, however, took the unusual approach by conducting a field exercise to find the actual conduct of MSIL. While awaiting the decision, an exploration into RPM based on simple economics provides interesting insights into the allegation of RPM. The mystery man is a management technique of ensuring a uniform behavioral pattern across the country. I have known friends coming to Delhi from Hyderabad to buy a car in days when there was no uniform GST. They did not consider the transaction costs of traveling and stay. The recent decision of CCI in Suo Motu Case No. 01 of 2019 In Re: Alleged anti-competitive conduct by Maruti Suzuki India Limited in implementing discount control policy vis-à-vis dealers.

In the case of manufacturer and dealers, the slim possibility of dealer power arises when there is only one dealer to service a region the arrangements are of exclusive distribution agreement and resale price maintenance (RPM). Strict controls over dealer pricing and over discounts are part of retail supply agreements to avoid double marginalization. A single dealer cannot price higher than others in the dealership arrangement and book higher profits, out of alignment with other suppliers. The producer–dealer equation is of joint profit maximization.

2.2.10 *Double Marginalization and RPM*

Double marginalization occurs if the dealer sets a price according to his marginal cost and the manufacturer on the basis of his marginal costs. Consumers are then bearing the double marginal costs. To avoid the possibility of double marginalization fix, the permissible level of dealer discount and of capping retail price, the pro-competitive vertical restraints of RPM are vertical restraints imposed on dealers.

Normally in the upstream relation of the manufacturer and the dealer, a common complaint is that dealers are not allowed to offer discounts. The common laymans' argument is that dealer discounts allow for enhancing consumer welfare. In cases of vertical agreements, the relationship between a manufacturer and a dealer is not of wholesaler and retailer as in the case of common items. The manufacturer appoints dealers as points of sale and are part of the entire vertical arrangements of OEM and OES and the dealer is another OES. For a manufacturer, there are several dealers covering different parts of the country. This necessitates a common retail price. There would otherwise be the piquant situation that a dealer in Mumbai Fort offering higher discounts gets more customers than a dealer say in Nava Mumbai both are localities in the area of Mumbai state of Maharashtra. Or dealers in Delhi offer different retail prices. Dealers are also often the service centers of cars. Normally, there would be two or three dealers in a city depending on the size of the population and demand. Under these circumstances, the manufacturer fixes two conditions. They are (i) dealers are not entitled to be multi-dears of all cars and (ii) the fixation of RPM.

Pricing of final product which includes the dealers' margin referred to as double marginalization referred to as vertical externality. In the above case of car pricing, consumers are bearing the marginal cost of the manufacturer and also of the retailer both priced at their respective marginal cost. The vertical restraint is pro-competitive at the point where the combined marginal costs cut the industry demand curve. Dealer power occurs when there is a single dealer for a region if the final price can be manipulated. It is, however, unlikely for consumer products for which there is demand.. The importance of resale price maintenance (RPM) is the mechanism to prevent double marginalization and control on account of dealer power.

Other factors considered in the assessment of pricing deviations of dealers is the scope afforded for free riding where investments of one dealer say in advertisements are taken advantage by other dealers which covers expansion of market frontiers expansion. Mitigating the impact of double marginalization where higher prices charged by retailers keep sales below the level which maximizes joint profit maximization underlies the RPM mechanism (Fig. 2).

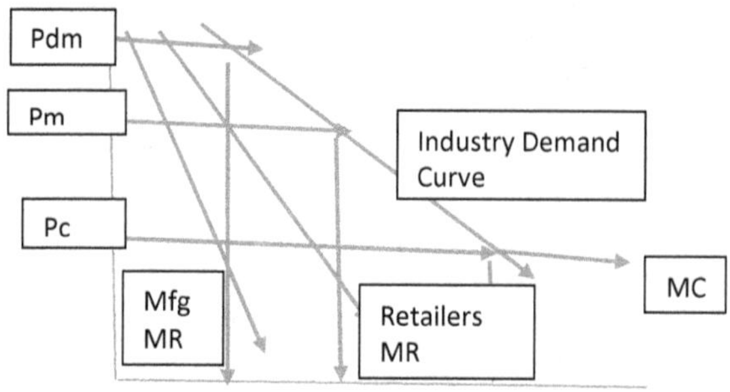

Fig. 2 Nash equilibrium for prisoners dilemma Price and output under double marginalization (*Source* Bishop and Walker, The Economics of EC Competition Law)

2.2.11 Tie-In Arrangement

An unusual case was Case Nos. 36 Fx Enterprise Solutions India Pvt. Ltd v Hyundai Motor India Ltd & CaseNo. 82 of 2014 St. Antony's Cars Pvt. Ltd. Vs Hyundai Motor India Lt. I refer to the two cases because of some of the fundamental clarifications issued by CCI in its Order.

This was a case where the reference is only to Section 3(4) i.e., without conflation. The allegations pertained to RPM and more significantly to tie-in arrangements. The informant claimed that Hyundai tended to push vehicles of lower quality. The DG under the broad market definition of 'market for passenger cars' defined markets for each of the contraventions identified eventually moving to conflation of Section 3(4) with Section 4. In his report, finding violation on all counts of Section 3(4)(a) more specifically on the allegation of tie-in arrangement clause 5(iii) on the insistence of Hyundai Motors India Ltd on purchase of high-end cars as a condition of purchase of tie-in arrangement. As discussed in Case No 3 of 2011, tie-in arrangement is antithetical to increasing business in terms of sale of cars.[85]

The importance of this case is that in its decision the Commissions gave clear indications that conflation of sections was not acceptable. The case pertained to abuses associated with Section 3(4) and not of Section 4. Further, multiple definitions of the market to each harm or abuse is of no consequence for establishing anti-competitive behavior. Reference was made to the *Competition Commission of India* v. *Steel Authority of India & Ors.,* Civil Appeal No. 7779 of 2010 that any investigation can proceed only after receiving directions from the Commission. The Commission also pointed out that clause 5(iii) of the Dealership Agreement was more in the nature of permission clause prior to setting up multi-product dealership.

2.2.12 Vertical Arrangements in Hospitals–Harvesting Stem Cell
Modern hospitals are arranged along verticals and it is important to examine antitrust abuses of vertical integration for hospitals that are profit-making organizations in the private sector. A new concept effort at examining verticals in hospitals was of Ramakant Kini v Dr. L. H. Hiranandani Hospitals (Case No, 39 of 2012).[86] The case related to harvesting stem cell of the new born by Life Cell India Ltd which was not part of the verticals of the hospitals. The patient was requested to use the services of Cryobanks International India which was a vertical of the hospital. The OP had argued that that the relationship between a hospital and stem cell are neither vertical nor horizontal. It was a case of horizontal with vertical links that prompted CLRC in suggesting in its report a wider definition of agreements which are neither horizontal nor vertical. [87]Allegations related to both Section 3(4) and Section (4).

Verticals in a hospital is an organizational structure that represents the different services offered in a hospital selected by a competitive process in each market. For example, in the selection of the labs and the stem cell center, there is a market-based competitive process. A vertical can then be envisaged as the end process of a long chain of market selection process. A hospital could specialize in a single vertical or it can consist of multiple verticals. My dissent on the majority Order arose from the fact that modern hospitals are a set of contracts between physicians, doctors and laboratories organized into verticals. A modern hospital is a platform for the provision of medical services of vertical agreements and come within the ambit of Section 3(4). As explained in my Order, a hospital platform is organized along different verticals (treatment areas) and transactions between a hospital and health care in each vertical consist of several layers of contracts which are vertical arrangements, a departure from earlier expansion in hospital services that were horizontal in their arrangement. These arrangements and contracts in the healthcare market give rise to vertical relations that are inherent to the tendering process of selected verticals.[88]

The allegation was that the competitive process was not followed in the selection of Cryobanks International India in the subsequent rounds of tendering. As argued by the informant, the allegation was regarding the refusal to deal arising out of the exclusive supply agreement between Hiranandani Hospitals and Cryobanks and submitted that competitors of Cryobanks are not allowed to approach prospective consumers who are taking maternity services from the Hospital.[89] At the time the case was filed, there were only two labs that undertook the job. This could have been an antitrust concern in a traditional non-platform market but not anymore.

The antitrust concern was more on expenditure per consumer using hospital facilities. Interactions among verticals are horizontal in that they are across verticals. The relationship, however, of each vertical to the hospital and across verticals is of complements and not of substitutes an important distinction that has been ignored. CCI in its study on Making Markets work for Healthcare has highlighted this dimension. This suggests that prices of service offered by the hospital should be lower contrary to experience. The evidence is not clear. It is difficult to estimate value of proper health care in terms of traditional economics of utility maximization and pricing policies in terms of fee-based pricing to value-based pricing. Costing of health care is of insurance companies who again compete to be the insurer of big hospitals.[90]

The concept of a platform market is familiar online but are common offline. They play an important role of aggregation s in platforms online. The idea is to provide all services at one place as one entity defined as Integrated Delivery Network ("IDN") which includes labs, insurance, etc. Two features stand out in hospital practices in India. Firstly, physicians charge a higher rate as they are not allowed to practice outside the hospital. The contract stipulates this condition. Consider a hospital acquisition of a physician practice that allows the new entity to bill some of the practice's services at the hospital's higher rates. In the first instance, this may simply reflect the new entity taking advantage of a contractual loophole. But if the increase persists into new, renegotiated contracts, then it more likely reflects an exercise of market power. Reverting to the findings of a workshop was organized on by CCI on *Making Markets Work for Affordable Healthcare*' (CCI, policy note 2018) I refer to the third factor: "Vertical arrangements in healthcare services-with incentive-based referral system tends to effect consumer choice". No doubt costs to consumers are higher on account of higher expenditures per consumers as compared to pure physician-owned hospitals. Private hospitals as 'not for profit' venture need a rethink.

Perhaps a more detailed enquiry by CCI is in the offing for issue of Guidelines similar to the 2020 Department of Justice and Federal Trade Commission issued the *Vertical Merger Guidelines.*

3 Conclusion

There are two running threads in this chapter on horizontal agreements and vertical agreements. The first thread is the legal approach to Agreements arising out of conflation and *de hors*. The second thread is on analyzing cases of the Competition Commission of India from the prism of economic tools of analysis of competition.

Conflation is commonly observed in all cases filed with CCI in combining Section 3(4) and Section 4. Lawyers are comfortable with it as civil law or criminal law see lawyers referring to several section. Dominance in vertical agreements with reference to the original manufacturer as in the cars in the automotive spare parts case is axiomatic. Even in the Hiranandani case of verticals of hospitals, the selection of vertical is through a process of competitive market selection process. On the other hand, dominance in Section 4 is with reference to market share and the possibility of exerting exclusionary or extortionary abuses. There can, however, be blending of horizontal and vertical arrangements which is not conflation.

De hors is the rule of applicability to organizational structures of vertical arrangements. While the debate in the Commission on inapplicability of *de hors* for Hiranandani Hospital and the verticals for applying Section 3(1) to prove AAEC, I hold the view that verticals in a hospital are the end manifestation of a longer chain of competitive market selection process of physicians, labs, etc.

The second thread of economic analytics highlights three critical lines of enquiry. The first and foremost concern in evaluating cartels is in finding the trigger point that can cause the cartel to break up. This applies in the case of the cement cartel. A new cement producer or a producer with unutilized capacity may just lower prices to make more sales and profits. Trigger points are important for an Authority as they are points to monitor. In the case of the onion trade market, even if traders are of the same caste class background an open process of bidding combined with information flows available to farmer of all urban mandis are the most effective triggers in agricultural products such as onions, tomatoes and potatoes. Information asymmetry was cited in the study by CCI of high hospital charges and rates.

Cartels in the Drugs and Chemists Association is of government intervention going awry. The Drugs regulator in this case was perhaps the inappropriate regulator for ensuring competition. By controlling discounts, permissible consumers were harmed. Resale Price Maintenance in the car market is a competitive restraint.

Defining a market while required for vertical arrangements may perhaps be required for horizontal arrangements. Cartels may operate in only segment of multi-product firms. Market sieving is now gaining credence.

The importance of distinguishing between complements and substitutes in vertical arrangements can lead to obfuscation of cause and outcomes. This again is not a distinction that lawyer maintains. Recognition that competition law is an economics-based law has been ignored with courts preferring representation only by lawmakers. A discernible feature is the maturing of CCI.

Notes

1. A point emphasized by my colleague Tayal in his dissent supplementary order on Case No. 39 of 2012 Mr. Ramakant Kini v Dr. L H Hiranandani Hospital, dated 24.02.2014.; Competition Commission of India v. Steel Authority of India & Ors., Civil Appeal No. 7779 of 2010/. See also Yogesh Pai and Nitesh Daryanani., Patents and Competition Law in India: CCI's Reductionist Approach in Evaluating Competitive Harm. *Journal of Antitrust Enforcement*, 2017, Vol. 5, pp. 299–327.
2. Report of the Competition Law Review Committee, Ministry of Corporate Affairs, Government of India, July 2019.
3. I would recommend my readers to either read the book or see the movie "Mafiosi' which deals with the investigations in to the drug racket of Mexico and USA.
4. Avner Grief, Contract Enforceability and Economic Institutions in Early Trade: The Maghribi Traders Coalition. *American Economic Review*, June 1993, Vol. 83, No. 3(June, 1993), pp. 525–548 downloaded on JSTOR 202.70.131.9 on Friday 26 March 2021.
5. Elinor Ostrom, *Governing the Commons*, Cambridge, Harvard University Press, 1990.
6. The EU Commission, Competition Market Authority in UK, the FTC and DoJ have come out with Guidelines on Mergers that relate to clearances of mergers leading to cartel.

7. Bill for Modification of the Competition Act, 2003 in Parliament. Report of the Competition Law Review Committee (CLRC), Ministry of Corporate Affairs, Government of India, July 2019.
8. Section 19(3) of the Competition Act: The Commission shall, while determining whether an agreement has an appreciable adverse effect on competition under Section 3, have due regard to all or any of the following factors, namely: —

    (a) creation of barriers to new entrants in the market;
    (b) driving existing competitors out of the market;
    (c) foreclosure of competition by hindering entry into the market;
    (d) accrual of benefits to consumers;
    (e) improvements in production or distribution of goods or provision of services; and
    (f) promotion of technical, scientific and economic development by means of production or distribution of goods or provision of services.

    Some of my colleagues have argued that Section 19(3) applies only to vertical agreements as Section 3(3) is a quasi per se rule not requiring analyzing the costs and benefits of cartel formation, a view I am not in conformity.

    Bhattacharjee and De posit in their analysis of cartels and the competition law that while Sec 3 was modeled after Section 101(1) of the Treaty on the Functioning of the European Union (TFEU), the mandatory requirements of 101(3) was not covered under Section 19(3) of the Act. In fact, they refer to Section 19(3) as a 'distraction' even in the case of hard core cartels.
9. Bhatacharjea A, and De. Cartels and the Competition Commission, Economic and Political Weekly, Vol. 47 Issue No. 35, 01,2012
10. A detailed report on cartels was prepared by CCI for ICN as a special Project Cartel Enforcement and Competition in 2018. The report notes that "the highest number of infringement decisions (15) took place in the entertainment sector, which is not usually regarded as being prone to cartelisation. Another unconventional sector is pharmaceuticals distribution, with thirteen (13) cases and eleven (11) infringements. Public procurement through online tendering saw fifteen (15) cases with eight (8) infringement findings, and transport (excluding railways) saw fourteen (14) cases with seven (7) infringements findings. Of the sectors which are internationally regarded as hotspots of cartel activity 9, public procurement, construction/cement and agriculture/agro processing have seen infringement decisions in India. Two (2) sectors, real estate and banking/finance, have seen a lot of antitrust activity, but almost no findings of infringement. In the real estate sector, there were eleven (11) cases out of which ten (10) were dismissed at the prima facie stage. The

banking / finance sector saw sixteen (16) cases, but only one (1) infringement finding. Therefore, purely based on the cases thus far, these sectors cannot be said to be "prone" to cartelisation in India. However, given the high number of cases brought before the CCI, they also merit attention."

11. Geeta Gouri. (edited) Towards Equity: New Economic Policy and Equity: New Economic Policies and Initiatives for Government Intervention, Oxford & IBH, New Delhi, 1995
12. Op. cit.
13. Bhatacharjee and De posit in their analysis of cartels and the competition law that while Sec 3 was modeled after Section 101(1) of the Treaty on the Functioning of the European Union (TFEU), the mandatory requirements of 101(3) was not covered under Section 19(3) of the Act. In fact they refer to Section 19(3) as a 'distraction' even in the case of hard core cartels.
14. Competition Act, 2002. The review committee on competition law has included the concept of 'hub and spoke' n which a third party a hub facilitates cartels in the spokes. Platform markets are good examples of a hub used by market players as in the Uber case (Case No.37 of 2018).
15. Geeta Gouri, Covid Advisories from the Competition Commission of India., Competition Policy International, July 19, 2020
16. NCLAT decision on written poofs only to be considered as Agreements.
17. Op. cit CLRC.
18. Competition Policy International, the need for defining the market and product clearly was brought out in the European judgment on cartels on underground cables. In this case ABB got away on the basis of leniency application as the market was not defined.

    The Court of Justice disagreed with that analysis and argued that the General Court had committed an error of law in misapplying the rules relating to the burden of proof imposed on the Commission. According to the Court of Justice, "it should be borne in mind that, according to the case law of the Court of Justice, in the field of competition law, where there is a dispute as to the existence of an infringement, it is for the Commission to prove the infringements found by it and to adduce evidence capable of demonstrating to the requisite legal standard the existence of the circumstances constituting an infringement."14 That principle implies that the Commission has to prove the existence or extension of the cartel agreement to the particular products concerned.
19. A mimeographed copy of the presentation by Jyothi Jindgar, Advisor CCI on screen tests available on the net gives clear picture of screen tests.
20. Mehra S, Antitrust and the Robo-Seller: Competition in the Time of Algorithms Minnesota Law Review, Vol. 100, Temple University Legal Studies Research Paper No. 2015-15.

21. *American Natural Soda Ash Corporation (ANSAC) vs. Alkali Manufacturers Association of India (AMAI) and others* (1998) 3 CompLJ 152 MRTPC.
22. Competition Commission of India, *The Competition Commission of India (lesser Penalty) Regulations* (2009), Manas Kumar Chaudhuri, Changing phases of standard of proof in defining 'agreement' Published on August 25, 2020.
23. Draft Note Review of the extant Confidentiality Regime as provided in Regulation 35 of the Competition Commission of India (General) Regulations, 2009. In this proposed regulation the suggestion is of Creation of a Confidentiality Ring, which would include internal as well as external members of the party. This would ensure that all parties would have access to entire records submitted. The opposite parties often complained of lack of information and records submitted which had lead to formulating Regulation 35. The intent of the modification is to hasten the process of inquiry and more important starting the process of self-regulation.
24. 'Confidentiality Ring'.
25. *American Natural Soda Ash Corporation (ANSAC) vs. Alkali Manufacturers Association of India (AMAI) and others* (1998) 3 CompLJ 152 MRTPC.
26. In a recent article by a young student Sherrril caught my attention.Sherrill uses a simple relationship of 3 × Damages [p(t) | Id)] > Litigation Costs + Id + [R | Id] + R(c) where I = investment; d = detection; Id = the cost of investment into detection R = damage to relationship; c = filing a complaint; Relationship costs = [R | Id] + R(c) (Sherrill,2020) Miranda Cherkas Sherrill Antitrust Writing Competition Student Paper Submission 2019.Concurence.
27. At CCI we commissioned several primers to India Development Foundation (IDF) which were extremely useful in developing the basic steps. I have taken from these primers whenever required as each primer was discussed in detail in CCI with presentations. The study on cartels DRU-IDF., Shubhashis Gangopadhya and Alisha Madaan, The Use of Economic Tools of Cartel Detection: A Primer., March 2014.
28. Ibid.
29. Geeta Gouri, COVID Advisories from the Competition Commission of India, Competition Policy International, July 2020.
30. Case no 29 of 2010, Builders Association of India and 12 cement companies including Cement Manufacturers' Association. The list apart from CMA consists of: Associated Cement Co. Ltd.; Gujarat Ambuja Cement Ltd.; Grasim Cement.; Ultratech Cement Ltd.; Jaypee Cement; The India Cements Ltd.; J.K Cements (JI < Group); Century Textiles & Industries Ltd.(Century Cement); Madras Cement Ltd.; Binani Cement Ltd.;

Lafarge India Pvt. The role of the sector regulator and of the Competition Commission need redesigning and will be studied in another chapter. Ltd. Two Orders were issued. First Order dated 20.06.2012 and second Order dated 31.08.2016.

31. The contentions of the parties were: (i) permission for cross-examination of witnesses who had deposed before the Commission was not given; (ii) access to documents submitted by other parties to DG was not permitted; and (iii) use of historic data. On these grounds COMPAT remitted the case back to CCI. The Order dated 31.08.2016 gives very appropriate responses to the arguments on the aspect of natural justice. The Competition Act does not stipulate the requirements of cross examination as all evidence are submitted to the Commission in a written form. The requirement of hearing the parties depose before the Commission is not mandated under the Act. We had permitted the parties to apply for permission to scrutinize all documents submitted to the Commission.
32. Presentation to Competition Commission of India by Shubhashis Gangopadhyay and Madaan Alisha, Economic Analysis of Collusion, 6 February 2013.
33. These points were dismissed by the companies in their replies to the DG Report. CCI found no counter evidence to accept lower growth rates in GDP and construction activity.
34. Compliance Manual for Enterprises, Competition Commission of India, 2017.
35. In this connection, the Commission also takes cognizance of the fact that CMA issues several publications such as 'Executive Summary-Cement Industry' and 'Cement Statistics-Interregional Movement of Cement' which give details of production and dispatch of each company. Such documents are circulated among its members. The sharing of such sensitive information makes co-ordination easier among the Opposite Parties. (para 202,p108), (Order, 31.08.2016).
36. A sample is given below of the coefficient matrix table for UP for the period September 2008 to 2011 by the Commission over and above the coefficients calculated by DG (p130) of Order dated 31.08.2016).
37. Op. cit. Primer from DRU.
38. Subhashish explained the game with reference to the alliance between Jet Airways and Kingfisher airlines. Its applicability in the games shown apply to undifferentiated products only.
39. Andrey Shastitko in his foreword as guest editor to the issue Antitrust in BRICS: Agenda and achievements in comparative perspective, Russian Journal of Economics, Volume 6,Number 3, September 2020 aptly summarises the requirements of making the presence of the Authority.
40. Recent Press release "Price Cartelisation charge: CCI raids major cement cos." Indian Express, 11 December 2020, New Delhi.

41. Geeta Gouri, Competition Law and Competition Policy in India: How the Competition Commission Has Dealt with Anticompetitive Restraints by Government Entities, with Aditya Bhattacharjea and Oindrilla De, Review of Industrial Organization, Jun 2018 online release.
42. See J. M. Connor, Cartel detection and duration worldwide, Competition Policy International Antitrust Chronicle, 2.10.2011.
43. A comprehensive reference to trade association from the legal dimension especially the use of legal terms in the Act and as an entity that comes under the jurisdiction of competition law is clearly discussed in several Orders of the Commission. Suo moto Case No. 02 of 2012 and Ref. Case No. 01 of 2013. In Re: Bengal Chemist and Druggist Association and Re: Reference Case No. 01 of 2013 filed under Section 19(1)(b) of the Competition Act, 2002 by Dr. Chintamoni Ghosh, Director, Directorate of Drugs. Dhanendra Kumar and Rahul Singh have expanded on the point in, Chilling competition? Trade associations & the Indian competition regime, have argued in Journal Indian Law Review, Vol 4,2020, Issue 3.
44. Balancing the positive with the negative aspects of horizontal agreements was not attempted.
45. Report of the Expert Committee on a Comprehensive Examination of Drug Regulatory Issues, Including the Problem of Spurious Drugs, Ministry of Health and Family Welfare Government of India, November 2003.
46. A recent article In Competition Policy International By Eduardo Frade on Professional and Trade Associations Back on the Antitrust Front, November 10, 2020 makes the point of countervailing power of Associations. Competition issues in the onion market in Maharashtra and Karnataka93: The study highlighted many findings and recommendations including indications of collusion among traders in selected markets in Maharashtra and Karnataka that may cause high prices of onion. The study also set out policy recommendations that aim at improving efficiency of market through competition.
47. As per the Mashelkar Committee Report " It was found that as against the frequently quoted figure of about 20,000 manufacturing units. The actual number of drug manufacturing licenses issued was - bulk drugs (1333), formulations (4534), large volume parenterals (134) and vaccines (56). Thus, the total number of manufacturing units engaged in the production of bulk drugs and formulations is not more than 5877. Besides there are 199 medical devices units, 638 surgical dressings and 272 disinfectant units, 4645 loan licences and 318 repacking units, 1806 blood banks, 2228 cosmetics units and 287other units not covered in the above categories."
48. Aditya Bhatacharje and Oindrilla De have made a pithy comment on the state of affairs." These cases reveal a truly Lilliputian situation in which

thousands of small regional distributors had for decades collectively tied down and dictated terms to the giants of the pharmaceutical industry, enforcing several blatantly anti-competitive practices all over the country." P13., Cartel Regulation in India, JAE, 21st December.

49. The Insurance Regulator was established to regulate health insurance.
50. AIOCD, instead of trying to correct the situation, has been trying to put the blame on regulators and trying to lobby that pharmacist should not be mandatory at ret AIOCD, instead of trying to correct the situation, has been trying to put the blame on regulators and trying to lobby that pharmacist should not be mandatory at retail pharmacies. This is dangerous for the patients and is a precedent not seen anywhere else in the world. In 2013, as reported by Pharmabiz, they even went on a nationwide strike and wanted the government to permit the partner or the proprietor of a drug store as a qualified person to dispense the medicines taking into account the shortage of qualified pharmacists. 'Renting' a pharmacist license, without having an actual pharmacist actually dispensing has become the standard and acceptable practice in retail pharmacies. Progressive trade associations like AIOCD should pro-actively address such pertinent sector issues as it compromises the safety of the patient.

    Technology-driven learning solutions can be deployed to meet the specific and lifelong learning needs of individual pharmacists, ultimately improving patient and public health outcomes. E-Pharmacies, on the other hand, are meticulous in employing pharmacists for validating the prescriptions and dispensing medicines in tamper proof containers as per Pharmacy Act 2015.
51. Ibid.
52. Op. cit ICN, 2018.
53. Patrick Rey and Joseph Stiglitz, *The Role of Exclusive Territories in Producers' Competition*, *The RAND Journal of Economics*, Vol. 26 (1995), p. 431.
54. Geeta Gouri, COVID Advisories from the Competition Commission of India, Competition Policy International, July 2020.
55. Ashok Sanjay Guha, *Economics without Tears, A New approach to an old Discipline*, Penguin 2016,
56. Avner Grief, Contract Enforceability and Economic Institutions in Early Trade: The Maghribi Traders Coalition. *American Economic Review*, June 1993, Vol. 83, No. 3(June, 1993), pp. 525–548 downloaded on JSTOR 202.70.131.9 on Friday 26 March, 2021.
57. Elinor Ostrom, *Governing the Commons*, Cambridge, Harvard University Press, 1990.
58. The Competition Commission of India commissioned a study on the onion market by Indian School of Economics and Social Science.

59. The late Prof George Rosen pointed the inappropriate suffix of formal or informal to market or to the economy.. Markets are where buyers and sellers interact.
60. Kaushak Basu quoted in the Economic Times of 06.01.2011, "there are forms of implicit cartel working among traders that block the movement of new entry, the appearance of new players" para 2.2 Sumo Mot Case of 01.2011, Order dated 10 April 2012 in the case of Rise in Onion Prices.
61. A.P. Kulkarni and Prema Basargekar, Factors Influencing Onion Prices in India, *Journal of Indian School of Political Economy*, Vol. 1X, No. 3(1997), pp. 463–489.
62. Ibid.
63. Please see ....
64. J.V.Meenakshi and Banerjee, J. The Unsupportable Support Price: An Analysis of Collusion and Government Intervention in Paddy Auction Markets in North India. *Journal of Development Economics*, Vol. 76, No. 2(2005), pp. 337–403.
65. Sameeta Sareen.
66. Chengappa, P.C., A.V. Manjunatha, Vikas Dimple and Khalil Shah, Competitive Assessments of Onion Markets in India, Agricultural Development and Rural Transformation Centre, Institute for Social and Economic Change, study commissioned by Competition Commission of India., 2012.
67. Ibid., Table 2, 9, p. 11.
68. See the Quarterly Newsletter of Competition Commission of India, Fair Play, Public Procurement and Competition Law, Vol. 12 January-March, 2016. In-Fous: Bid-Rigging in Public Procurement, Vol. 26, July–September, 2018. Seminars and Workshops on the subject are organized as part of advocacy programme of the Commission.
69. Ibid., Vol. 12.
70. The joke in the Commission is that government officers are worried about three C's. The Central Bureau of Investigation (CBI); Central Vigilance Commission (CVC); and the Competition Commission of India (CCI).
71. Kin Binmore, *Game Theory: A Very Short Introduction*, Oxford University Press, 2007. p. 17.
72. Vickrey, William, Counterspeculation, Auctions, and Competitive Sealed Tenders. *The Journal of Finance*, Vol. 16, No. 1(1961), pp. 8–37. 10. 1111/j.1540-6261.1961.
73. Geeta Gouri, COVID Advisories from the Competition Commission of India, Competition Policy International, July 2020.
74. This despite reference in Section 19(4) to acquisition of dominant position on account of vertical arrangements as a mitigating factor.
75. Op. cit. i.
76. Competition Act, 2002.

Section 4(2)(a):	(i) directly or indirectly,imposes unfair or discriminatory—
	(ii) price in purchase of sale (including predatory price) of goods and services.
Section 4(2)(b): limits or restricts—	(i) production of goods or provision of services or market therefore; or
	(ii) technical or scientific development relating to goods or services in the prejudice of consumers;
Section 4(2)(c):	indulges in practice or practices resulting in denial of market access (in any manner);
Section 4(2)(d):	makes conclusion of contracts subject to acceptance by other parties of supplementary obligations which, by their nature or according to commercial usage, have no connection with the subject of such contracts;
Section 4(2)(e):	uses its dominant position in one market to enter into, or protect other relevant market.

77. Ibid.
78. Eastman Kodak Company v Image Technical Services inc., et al. 112 S.Ct. 2072(1992) quoted in Carl Shapiro and David Teece, Systems Competition and Aftermarkets: An Economic Analysis of Kodak, Antitrust Bulletin, Spring 1994 39 n1 pp. 135–162.
79. Competition Act, 2002.The Competition Law Review Committee have suggested modifications to Section 3(4) which for Section 3(4) are:

    (i) Section 4 to comprehensively cover all kinds of anti-competitive agreements that may not strictly fall within the categorization of either a horizontal or a vertical agreement.
    (ii) In the case of tie-in arrangements in the explanation to insert the word 'distinct' to expressly clarify that the tied and tying products must be distinct or separate goods and services;
    (iii) With regard to 'exclusive supply agreement' to be replaced by ' exclusive dealing' expressly recognize the imposing of exclusivity both from sellers' as well as from the buyers side;
    (iv) In resale price maintenance to insert the words 'direct and indirect' to expressly clarify the ability of the CCI to penalize both direct and indirect means of imposition of RPM.

    - To expand the scope of Section 19(3)(g) t make the list of factors provided therein for determining AAEC inclusive.

- Section 19 (3)(c) delete the words "hindering entry int the market" with 'foreclosure of competition 'which takes into account situations such as lessening f existing competition, barriers to expansion in the market etc.,
- To include 'consumer harm' in Section 19(3)(d) as a factor for assessing AAEC.

80. Eastman Kodak Company v Image Technical Services inc., et al. 112 S.Ct. 2072(1992) quoted in Carl Shapiro and David Teece, *Systems Competition and Aftermarkets: An Economic Analysis of Kodak*, Antitrust Bulletin, Spring 1994 39 nl pp. 135–162.
81. I had demitted from the Commission a few months before the Order was passed. The DGs definition I had argued was based on a lack of understanding of vertical agreements and vertical integration of firms. The economics division did endorse my understand.
82. Based on discussions with the economics division.
83. Op. cit.
84. My younger colleagues reminded me of some of the discussions at the division.
85. Similarly the report of CLRC suggested that the abuse of tie-in arrangements in Section 3(4) must explicitly state that the arrangement between the two goods should be of distinction and separate products.
86. Case No. 30 of 2012, Ramakant Kini v Dr. L.H. Hiranandani Hospitals, op. cit.1 Ramakant Kini v Dr. L.H. Hiranandani Hospitals. This case is now pending before the Supreme Court.
87. The CLRC has suggested amending the present Act to include "other agreements" over and above vertical agreements that lead to AAEC. The modification was the minority decision in the Hiranandani case.
88. Clarification of the importance of *de hors* was pointed out by my colleague in his dissent order (Member T), ibid.
89. Order (Member G), ibid.
90. A recent issue of Competition Policy International (CPI 2021) provides fresh insights from the accepted standard argument of complements and of lower prices and calls for a structured analysis. Cory Capps, Nitin Dua, Tetyana Shvydko, Zenon Zabinski Stacking the Blocks: Integration and Antitrust in the Healthcare Industry., Competition Policy International–May 11, 2021.

References

CCI, Making Markets Work for Affordable Health Care.

CCI-ICN report on Cartels.

Hazari Committee Report on Industrial Licensing, Government of India, 1967.

Indian Institute of Corporate Affairs, Modules on Competition Law.

Institute for Social and Economic Change, Competitive Assessments of Onion Markets in India study commissioned by Competition Commission of India., 2012.

Mashelkar Committee Report, Report of the Expert Committee on a Comprehensive Examination of Drug Regulatory Issues, Including the Problem of Spurious Drugs, Ministry of Health and Family Welfare Government of India, November 2003.

OECD, Cartel Detection.

Raghavan Committee Report.

Report of the Competition Law Review Committee, Ministry of Commerce,Government of India, 2019.

CHAPTER 5

Dynamics of Competition: Dominance, Platforms and Antitrust Abuse

The presumption that a dominant enterprise can exert market power central to market regulation stands contested. Dominance occurs due to several factors. It could be an outcome of industrial policy a historical legacy; it maybe a manifestation of horizontal and vertical agreements among enterprises, or of high technology and of platform markets. Exerting market power is no longer a per se conclusion. Exertion of market power is a possibility when competitive constraints are hindered. In exploring reasons for exercise of market power, the per se approach gave way to the 'rule of reason' or effects based from form-based approach. The assertion of market power and the tendency noted in the previous chapter of conflation of cartelization and of vertical arrangements to borrow a phrase "reductionist approach" of one large enterprise exerting market power is no longer passe'.[1] Small (in terms of size) enterprises can also assert market power in the market of ideas and patents.[2] The process of an enterprise acquiring dominance and remaining dominant under competitive market conditions is intimately connected with the ability to exert market power.

Dominance and antitrust abuses are divided into three sections in the Competition Act. They are Section 4 existing or ex poste 'abuse of dominance (AoD); acquired or created ex-ante in Sections 5 and 6; and cartelization and vertical agreements in Section 3. All three sections are distinguished by the nuanced differences in dominance. This is a marked

G. Gouri, *A Commissioner's Primer to Economics of Competition Law in India*, https://doi.org/10.1007/978-981-19-9476-0_5

change from the initial market regulatory framework the Monopolies and Restrictive Trade Practices Act (MRTP).

Given this divide the number of cases under ex poste abuse of dominance (AoD) is limited as compared to mergers and acquisitions where the decisions are prescient based on probability of possibilities. They belong to the process of creating dominance. Anything ex-ante can be taken up ex post which facilitates quick decisions to encourage much needed investments during period of crisis. Economics of assessing the market power of dominance have a lot of overlaps with merger analysis. Merger analysis has a wider canvas with inclusion of parameters such as parallel imports, possibility of a failing business and scope for innovations. These extensions distinguish the two sections.

The Act framed in the economics of traditional binaries of monopoly and competition with its emphasis on market share has limitations to competition enforcement where high-tech industries are involved. Standard indicators used in antitrust analysis fail to capture the dynamics of high-tech industries specifically platform markets. Technology and digital markets have provided a different understanding of dominance and abuse. It also raises the issue of dominance and innovation-dominant enterprise foster innovation.

The Indian consumer as elsewhere in the world enjoys the benefits from the ever-growing spate of inventions and innovations identified with the sector. But the same innovations that benefit consumers can also disrupt individual competitors. Competitors that lose or lag in the innovation race may resort to using regulatory process to stifle innovation and gain ground against leading enterprises. The Competition Commission of India therefore faces the challenge of sorting legitimate '*abuse of dominance*' claims from attempts to abuse the regulatory process to benefit individual competitors as in industries characterized by the presence of a few firms, where high market shares or other traditional indicia of competitive success suggest, often wrongly, dominance of a leading enterprise (Geeta Gouri, 2020, 2021).[3] Recent antitrust literature refers to 'deceptive dominance' particular reference to inaccurate or insufficient information provided by the enterprise where the reference is to Intel chip.[4] There is no finality as to its inclusion under Section 4. Inappropriate claims of dominance fall into the steps of measuring dominance. It will be examined in the chapter on patents and royalty payments in the market for ideas. It finally boils down to how much market power an enterprise can exert in the specified market and in this context defining the markets is critical to abuse by a dominant enterprise. Dominance and market are therefore to be combined in assessing anti-competitive outcomes.

Four steps rules are applied in assessing abuse of dominance. They are: (i) categorization of the conducts as abusive or not benefitting consumers; (ii) defining the relevant market; (iii) assessing dominance and market power; and (iv) assessing harm to competition. The sequence can change. In the Google case, it got reduced to three steps proceeding on the presumption that dominance leads to market abuse.

Defining a Dominant Enterprise

How does one define a dominant enterprise? [5] The entire Competition Act is on dominance. Section 4 in the *explanation* defines a "dominant position" as (i) the ability to operate independently of competitive forces prevailing in the relevant market; (ii) affect its competitors or consumers or the relevant market in its favor. In traditional product markets, a dominant enterprise is defined in terms of size (market capitalization, capital investment) in the defined market and market share of the enterprise. Size as a factor of dominance may not always capture the major attribute of dominance as a position of strength. Critical software packages or precision instruments in terms of traditional parameters of size maybe small but dominate in niche areas while creating value for other activities. This gives the power to dominate.

Besides the two factors, size and share of the market 11 additional factors are listed in Section 19(4) for defining the dominant position of an enterprise. The list of 13 factors are given below and covers:

(a) market share of the enterprise;
(b) size and resources of the enterprise;
(c) size and importance of the competitors;
(d) economic power of the enterprise including commercial advantages over competitors;
(e) vertical integration of the enterprises or sale or service network of such enterprises;
(f) dependence of consumers on the enterprise;
(g) monopoly or dominant position whether acquired as a result of any statute or by virtue of being a government company or a public sector undertaking or otherwise;

(h) entry barriers including barriers such as regulatory barriers, financial risk, high capital cost of entry, marketing entry barriers, technical entry barriers, economies of scale, high cost of substitutable goods or service for consumers;
(i) countervailing buying power;
(j) market structure and size of market;
(k) social obligations and social costs;
(l) relative advantage, by way of the contribution to the economic development, by the enterprise enjoying a dominant position having or likely to have an appreciable adverse effect on competition; and
(m) any other factor which the Commission may consider relevant for the inquiry.

Let me also draw attention to three other factors in the list (e), (g) and (m) frequently referred to cases filed in the Commission. Factor (e) refers to '*vertical integration of the enterprises or sale or services network of such enterprises*' of dominance and lies behind the tendency toward conflation of Section 3(4) and Section (4) that we observed in the previous chapter. Factor (g) is on creation of entry barriers with reference to sunk costs of large projects. In India on account of large sunk costs and high financial risk, these sectors were reserved for state-owned enterprises (SOEs). In my view, factor (g) refers to the dominance of SOEs which are legally created enterprises resulting in an overlap between dominance and that of dominance created by statute. Post-liberalization exclusion of private enterprises in sectors involving high costs, high financial risks are now open to the private sector. Their response is limited. The number of firms in capital intensive sectors are invariably limited as economies of scale come into play. We shall look at a case of a dominant SOE and dominant private enterprise which in CCI are of one private sector pitted against an SOE.

The last factor (m) is a catchall phrase '*any other factor which the Commission may consider relevant for the inquiry*'. This is an open or a no-holds barred feature. My understanding is that the term 'any other factor' connotes 'public interest' and is as defined by the government (Gouri, 2020).[6] It includes the concept of 'essential facilities' which are outside the purview of competition law. Reference of dominant position is to the "group" and draws from the definition in Section 5. The 'group' includes all units and subsidiaries of the enterprise on which it exercises control singly or jointly over another enterprise or group. Group as per the Act covers two or more enterprises which directly or indirectly exercise 26% of the voting right over the other group and appoints more than fifty percent of the members of the board. It also exercises control over the management or affairs of the other enterprises in the group. Provisions of Section 4 apply only to the enterprise and not to the group.

There is no reference to collective dominance unlike EU competition law. The omission of collective dominance was discussed, and the consensus in the Commission was that collective dominance would fall under the category of cartel.

Consumer Harm

Consumer is an amorphous group, non-specific and general like the term 'public'. Assessment of anti-competitive effects of unilateral conduct is on consumer harm which will have to be specific in terms of which group of consumers are all consumers affected. An enterprise in monopolistic or oligopolistic market conditions may or may not be in a position to exert consumer harm a core area for economic analysis of competition law. In terms of classical economics of product markets, maximization of total welfare is maximization of producer and consumer surplus as discussed in Chapter 2. Domain impact of competition law is on business and on economic activity and in this scenario welfare maximization by CCI was seen more from the lens of maximization of producers' welfare. Evaluating anti-competitive effects focused on producer surplus rests on the given understanding that more producers in monopolistic markets create competition and ensure public interest. Section 4(1) of the Act states that '[n]o enterprise or group shall abuse its dominant position' with the use of the modal verb 'shall' rather than 'may' a quasi per se approach than an effects-based approach toward monopolistic markets.[7] Ultimately, in assessing abuses of dominance the Commission always considers the yardstick of meeting competition.

The aspect of consumer harm needs probing for the manner in which a consumer is defined for which it determines the effectiveness of intervention by the Authority. In platform markets, the importance of consumer comes to the forefront unlike in product markets. Consumer benefits and satisfaction define their success dependent as these markets are in harnessing network effects. Strategies followed by platform markets to attract and sustain consumers are often reckoned as anti-competitive even if consumers gain. Consumer addiction to a market have been cited especially by the European Commission as restricting consumers from shifting from one platform to another responsible for entry barriers on account of higher switching costs.

The Competition Act, 2002, defines a 'consumer':

> 2(f) consumer means any person who
>
> a. buys any goods for a consideration which has been paid or promised or partly paid and partly promised
> b. hires or avails of any services for a consideration which has been paid or promised or partly paid and partly promised

Consumer is broadly defined. It includes both who buy goods and those who hire or avail of services. A large number of cases are to consumer defined under 2(f)(b) which includes the informant who files a complaint. CCI deals only with class complaint of individual consumers as defined under 2(f)(a) and not of individual consumers. Consumer harm is not defined. CLRC also noted the gap in CA02, but no specific suggestions were made for incorporating changes in the Act.

Defining the Relevant Market

In the assessment of dominance, the parameters of the relevant market have to be defined. Delineation of relevant market is to specify the product and geographic scope within which the competitive effects of a particular business conduct are to be assessed for antitrust purposes. The process of defining the relevant market is in essence a process of determining closely substitutable commodities, and the geographical scope within which such commodities compete. Because real-world product and geographic markets are multidimensional and complex, the definition more often than not involves blurred or shaded edges with close substitutes on the inside and varying degrees of partial substitutes on the outside.[8] However, notwithstanding the complexities, assessment of market power critically hinges on the scope of relevant market. An overly narrow market definition overstates market power; a broad definition understates market power. Imminent criticism has questioned whether there is even the necessity of defining the relevant market for in defining itself there could be tendency toward arbitrariness. Apprehensions for establishing abuse of market power' is to establish consistently reliable empirical criteria for determining the degree of substitutability among products/services.[9]

The widely accepted test for delineating the boundaries of a product market is the application of what is known as the "hypothetical monopolist" test commonly referred to as the "SSNIP" test (which refers to a small but significant non-transitory increase in price). The test as observed in the earlier chapter looks at shifts in demand when there is a small but non-transitory increase in prices as a measure of substitutability. The quantitative data needed to carry out the test are often not available and the Commission accordingly delineates the market boundaries based on qualitative analyses of characteristics, price and intended use. In most products, this is an acceptable proxy. I have found that it is important for economic analysis to derive elasticities of demand for assessing consumer harm. While attempts have been made to derive elasticities from NSS data as observed in Chapter 2, their applicability is limited because they apply to broad categories of consumer grains and to products but could be taken as proxy indicator.[10]

Price elasticities are critical for evaluating several price-related abuses such as price discrimination and predatory pricing. Estimating elasticities of demand for every product is time consuming but the results in applying them are often surprisingly contrary to the belief of consumer harm.[11] Among the abuses listed under this Section, predatory pricing and other price restrictions rate high as instruments of controlling entry, of high switching costs. Non-price competition pointed out by Lina Khan is gaining considerable credence among competition authorities including CCI.[12] The recent prima facie Order of the Commission is on non-price competition.[13] The Order also points to the fact as it did in earlier cases (Harshita V WhatsApp) on the use of SSNIP "it may be difficult to contextualize substitutability from SSNIP point of view for OTT (Over the Top) communication Apps as they do not levy monetary charge on the users".

Complementary to the SSNIP is the HHI index used in arriving at market share of the dominant enterprise followed by the Lerner Index as an index to measure market power (see Chapter 2). The Index is based on the price elasticity of demand.

As observed in Chapter 1, platform markets and their market structure on the other hand are completely different from product markets. To start with platform markets are two sided. Commercial markets are on one side and advertisements on the other side. They are mainly on the internets and online. As an aggregator of markets, all actions and outcomes of platforms are defined in terms of generating of network effects. An important feature of platforms is that interoperability between two consumers is not possible unless both are on the same platform. Platforms negotiate their equation with markets from the perspective of consumers. To marketing strategists this may seem a trivial distinction between market structures. To a competition, regulator customer-centric innovativeness within the multilayers of digital ecosystems is crucial. Spaces are created by platforms where interfaces between markets create depth (network effects) and attract consumers, and to generate network effects, critics argue that consumers are 'locked into the system'. Digital markets are shaped by technology and consumer-centric innovation. In the next section, high-tech sector and platform markets will be examined. Consumers are never defined neither is harm.

An unsettled matter is between online and offline markets. CCI tends to accept that online markets are not separate from offline markets post Ashish Ahuja v Snapdeal decision (Case No. 17 of 2014) that they could be different channels of distribution. A similar approach was maintained later on booking agents for travel offline v online. There is no finality to the distinction as observed in the CCI market study on e-commerce. An important reality is that the Indian digital ecosystem is the mobile digital ecosystem and is a factor that needs to be kept in mind while analyzing platform markets. The growth of use of internet on cheap smart phones in India is inexplicable and needs to be considered in assessing anti-competitive activities of platform markets.[14] On date, it is estimated there are 900 million users on cheap smart phones and maybe more as each phone will have multiple users. Several companies have their own web sites.

1 Case Analysis of Product Markets

Case studies pertaining to AoD will be broadly divided into those that I label as traditional cases belonging to the category of traditional product markets and those that are on modern platform markets. Several of the decisions were divided but have selected those that went on the basis of economic reasoning, two-sided or multi-sided markets and networks effects. In the overlap of Sections 3(4) and 4, the cases will be with reference to the abuses listed under AoD which broadly cover predatory pricing, leveraging to enter into another market and entry barriers.

- DLF Real Estate–Steps in assessing anti-competitiveness: Unfair or Discriminatory Conditions and Pricing
- Springer India–Insignificance of defining Geographic Market qua relevant market definition
- BCCI–Conundrums of an administrator rolled into a regulator: Anti-competitive in conflict of interest
- Jindal and Steel Authority of India (SAIL)–Competitive Neutrality: State-Owned Enterprise v private enterprise
- MCX-SX v NSE–predatory and leveraging in a nascent platform market
- Matrimony.com Google India–Protecting Competition versus Protecting Competitors

1.1 Real Estate and Services of Builders: Steps in Assessing Anti-competitiveness: Unfair or Discriminatory Conditions and Pricing

A significant antitrust case that raises several difficult issues was in the real estate sector pertaining to services of builders Case No. 19/2010, *Belaire Owner's Association v. DLF Limited, Haryana Urban Development Authority, and Department of Town and Country Planning, State of Haryana*): firstly, how is service to be defined in terms of *'interchangeabilityand substitutability'* in identifying the product market of a real estate developer; secondly, defining the geographic market of the real estate developer; and thirdly, establishing abuse by the dominant enterprise.[15]The real estate market has been in the limelight for several controversies in a country where demand for affordable housing is high and land acquisition a cumbersome process (Gouri, 2012). [16] A group of flat owners alleged that DLF had imposed arbitrary, unfair and unreasonable conditions on apartments allotted to them in the Housing Complex "*the Belaire*". DLF is a large real estate company that bought land to build flats then sold to buyers. Belaire is situated in DLF City, Phase-V, Gurgaon and forms part of Greater Delhi. [17] At the time the case was filed, the apartment complex was being constructed by DLF. The usual process of apartment builders is to build these apartments on the basis of advance from owners who have registered for the flats. Payment is on installment basis expected to be aligned with progress in construction. The alignment was not observed by builders compounded by the fact that the agreements were loaded in favor of builders.

The informant Belaire Owners' Association, an association formed by the apartment allotters of Belaire, raised the inequity in payment of installment and the related progress in construction. The equated installment payment mechanism is a well-known mechanism for purchase of high-value consumer goods such as cars and housing apartments. The complaint pertained to the skewness in the relationship between payments and access to possession. High interest rates charged on default payment were not applicable to delay in completion of flats and handing over ownership. This skewed inequity in payment and delivery with a one-sided default payment was combined with changes in technical specification of ownership and rights of property ownership such inclusive of club membership, common area, etc. DLF has access to funds at zero interest with no matching responsibility. Prima facie DLF had abused its dominant position in violation of Section 4 of the Act in the Apartment Buyers Agreement (ABA).

An important question to understand is the filing of the case as an abuse of dominance with CCI rather than with the Consumer Commission of India. A class action CCI examines specific consumer complaints but they need to be considered as hindering competition. The informant's argument for filing with CCI was mainly on account of the speed with which decisions are taken as compared to consumer courts that are overloaded with complaints. Furthermore, the case was filed under Section 4 and not under Section 3 which is on Agreements that cause AAEC. Section 3 is with regard to cartelisation and of agreements between builders requiring evidence that Belaire Owners were not in a position to provide.

1.1.1 Defining the Relevant Market

The relevant market in DLF was the *services of a real estate developer* ("*services*" as defined under Section 2(u) of the Act), and consumer is the person who avails of these services 2(f) (b) The point of determination is whether DLF real estate developer provides services, that are distinct in nature "*by reason of characteristics ... their prices and intended use*" as stipulated in Section 2(t) of the Act The Commission noted from the DG's investigation report that the nature of service being provided by DLF in the context of the present case was described as services of developer / builder in respect of "*high-end*" residential accommodation in Gurgaon with two distinct features based on the characteristics of the underlying physical asset namely "*high-end*" nature of the product provided by DFL and for "*residential accommodation*". The Commission then went on to define "high end" and to include terms such as "premium" and "affordable" as these are subjective terms,[18] defining high-end demarcate DLF services market to residential accommodation in the premium segment ruling out their services in non-premium residential accommodation.

Terms such as "*high-end*", "*premium*" or "*affordable*" are relatively subjective and therefore it was felt necessary to establish a clear and logical interpretation of the term "*high-end*". The Commission noted that "*high-end*" is not a function of size alone. It is a complex mix of factors, such as size, reputation of the location, characteristics of neighborhood, quality of construction, etc., that qualify a dwelling unit as "*high-end*" or otherwise. However, the most significant characteristic of a "*high-end*" dwelling unit has to be the characteristics desired by actual customers and, among all objective differentiators of a customer's preferences, is his or her capacity to pay as demand is desire backed by the ability to pay. Apart from physical attributes, these categorizations also take into account income or expenditure levels of the customer base. Together, these factors create a distinctly identifiable residential unit that is not substitutable in an economic sense.

Users/buyers of "*high-end*" accommodation demand quality and the ambience of a distinctly higher level, and are willing to pay significantly higher prices to meet their requirements. Taking into account the current prices of High Income Group accommodation provided by the development authorities in India, as also the demands and paying capacity of the growing upper middle and rich classes in society, from the cost perspective, the Commission found it quite logical to accept an apartment costing between INR 2–2.5 crores (approx. USD 20–25 million) as "*high-end*" in the Indian socioeconomic reality.[19]

The distinction between "*high-end*" and "*mid-group*" as constituting separate markets based on price and consumer preferences has come under considerable criticism primarily on the delineation of the relevant geographic market. A related criticism was that the data used by the Commission made nothing between the product market and the geographic markets on the basis of value rather than stock.

The relevant geographic market was taken as Gurgaon which is part of the National Capital Region and the allegation pertain to DLF services in

Gurgaon. This geographic market limited to a small locality within a small state of NCR was justified on the specious argument that a decision to purchase a high-end apartment in Gurgaon is not easily substitutable by a decision to purchase a similar apartment in any other geographic location. Gurgaon is known to possess certain unique geographical characteristics, such as its proximity to Delhi, proximity to the airport and a distinct brand image as a destination for upwardly mobile families.

Defining a geographic market especially with reference to services can be contentious. In the case of goods, the relevant geographic market is bounded by the limits of the Act in terms of its applicability where conditions of supply of a service are distinctly homogenous from the conditions in neighboring areas. Contentious relevant geographic markets, which first arose in the *DLF* case in terms of defining a market that is exclusive and non-interchangeable or substitutable, point to the way cities are divided into localities that are exclusive and those which are more pedestrian or plebian. Several dissenting orders passed at the *prima facie* stage reflect the contentions that have arisen in relation to relevant geographic market definitions in the real estate sector.[20]

No SSNIP test was attempted although in a differentiated product market consumer surveys are important for distinguishing between different types of residential apartments.

1.1.2 Dominance and Its Abuse

Dominance in a relevant market defined within the narrow geographic boundaries of "*Gurgaon*" is almost axiomatic. The market definition was vigorously discussed in the Commission meetings. Several agreements of real estate developers were examined and it was found that all followed the practice of unequal agreements. The Commission was of the opinion that such agreements were clearly anti-competitive and DLF, on account of historic factors, was the first real estate developer in and around Delhi (including Gurgaon) and set the trend in ABAs and in developing premium real estate conclaves through acquisitions early in its formation of large land banks. The abuse inherent in the unequal agreement between buyers of apartments and the real estate developer was clearly anti-competitive. Criticism that a "*one-sided*" agreement entered into by a dominant enterprise with its customers is anti-competitive which in itself tends to prevail.

The *DLF* case spawned a large number of complaints in the real estate industry to the Commission. It suggests that the debate on defining the relevant market (in particular, the geographic scope of the market) and its abuse in the real estate sector has yet to evolve rigorous, consistent tools of analysis and measurement. Subsequent to the order, the Real Estate Regulatory Authority (RERA) was established.

The important conclusions of anti-competition from the DLF case are:

I. Whether abuse is more important than rigorous definition of markets and its geographic demarcation, this is treading dangerous ground as there is always the fear of finding abuse not in dominance;
II. The debate on defining the relevant market (in particular, the geographic scope of the market) remains inconclusive;
III. Abuses in DLF Apartment Buyers Agreement were the policy of all real estate developers and DLF was the trend setter. Dominance is defined by non-economic and non-parametric factors as evidenced by several minority orders of the Commission in this sector; and.
IV. Does this lend to regulatory authorities the powers of regulating rather than facilitating market functioning.

1.2 Springer India: Insignificance of Defining Geographic Market qua Relevant Market Definition

Prints India v. Springer India Private Limited & Ors (Case No. 16, 2010) was the first case of the Commission of AoD involving internet markets. It required defining the relevant geographic market involving transactions on the internet and outside national political boundaries. Surprisingly, Prints India v Springer India has rarely been referred in the literature on antitrust abuses in India although there are 3 Orders on the case from the side of the Commission.[21]

The case related to the publication and distribution of scientific and technical books and journals. Prints India was a distributor of STM (Scientific, Technical and Medicine) of journals printed in-house by the scientific and technical management institutes in India. Springer India is part of the larger international publishing firm Spring-Verlag which is ranked high in STM journals. They publish and distribute journals. In-house publishing unit becomes a distraction and costs for scientific and technical institutes. Academia would prefer to concentrate on their work and publish their papers in journals which are peer reviewed and of international standing. They are not into the business of publishing and distribution. Expertise of publishing and circulation internationally prompted many to shift from Prints India to Springer India. Sticking to the core is not the subject of competition authorities nor the argument on domestic distributors versus international publishing firms. The importance of the case rested on defining the geographic market and not the product market which was well defined. The geographic market remained undefined.

The relevant market under the Act as noted is split into the product market and the geographic market. Geographic market is usually complimentary to product market, and in mapping, the geographic market logistic of transport and transition costs on consumer demand are considered notwithstanding that the Act is applicable only to India. The Act in the definition of the "relevant market" (Section 2(r) "*means the market which may be determined by the Commission with reference to the relevant product market or the relevant geographic market or with reference to both the markets.*" In Section 19(5), reference is to both the 'relevant geographic market' and 'relevant product market'. In virtual markets, the need for defining the relevant market and its two dimensions, namely product market and geography, the standard steps followed in assessing anti-competitive practices maybe diluted.

The allegation of Prints India, a bricks and mortar publishing house, pertained to unfair practices indulged by Springer, an international publishing firm, in the (STM) journal segment in India as an abuse of the dominant position. Publishing is now an online business, and each business house is an online platform that seamlessly connects authors and readers worldwide. It also facilitates peer reviews, archival facility and most important a wider reach of readers' world-over drawing attention to mapping dominance in the larger geographic market. The geographic market left undefined the majority view was that the resolution would be with reference to publishing houses on the internet. In terms of the product market, Springer could not be classified as dominant. There were other publishing houses such as Elsevier.

Several cases of dominance on the internet are under investigation with the Commission. Clarity as regards the relevant market, both product and geographic and of dominance, is yet to emerge. Recent decisions in the e-commerce segment see a digression from defining the relevant product to splitting the market as consisting of both brick and mortar and virtual markets departing from the approach taken in the Prints India v/s Springer case. Certain aspects of Google's activities in India are also under investigation, including practices related to its advertising platform. There are issues with regard to virtual markets primarily arising out of defining the market when consumers pay no price. Assessing dominance in virtual markets is difficult and will be examined in the next section.

Challenges of antitrust enforcement in hi-tech sectors are characterized by intense and rapid innovation, assessing dominance solely through "market" shares that can be misleading. Superficially, market shares may appear high, but market shares are dependent on clear market boundaries and with technology sectors, and in particular with the internet, market boundaries often cannot be well defined. Both the products and services available over the internet and consumer usage and expectation of them are evolving rapidly. As such, both market boundaries and market shares can be transient in many technology sectors. For competition authorities like the CCI facing the technology sector, it is important to examine the actual competitive constraints on a firm with an apparently high market share and consider the prevailing market conditions in which it operates, including presence of barriers to entry and expansion, the ease of switching and potential competitive threats for emerging technologies.

The underlying understanding that dominant companies have the potential to distort competition need relooking once the geographic market is widened. Recent debates questioning the need for establishing dominance and to rather look at abuse while still inconclusive make it imperative for a competition commission to go beyond the black letter of law.

Conclusions on anti-competitive effects from the Prints India v Springer case are:

1. A rethink on defining the relevant market as necessary for application of competition law. In leaving the geographic market undefined, the first step was taken toward global inclusion of competition.
2. The geographic market on the internet is drawing market boundaries within the confines of political boundaries of a nation state that have limitations of jurisdiction in case of AoD.
3. Jurisdictional issues requiring clearances from all Authorities where the enterprise has business which is applicable only to mergers clearances.

4. Defining relevant product market in the case of platform markets is also problematic leading the Commission to define multiple markets in all cases related to internet markets including search engines.
5. Emphasis in the product market on substitutability and interchangeability. is not possible in the case of internet based two-sided markets as there would be several markets on the platform.

1.3 BCCI: Conundrums of an Administrator Rolled into a Regulator: Anti-competitive in Conflict of Interest

An administrator acting as a regulator raises suspicion in any activity that is commercial and market driven. The right of approval is with the regulator an Umpire and player rolled into. Aa a case of conflict of interest, this was my first reaction to the Board of Control of Cricket in India (BCCI) and its dual role when the case was filed with the advent of league matches in cricket.[22] Cricket is an obsession in India, and this obsession saw the emergence of new league matches the Indian Premier League (IPL) a paradigm shift from the legacy of the 'Raj' of five-day test matches under the aegis of The Board of Control for Cricket in India (BCCI). League matches are a business proposition, a commercial venture and constitute an economic activity whereby falling under the scrutiny of CCI. IPL was conceived by the Board managed by the IPL council in which the BCCI has a controlling interest.

In the literature on sports and antitrust in league matches, two aspects raise concern: first the rules of the game for instance how many overs, how many players, etc.; second, governance of rules such as legal structures, financial rules, etc.[23] The present case is of irregularities in the framing of rules and regulation and in its governance. Conflict of interest is not within the purview of the Act but anti-competitive activities falls squarely in the domain of CCI. The 3 separate Orders and one divided opinion reflect the inhibition of role demarcation between an administrator and a regulator. Regulators come to the forefront in market activities where administrators trained to administer attempt to regulate.[24]

As Makan Delrahim, former U.S. Solicitor General, observed in his outgoing speech referring to sports, it is now a big and new area of antitrust analysis, an uncharted area that needs to be explored. [25] IPL and the anti-competitive activities of BCCI are also uncharted areas where the Commission first ventured in CASE NO.61/2010 Surinder Singh Barmi v BCCI Orders dated 08,02,2013 and 29.11. 2017. Fundamental questions get raised which hitherto were taken as granted. Can a regulator like BCCI be an enterprise as defined under Section 2(h)? As an enterprise if BCCI is involved in business and commercial ventures then how are the two roles demarcated? decisions. Are national sports commercial ventures with BCCI controlling both national cricket and commercial league cricket?

League matches are managed by the IPL Council an offshoot of BCCI similar to what is followed in Britain as regards ICL and ICCI. BCCI as founding member controls the IPL Council. Full members of IPL are the governing bodies of the cricket associations in India all members of BCCI. As a commercial venture, the most favorite sport in India was ripe for monetizing the game, the name and brand of the franchisee with several doyens of industry bid for the franchisee of a team. Team franchising is the format adopted in all League matches. The bidding process is based on the composition of the team, brand name and past history of winning matches a format common to all League matches in every sport.

The allegations raised by the informant was on irregularities in the: (i) grant of ownership for franchisee rights; (ii) grants in media rights for the IPL match coverage; and (iii) award of sponsorship rights and other local grants. The case was not on conflict of interest which does not fall within the purview of the Act but on award of rights as decided by the Board which create entry barriers and entry restrictions. Pending its hearing at the Supreme Court the decision of CCI did not get attention to generate debate on sports administration in India. League matches are now important in several games including chess.

1.3.1 Parameters for Competition Assessment

A major point of discussion was on whether BCCI is an enterprise as defined under Section 2(h) of the Act in terms of the nature of its activity. Only an enterprise and its activities come under the purview of competition law. The definition in Section 2(h) of an enterprise is a functional decision and as noted in the majority Order "It is in substance the nature of activity that would decide whether the entity is an enterprise for the purpose of the Act or not". Claims by BCCI as a 'not-for-profit' status of the Board do not dilute its activities as an enterprise. The ECJ held a similar view on ELPA the Association for organizing motor cycling and other sports events.

The business of BCCI further strengthens its status as an enterprise by promoting commercial cricket Revenue is the primary consideration in Private Professional Leagues. The arguments of BCCI that its sole interest is in nurturing the game by reploughing the profits is what a profitable enterprise undertakes.

The relevant market was defined as Organization of Private Professional Cricket Leagues/Events in India. Given India's obsession with cricket, a SSNIP was not even considered as the possibility of substituting cricket matches with other forms of entertainment which is low in India. This assessment was based on the TRP ratings of TV and during semi finals and finals of IPL matches the rating exceed 10 (Order 61, 2010). Among other sports events, the DG finds that cricket scores the highest TAM ratings.

1.3.2 *Rights and Rewards*

League matches consist of Franchisee and Ownership Rights, Media Rights and Sponsorship Rights. These rights are awarded through a process of calling for tenders, evaluating the bids and then granted to the winning party. If due process has been followed, then it can be argued that the allegation of irregularity in the bidding process does not hold scrutiny.[26] The irregularities in the case of BCCI is, however, inbuilt within the Agreement in the award of Rights referred to as the *Louis Schmelling Paradox* the '*Peculiarity of Sports League*'.[27]

The Louis Schmelling Paradox is based on the understanding that for league matches revenue receipts are crucial and depend upon competition among the teams and not about business competition among the firms running the contenders. There can therefore be many leagues and league matches. Having eliminated, ICL BCCI ensured a monopolistic position for IPL in commercial cricket. Modeling of league matches emphasize the commercial dimension with demand as a function of gate receipts. Competitive balance is an important component of demand for each league series of matches. It is an acronym for closeness of competing teams in terms of winning capabilities. Matches are exciting when teams are balanced. Pitched against competitive balance is the uncertainty of the match winner. Demand for league matches is stylized (Treble, 2006) by the two factors' competitive balance and uncertainty. The two factors capture other considerations that define demand. Formalized in this manner, the model is a pure betting or gambling model where gate receipts depend on the weights placed on the two factors—the balanced team in a league or the unexpected outlier. An important factor to note is that each team in a league is run by a profit-maximizing entrepreneur. BBCI controls who gets into this exclusive club of lucrative earnings in the award the three rights.

Each of the rights as claimed by BCCI no doubt have their different price, demand function and end users and are not substitutable with each other. As an administrator, BCCI designed the rules of award of rights by defining the price, determined the competitive balance and minimized uncertainty by defining the terms of the Agreement. First and foremost, BCCI ensured there was no other league except IPL. ICL an attempt to form a league was thwarted in the begining itself. Any League match has to be cleared by BCCI as the regulator.

The design of the Agreements and the governance rules were framed by BCCI the administrator as a regulator. Firstly, franchise and ownership rights were to be held in perpetuity. BCCI fixed the minimum bid price for a franchisee and ownership rights at US 50 million. Sale was permitted after a minimum lock in period of three years but with permission from BCCI. Associate sponsorship was permitted without following due process. The size of the Agreement was Rs. 444 crs. (Order, Para 6.1). These are sponsorships rights for cold drink, food, etc. There was no time limit and could be changed with every season. Secondly, Clause 9,1(c)(1) is a guarantee by the BCCI to all contracts awarded that as follows: "*BCCI represents and warrants that it shall not organize, sanction, recognize, or support during the Rights period another professional domestic Indian T20 competition that is competitive to the league*". Lastly, in the media and communication rights the position taken by BCCI was that a second auction required no tendering process with no change in the terms of the franchisee.

The conditions of perpetuity, Board guarantee of maintaining monopolistic status and discretion in the award of contracts in the second auction were clearly abuse of dominance. The rule of the games and their governance by BBCI were violations of Sections 4(2)(a)(i), 4(2)(b)(i) and 4(2)(c) of the Act. It was creation of entry barriers, foreclosure of competition in the most popular game of sport in India. There will be an abuse of dominant position if the enterprise imposes discriminatory or unfair conditions, restricts the services (production) in the market and indulges in practices that result in denial of market access.

The conclusions I draw from the case is that competition in any arena including sports is the expertise of CCI. The counter argument that league matches can sustain only one league is a market decision. BBCI can only be a promoter of the game and not even an administrator as the dividing role between regulator and administrator is a blurred division. A mere promoter of the game perhaps is also redundant in commercial cricket as the market contends with the Louis Schmelling Paradox.

1.4 Long-Term Supply Agreement: Jindal Steel v Steel Authority of India

This case (Case No. 11/2009) was on long-term supply agreements of bilateral monopoly between a monopolist and a monopsonist. If the agreement is representative of buyers choice on rational economic considerations, competition authorities do not intervene. An interesting case (Case No.11 of 2009) that came up before the Commission was of Jindal Steel & Power Limited v Steel Authority of India (SAIL) regarding exclusive supply agreement of SAIL with Indian Railways (IR) in the supply of rails a safe harbor agreement. This was a case involving two large public sectors units. State-Owned Enterprises (SOEs) are statutory corporations set up by an act of Parliament and fully owned by government. IR is completely owned by the Government.

SAIL is the umbrella for the steel plants in the public sector. These are legally created monopolies as against natural monopolies. Entry was restricted to the private sector excepting those that already existed as in the case of Tata Steel in Jamshedpur. Large capital investment lead to monopolistic competition. Given their dominant position, SoEs are liable to contravene Section 4 of the Act. Trade liberalization and removal of trade barriers is the best mechanism for ensuring competition.

The exclusive supply agreement of SAIL with IR has a long history of supplying rails of required lengths giving rise to the allegation that an exclusive long-term agreement between a buyer (monopsonist) and a seller (monopolist) violates Sections 3(4) and 4(2). Defined as a 'bilateral monopolist', antitrust literature emphasizes the importance of long-term agreements in these circumstances endorsing 'buyers choice' inherent in them. The economic rationale for the endorsement is based on considerations of availability of essential supplies on a continuous basis to ensure that the railways are not restrained in their services.

It was primarily the requirement of rail movements that a dedicated unit for producing rails in one of the steel plants was taken therein ensuring no stoppage. Shifting from structural products to rails is an expensive and time-consuming process. These rails were endorsed by the RDSO of IR while Jindal as a new entrant to rails from producing structurals still awaited RDSO clearance at the time the tender was issued by railways. Imports were ruled out as the rails were not standardized in length requirement of IR, and since SAIL was ordered to produce rails, it was bounden on IR to provide the comfort of a secure contract. The Jindal rails were shorter and had a lucrative export market but not a domestic market.

The Commission examined the long-term supply agreement of IR and SAIL as such agreements reduces the size of the potential entrants and of future competitors.[28] Economists who have studied bilateral monopolies while endorsing the importance of supply assurance emphasize the importance of non-exclusionary tender documents provided they are subject to periodical reviews and open to review.[29] In a bilateral monopoly as noted by the Commission in this case, buyer's choice was respected equilibrium price and quantity is indeterminate. Nash bargaining as it was pointed out enables the derivation of price-quantity equilibrium solution compatible to both parties (Para 121). The required additional factors of openness, fairness and periodical reviews persuaded the Commission that the long-term agreement was not anti-competitive. Moreover, data on non-IR sales of rails was about 25% of the rail markets. Scope for exports was additional factor that weighed in the Commissions' decision.

2 What We Understood and What We Missed: Beginnings of Platform Market

2.1 *The Learning Process*

The peculiarities of platform markets were not conceptualized in the Competition Act, 2002. They were examined in the review of the Act by the Committee set up by the Government of India in July 2019. On review, the Committee opined that the prevailing structure on dominance and its abuse was wide and all encompassing requiring no change in the prevailing Section 4 of the Act. In a separate chapter analysis of technology and new age markets, the Committee deferred introducing any modifications on the premise that prevailing conditions did not warrant a change in the clauses of the Act. It is perhaps a premature response based on incomplete understanding of the underling economics of changing markets structures persuaded more by legalese of parties arguing before the Commission. Staying within the framework of traditional product market, the decisions remained sterile. The divide between economics and law is stark. An important modification was introduced by the Committee, and in my opinion, a significant change was the acceptance of the power to dominate by small innovative firms. It suggests softening the primary emphasis on size as a factor of dominance and abuse suggesting caution in the merger of large firms with these small technology enterprises. I prefer to rechristen the new age markets as platform market to captures the economics of these markets more effectively. MCX-SX v NSE and Matrimony.com, CUTs v Google India as two major Orders selected missed comprehending shifts in market structures. The importance for competition analysis stems from delineating the two markets as pointed out in Chapter 2. The selected two cases illustrate deficiencies in antitrust analysis of both exclusionary and extortionary abuses if market differences are not taken into consideration. Platform markets bring to the forefront the importance of consumer harm as the litmus test of abuse of dominance much more sharply than the 13 factors listed in Section 19(4). In fact, in platform markets all 13 factors get subsumed under consumer harm.

2.2 *MCX-SX v NSE: Predatory and Leveraging in a Nascent Platform Market*

Stock exchanges are at the most two in country meant for listing of shares, debentures and trading in stocks. The MCX-SX v National Stock Exchange (NSE) (Case No. 13 of 2009) was CCI's first exposure to a stock exchange. It was also among its earliest exposure to platform market. Stock exchanges have several verticals on the platform for each trade two-sided with buyers and sellers on either side and dominant. Competition authorities have always been bothered about platform markets as too big to leave unregulated. In this case, the main hurdle was conceptual. The majority decision rested on dominance of NSE as a stock exchange and not dominance of two-sided platform market.[30]

Dominance is a given for stock exchange. NSE is the largest stock exchange in India as against the other stock exchange that of Bombay Stock Exchange, in terms of volumes of transaction and value of trades at the aggregate on the exchange. There are only two stock exchanges. MCX-SX is an exchange in the commodities of products interested in securing a license from RBI for currency derivative (CD) vertical. There is no separate exchange for derivatives as in the US. The carry-over of dominance by a stock in the platform network markets defines a shift from traditional product market to platform markets, a shift that has significant impact on competition analysis and application of a law that is designed for traditional markets.[31]

Allegations of predatory pricing by NSE Section 4(a)(i) was premised on waiving of the transaction fees (zero transaction fee) for trades in currency derivatives (CD). MCX-SX's claim rested on its inability to levy zero fee in its single segment stock exchange, i.e., the CD segment resulting in losses for the nascent exchange. Zero transactions' costs were permitted by the other two regulators SEBI and RBI as an introductory offer to encourage exporters to shift from banks and for creating depth in the market. The allegation of leveraging by NSE Section 4(2)(e) to enter and monopolize the CD market was a follow-up on the allegation of predatory pricing. In fact, the market share of MCX-SX was higher than NSE in the CD market except that reference was to the total volume of trade in stocks.

2.2.1 *Economics of Predatory Pricing and Leveraging*

Predatory pricing is of pricing a product or service below its cost of production (marginal cost) as given in Explanation to Section 4:

> means the sale of goods or provision of services, at a. price which is below the cost, as may be determined by regulations, of production of the goods or provision of services, with a view to reduce competition or eliminate the competitors.

In the traditional product market framework, zero pricing or pricing below marginal cost is clearly an abuse of dominance. In platform markets, there are several reasons for following pricing strategies at zero or below cost and not just as an introductory offer. Firstly, and in my opinion the main force behind pricing schemes is the requirement of generating network economies. This requires attracting customers and traders to the exchange. Zero pricing is more often the strategy for networks to build up often referred to in 2-sided markets as the 'positive feedback loop effects'. Apart from waiver of transaction fees, membership fee in the CD segment was also waived. There were the small fees waived such as data fee. [32] Secondly, a two-sided market revenue can be generated from either side. Thirdly, in pricing below MC, it is possible that the firm is left with only variable costs which in a digital market may be very insignificant.

Leveraging the other allegation under competition law to be considered anti-competitive is very specific in the use of the term. The basic condition for leveraging is the requirement of two markets where dominance in one market is used to protect the other market provided there are strategic gains to be realized. Leveraging leading to foreclosure is when a firm in one stage say manufacturing leverages to enter into another firms market say of an input denying other firms the access to a critical resource. Foreclosure would happen if the two markets are in different stages of production which was not so in the MCX and NSE CD market. Or when there are links between the different segments of a stock exchange between equity derivative and currency derivative or between equity, debt and currency derivatives. This is not so as trades and instruments in each market segment of the exchange are separate in terms of objectives and risk.

Currency derivatives are instruments of hedging for exporters to hedge against their foreign exchange risk. Earlier banks would provide for coverage on foreign exchange risk except they treat all transactions on similar footing charging the same bank rate on forward dealings. On the other hand on the exchange, a variety of derivative instruments are available to suit individual requirements of each exporter. Financial markets, however, require depth to attract trades as consumers gain from instruments of different lengths of contract and varying discount rates. These are the network economies that lie behind pricing strategies. To sustain the arguments of predatory pricing and leveraging requires large amounts of data on costs and prices.

2.2.2 Relevant Market

The relevant market in the both majority and minority Orders was defined as "*the stock exchange services in respect of the CD segsment in India*". The market defined as 'the stock exchange services in respect of the CD segment in India'. Interestingly, it is important to note that the Order adopted a wider definition of dominance than the reference to the market defined capturing the essence of *Explanation* of dominance in Section 4 of CA02.

Quote:

> In terms of explanation (a) of Section 4 of the Competition Act, 'the position of strength' is not some objective attribute that can be measured along a prescribed mathematical index or equation. Rather, it has to be a rational consideration of relevant facts, holistic interpretation of (at times) seemingly unconnected statistics or information and application of several aspects of the Indian economy. What has to be seen is whether a particular player in a relevant market has clear comparative advantages in terms of financial resources, technical capabilities, brand value, historical legacy etc. to be able to do things which would affect its competitors who, in turn, would be unable to do or would find it extremely difficult to do so on a sustained basis. The reason is that such an enterprise can force its competitors into taking a certain position in the market which would make the market and consumers respond or react in a certain manner which is beneficial to the dominant enterprise but detrimental to the competitors.

End of Quote

The minority Order differed in treating the stock exchange as a platform and CD segment a vertical on the platform. And, in this difference, the analysis of abuse between the two Orders varied. The dominance of NSE, in the majority Order of MCX-SX v. NSE, was not based on NSE's market share in the CD segment rather, it premised on the dominant position of NSE in stock market services derived from the explanation of "dominant position" provided under Section 4, supported by an assessment of the factors set out in Section 19(4) of the Act. MCX-SX in fact had a slightly higher market share in the CD segment than the other two stock exchanges. The majority decision was per se premised on zero transaction costs as 'unfair price' and not on predatory pricing.[33] The rationale of zero pricing in platforms seeking to provide consumers (traders) the benefits of network economies was not considered in the decision purely on account of reluctance to appreciate the nuances of network economics where zero transaction costs as the method adopted by NSE to create depth in the newly launched CD market. The argument carried no weight in the majority decision. Zero transaction costs as an introductory offer surmised if extended beyond a period which would lead to foreclosure of competition in the CD market, and other CD exchanges would have to exit the market despite the complainant MCX-SX having a larger share of the currency derivate trades. The perception of competition was on numbers and not on consumer harm. The views of the consumer were not sought. The allegation of leveraging was a natural corollary to the given theory of competition.

The minority decision analyzed the economics of both zero transaction costs and leveraging in the framework of platforms and of network economics. The order found no violation of the law and the allegations as anti-competitive were not accepted.

The challenge for competition authorities in platforms where network effects are important and to be realized the minority Order emphasized the benefit to consumers of zero transaction costs. Counter factual evidence was presented to emphasize the revenue earning tactics of large platform market. Ensuring prevalence of competitive constraints than of penalizing zero transaction costs changes the construct of intervention by the Authority CCI. It is for competitors to be innovate with alternate pricing mechanism and not seek the support of the competition authority.

Defining to distinguish the market was important for a critical appreciation of competition in stock exchanges. The Order failed to appreciate the significance of platforms and two-sided market. Pricing schemes in these markets permit innovative mechanisms with the flexibility of recovery of costs from one side of the market. Is the stock exchange a platform for all services or is it a platform for several verticals where currency derivative is one vertical as are other verticals such as equity, debt, foreign exchange derivate, etc. Are stock exchanges feasible and viable when they have multiple verticals or is a vertical viable with multiple products and instruments of exchange? How to define consumer harm in the presence of network economies?

The MCX-SX v/s National Stock Exchange (NSE) (Case No. 13/2009) was the first case in the genre of high technology. Stock exchange is a regulated business. Permitted trades on specific stocks and instruments are on the basis of license from the Reserve Bank of India. Trade in currency derivatives was initially licensed to NSE, MCX-SX and United Stock Exchange of India (USE). NSE and USE are stock exchanges while MCX-SX is part of the Commodity Exchange MCX.

The Order (Majority) preferred to stay within the confines of the Act. The Order upheld the allegations of zero pricing preferring to use the term 'unfair' rather than predatory pricing by NSE absolving the need to provide data on marginal costs or average costs as set out in the Regulation on Determination of Cost of Production. Zero pricing created exclusionary barriers for MCX to sustain itself leading to the allegation of leveraging by NSE. On hindsight, I think the economics of high technology was disruptive and difficult to conceptualize with the majority Order preferring instead to stay with economics of competition in terms of increasing numbers in a sector where single exchanges or one more is the rule.

The Minority Order premised on network economics. Complementarity between nodes (users) as seen in relation between buyers and sellers required to complete a transaction was the basis of classifying as a network industry. The stock exchange as a platform for providing trading facilities and the requirements of a minimum critical mass in terms of liquidity and trading activity drew attention to the economies of networks. All of us familiar with the financial markets know how critical depth in a market is required for innovative instruments to be offered. The attributes of network industry specifically on the allegations of 'zero pricing' was succinctly argued in the Order (paras 6.5 to 6.7) of the Minority Order.

Scope for divergent pricing schemes including zero price and of non-price competitive strategies is difficult to conceptualize. The analytical framework of network economies helped in conceptualizing that network industries as in the case of other high-tech industries consumer welfare is maximized from dynamic gains for which in the stock exchange market necessitated in the initial stage to create depth. Different pricing schemes and non-pricing competing strategies gain prominence. By licensing three CD segments, the strategy followed by NSE does not suggest the same be followed by MCX. The Order brought to attention that in network industry economic analysis has "brought attention the difficulty in developing standardized business strategies based on uniform behavioral principles".

NSE was fined. NSE levied a fee following the decision of CCI started to levy a transaction fee. Market share of MCX rose above the other two licensees NSE and USE.

2.2.3 *'What We Understood and What We Missed'*

- Did the Order address the key factor force of competition that of forcing competitors to compete and win customers be it price or non-price strategies? Innovative approaches in design of new instruments, of trade delivery and settlement of addressing variance of risk as between consumers are strategies that the informant could have considered have not been forthcoming. Rather, abuse was seen in terms of loss of the firm.
- Did consumers gain?
- Did consumers' traders and seller benefit from the decision of levying a fee on the transaction considering that the intent of

> having a CD segment was primarily to encourage small and MSME exporters as against the prevailing alternate of the banking sector perforce unimaginative. Exporters lost out in hedging instruments of currency derivatives in their choice of an exchange. Let the consumer decide between a zero fee and a small fee with innovative instruments.

Wrongly exercised the decision without a perspective on networks failed to release the potential for growth in exports that CD markets can harness. It also brought to focus consumer harm in an inappropriate assessment of markets and competition by simply failing to understand the finer distinction between product market and platform market and the underlying economics.

2.3 *Matrimony.com v Google India–Protecting Competition Versus Protecting Competitors*

Google is always in the forefront of cases filed as antitrust abuses. The myriad of decisions on each premised abuse makes it a fascinating case study. I have tried to raise several of the arguments in this section without attempting a definite conclusion leaving it to the reader to draw her own conclusions.

The primary aim of competition authorities is for protecting competition versus protecting competitors which is often missed in the opaque understanding that competition requires increasing the number of competitors.[34] Enforcement by CCI suggests the latter merits discussion. Google has always been at the center of antitrust analysis a '*prima donna*' of antitrust, and when two cases were filed (**Case Nos. 07 and 30 of 2012**) within a short span of each other, there was a perceptible feeling of acknowledgment within the Commission as an authority of reckoning. Further cases have been filed on Google and Android as possible new anti-competitive abuses emerge. I guess Google and Facebook will remain in the frontline of competition enforcement activity for a while. The divided decision in the first case of CCI is testimony to the fact that the jury is not yet out on Google and on platform markets

The case was premised on alleged bias of the search algorithms of Google toward its own "properties" and the algorithm used to calculate an advertisers quality in ranking of verticals violates competition statutes.

It was a divided decision. The majority decision following jurisprudence practice shifted the burden of rebuttable to Google.[35] It found Google abusing its dominant position in the market for internet search by promoting its own comparison services referring to travel services and fined Rs. 632 crs. The minority decision differed on the lack of substantive evidence on claims that the Google search engine played favorites.

The Google case raised several points which need careful scrutiny in each of the four steps rule of competition analysis of (1) categorization of the conduct, (2) market definition, (3) assessment of dominance or market power and (4) analysis of competitive effects.[36] The first step regarding categorization of conduct the presumption of dominance and abuse was overriding in assessment. India as with the EU Commission was not inclined to categorize the behavior as 'innovation in product design'.[37] The informant's complaint against Google was on two aspects as regards the search service. In combining its vertical search tools with organic content, the bias was inherent in the use of the two formats: (a) Universal Results and (b) One Boxes. The former is in response to a general query while the latter provides short factual notes to specific questions. Each search engine uses its own format essentially to satisfy the consumer in her search. These are innovations in product design that need to be acknowledged. The informants complaint to CCI was on the ranking of web sites and the search bias in favor of its own products by Google. To me and Salinger, it was an unusual challenge of proving that a competitive market is competitive (Salinger and Gouri, 2016).

The first case was filed by Matrimony.com a web site with its concern that in the Google web search the ranking of its matrimonial site was low. The second case by Consumer Unity Trust Society (CUTS) was filed as a public interest litigation case. Both cases were combined. Later, Make My Trip, a travel agency, joined as a party in providing evidence.

The majority decision CCI found Google India indulging in anti-competitive practices in the search intermediation agreement in the search services market.[38] The minority dissent decision pointed to the lack of substantive evidence to accept the allegations of the informants.

As an agreement, the abuse would fall under Section 3(4), but as a dominant, Section 4 is operative and the cases were filed under both sections. Google's conduct was found to be anti-competitive in terms of Section 4(2)(a)(i), Section 4(2)(b)(ii), Section 4(2)(c) and Section 4(2)(e) of the Act (CCI Order, 2018).

2.3.1 The Relevant Market

CUTS the petitioner averred that there are two markets '*online general search market*' and '*online search advertising services market*'. DG proceeded on the two-market classification as put forth by the informant '*online general search market*' and '*online search advertising services market*'.[39] Google is an intermediation service provider serving users with information they seek from surfing the platform. As a search engine, the market for Google relates to search blurring the distinction of two markets. Search is always specific to the user and the term general search engine perhaps is a reference to search for any subject.[40] Since search is free for users, Googles' earnings are from web sites or verticals that wish to advertise on the platform. But verticals which include You Tube, Google maps also form part of the search and it is in this loop that Google classification as a two-side platform is in dispute. As a search engine, Google combines its verticals which include Google Maps and You Tube and in a search, these verticals or web sites are part of the general or Organic search results (Salinger and Gouri, 2016) also pointed out by DG "*Online search advertising is linked to user-initiated search query*" in para 17 of the Order.

On what constitutes a market for evaluating unilateral conduct on search engine platform is blurred. The relevant market is defined on the basis of substitutability. Complementarity rather than substitutability of search and advertisement lead to CCI defining two markets. Two markets in the Google case lack the clarity of two side or multi-sides of e-commerce platforms. The abuse pertains to the search intermediation agreement services of verticals who wish to be on the Google platform. Doubts on whether general search can be a relevant market or does a market need specification in terms of the market of classes of search such as matrimony, travel, sport, etc. raises the basic question: Can there be abuse without a defined market a '*non-market*' abuse (Gouri, 2016).[41]

The operative market relevant for antitrust is the market of transactions where an enterprise is inclined to indulge in anti-competitive practices with the intent to reduce competition and maintain levels of profit.

Technological developments and changed paradigms of business as with platforms can cloud thinking between the way business is conducted and the defining of market. Earlier, a cement producer is in the cement market extendable to the market for building material. The classic case of a non-market is of aftermarkets. In the automotive sector, distinction is attempted between the automobile market and the aftermarket for spares. Are these two markets independent or are both segments of the larger automotive market? The aftermarket debate highlighted the importance of locating the relevant market in relation to the source of competitive constraints.

I find where platforms are involved there is greater blurring of the relevant market. Definition of the relevant market gets mired in an inexplicable controversy of two-sided and multi-sided platforms confusing markets with innovative business models. Uber a taxi aggregator is a two-sided platform business model with taxi hailers (riders) on one side and taxi owners on the other side. The market is 'radio taxi service' market (*Mega Cabs v ANI Technologies*). With greater use of mobiles and Apps, most taxi services are now attempting to offer the facility of taxi on call, but they are not aggregators on a platform with the felicity of innovative pricing schemes and of tracking.

The Commission in the case of Google identified the market by splitting into '*online general search engine*' and '*online search advertising services*' markets persuaded perhaps by the concept of multi-sided platforms. Google is a search engine or aggregator in the business of providing information to consumers.

It is still not clear why a second market was defined. As per the name 'Online Search Advertising Services', distinction is drawn between free search known as Organic and sponsored search which came in the wake of Commercial Units. Google Shopping and Google Flights are sponsored search catalogs. Increasing digital sales in these two areas and consumers searching for these sales' outlets make sense to have sponsored catalogs. *eMarketer* estimated that in India digital travel and related sales were expected to increase by 33% in 2017.

Firms pay to advertise on the net with a preference to be shown on sites that consumers visit regularly. The second market was of combining revenue sources with searches. It makes commercial sense, but does it merit the status of a relevant antitrust market. Antitrust agencies claim that these Commercial Units have the 'potential' to negatively affect the business of web-based commercial firms and definite candidates for likely unilateral conduct. A lot more explanation is required than provided in the Order for defining the relevant antitrust market.

Firstly, web sites of commercial firms are known as verticals on account of a second click on the Google box to access the relevant page which includes Google Flights. Google is a search engine and not a vertical.

To indulge in anti-competitive practices, Google has to be a vertical or have stakes in firms sponsoring Google Flight. An investigation report should have gathered such information to justify the enforcement decision. The focus of search engines is on satisfying consumers. Failure to do so would see reductions in business and revenue. History is replete with search engines reinventing themselves such as Bing, Duck Duck Go and Yahoo. Now Google chrome is a default search engine on Bing if your software is Microsoft Windows.

Secondly, the "Map Heat" test of Microsoft conducted in Europe 'stray-stay' eye movements of consumers on Google Flight is not convincing to establish consumer preferences. Indian consumers are price sensitive always on the lookout for deals in air tickets in shopping evident in the Amazon-Flipkart deal. In a survey conducted by the DG, it was found that 90% of Indian consumers scroll down to find an attractive price. The Google flight box at most remains a comparator.

Lastly, a quick check on the web (Google) showed that Make My Trip (MMT) (*Investor Presentation*) had gross bookings of USD 1.84 billion in 2016 expected to go further up in 2017. Yatra the closest rival showed gross bookings in 2017 of INR 69.1 billion (*Yatra, Investor Presentation*).

In a recent decision (Case No. 1 of 2020), MMT was in the docks for abusing its dominant position as the main online travel agency with Treebo a new chain of hotel management alleging MMT favoring its own comparison service OYO.

2.3.2 *Dominance Assessed*

Google as dominant was assessed on the fact that it had more than 60% of search market. Presence of competitors indicates a wide market and not amenable to unilateral conduct. Bing, Yahoo, Duck Duck Go and Qwant are some of the well-known search engines that are competitive constraints to Google. All web sites offering information including Wikipedia, Facebook and Amazon provide information. In a recent decision on the newly introduced vertical Google Meet, CCI (Case No. 39 of 2020) found no evidence of dominance and abuse in the online search vertical.[42]

The Google decision of CCI was influenced by the EU Commission decisions where it was argued that in the European Economic Area (EEA) Google was dominant in the internet search. Entry barriers were on account of both high investments and network effects. The EU competition law proceeds on the Ordo-liberal thinking that dominant companies have a responsibility to encourage other search engines and not abuse their dominant position. This approach was in keeping with India's historical socialist approach. The approach of FTC of 'innovation by design' was not sufficiently strong for CCI to take a lenient view of dominance. Consumer benefit or satisfaction was not factor in the decision.

2.3.3 'What We Understood and What We Missed'

The changing allegations on Google and of the remaining Big Five by competition authorities is aptly summarized in the phrase ' what we understood and what we missed'. As noted in the earlier MCX-x v NSE case in high-tech industries, the emphasis must necessarily be on consumer welfare. Another important learning is that competition and competitive constraints are not price dependent. Combining these two dimensions what we missed is the importance of innovations in product design in meeting consumer satisfaction. Innovations have their own cycles, and a frontier player can fall back to being a laggard. The rate of attrition is high, and sustainability capacity of established players is continuously on test. A small player with a new innovation is what competition authorities should not be swept in regulating the big players. The lessons of Microsoft and FTC intervention are oft quoted in antitrust literature of undue overenthusiasm. In our paper (Salinger and Gouri), we have tried to capture the design and redesign of products of search covering Universal Search, One Box, Ten Blue Links and verticals.

> In our opinion the notion than any competition authority can help Google design its search algorithms and displays inways that consumers will prefer is nothing short of preposterous. Microsoft appears to agree with us. It had been leading efforts to get competition authorities to sue Google, but it has no interest in making Google more attractive to searchers. That would hurt Bing.

The tendency of competitors to use CCI to file cases as noticed in all cases including the present is not prevalent in mature competition jurisdiction meriting us (Salinger and Gouri) to comment

> And, we would, observe it has not invited a similar inquiry by DG-Comp, the US FTC, or any other competition authority into Bing, so that it may benefit from their consulting advice on how to better satisfy users.

In punishing Google, there is no concern about consumers and their satisfaction. To reiterate in this case too, consumer identification and satisfaction were missed.

The understanding that verticals themselves in a search engine are web sites of advertisers in search of information to the query sought by the user is good business strategy. Advertisements are complements and not substitutes to the general search and persuaded the commission on two markets. Blurring boundaries of markets of the Google case are initial insights into the way algorithms which traverse across markets.

3 Conclusion

Definitions commonly understood in competition law require redefining emerged from the first Google case, defining dominance based on defining the markets itself. The argument is circular. Recent cases have been on Android, the software package in preference to Apple and Samsung. Platform markets are the fights of Titans. The new set of antitrust abuses is on algorithms which we examine in another chapter. The abuses related to both Section 3(4) and Section 4 and conflation of sections in the Google case draw attention to algorithms of search engines and of web sites and verticals.

Notes

1. Yogesh Pai and Nitesh Daryanani, Patents and competition law in India: CCI's reductionist approach in evaluating competitive harm, Journal of Antitrust Enforcement, 2017, 5, 299–327.
2. Market power and size is new disputed in Germany and France where there is a move to codify the prevalent competition law. Bundeskartellamt Paper on Platform Market Power–Results and Recommendations, Autorite de la concurrence of France. An interest article puts the arguments succinctly by Rahul Goel, Emerging Trends in Market Power: An Update, July 25, 2017, posted in COMPETITION.
3. See Geeta Gouri & Kalyani Pandya, The Indian competition law experience– its history and its (digital) future, Indian Law Review, Nov. 2020, pp. 276–300.

4. *Maurice E. Stucke*, How do (and should) competition authorities treat a dominant firm's deception? SMU law Review, Electronic copy available at: http://ssrn.com/abstract=1395076. Among the various alleged deceptive practices, Intel misrepresented industry benchmarks to favorably reflect the performance of its central processing units relative to its competitors' products, and it pressured independent software vendors to label their products as compatible with Intel and not to similarly label the names or logos of a competitor's products, even though these products were compatible.
5. I refer the readers to Report of the Competition Law Review Committee, Ministry of Corporate Affairs, Government of India, July 2019. The report in Chapter 6 discusses unilateral conduct in the present Competition Act and in this context provides the reader with case studies and competition law in other countries.
6. Geeta Gouri, "Convergence of competition policy, competition law and public interest in India", in Russian Journal of Economics Volume 6, Number 3, Special Issue: Antitrust in BRICS: Agenda and achievements in comparative perspective, Editor, Andrey E. Shastitko, September 2020, pp. 277–293.
7. In implementation of the law, a quasi-effects approach was applied rather than mere' per se'. The move toward a full effects analysis was a slow process in matured competition jurisdictions of EU and US.

   I draw attention to a very well-reasoned article on the use of 'shall' than 'may' in legal language. See Jyothi Sagar, "Shall" Shocked: The use of shall in legal documents", Bar & Bench, 19th Jun, 2021.
8. Invited by Competition Policy Research Centre (CPRC) of the Fair Trade Commission of Japan (JFTC) to deliver the special lecture "Making Markets Work Effectively in India", 10th International Symposium on "Role of Competition Policy in Emerging Economies', Tokyo, Feb 2013. Welfare maximization and the concept of deadweight loss have been discussed in detail in Chapter 2.
9. The Competition Act 2002 defines the Relevant Market and lays down the criteria/factors which are to be looked into while delineating the relevant product and geographic markets.

   Article 2(r), (s) and (t) of the Competition Act, 2002, define "relevant market" as:

   (r) "Relevant market" means the market which may be determined by the Commission with reference to the relevant product market or the relevant geographic market or with reference to both the markets;

   (s) "Relevant geographic market" means a market comprising the area in which the conditions of competition for supply of goods or provision of services or demand of goods or services are distinctly homogenous and can be distinguished from the conditions prevailing in the neighboring areas;

(t) "Relevant product market" means a market comprising all those products or services which are regarded as interchangeable or substitutable by the consumer, by reason of characteristics of the products or services, their prices and intended use.

10. Gaurav S Ghosh, Repurposing NSSO data for Market Definition, Economic and Political Weekly, Vol. LIII, No. 38, Sept. 22, 2018, pp. 67–73.
11. A young economist who started her career as an intern in CCI did a simple a consumer survey of Google Pay and found that several consumers choose their own UPI or unified payment mechanism which was against the argument that Google Pay dominated the market and created entry barriers. See Garima Sodhi, forthcoming in Competition Policy International.
12. Lina Khan, Amazon's Antitrust Paradox, The Yale Law Journal 126:710, 2017.
13. CCI suo moto Prima Facie on Updated Terms of Service and Privacy Policy for WhatsApp Users order dated 24.03.2021.
14. Geeta Gouri, Markets Platform Markets: The Antitrust Challenge in India, Competition Policy International, March 12,2021.
15. Referred to as the three steps of assessing unilateral conduct.
16. Geeta Gouri, Market Activism, Competition and Development of Markets in India, in Jenny, Frederic and Katsoulacos, Yannis, edited Competition Law Enforcement in BRICS and in Developing Countries, Legal and Economic Aspects, Springer,2016.
17. My colleague M(R) raised an interesting point of discussion on taking up DLF under Section 4 'abuse of dominance 'and not under Section 3 which assesses agreements and their impact on competition. DLF as pointed out was dominant among all the builders in the area, and as all builders have similar agreements, the case should be assessed under Section 4.
18. The Commission noted that "high end" is not a function of size alone. It is a complex mix of factors, such as size, reputation of the location, characteristics of neighborhood, quality of construction, etc., that qualify a dwelling unit as "high end" or otherwise. However, the most significant characteristic of a "high-end" dwelling unit has to be the characteristics desired by actual customers and, amongst all objective differentiators of a customer's preferences, is his or her capacity to pay as demand is desire backed by the ability to pay. Case No. 19/2010, *Belaire Owner's Association v. DLF Limited, Haryana Urban Development Authority, and Department of Town and Country Planning, State of Haryana*, p. 173.
19. ibid.
20. Case No. 21/2011, Dissenting Order, *Jagmohan Chhabra and Mrs. Shalini Chhabra v. M/s Unitech Ltd., Gurgaon*, Case No. 27/2011,

Dissenting Order, *Jagmohan Chhabra and Mrs. Shalini Chhabra v. M/s Unitech Ltd., Gurgaon*, Case No. 67/2011, Dissenting Order, *Geogi Kuruvilla, Chennai & Ors. v. M/s Hirco Developments Pvt. Ltd., Mumbai & Ors.* and Case No. 55/2011, Dissenting Order, *Kolkata West International City Buyers Welfare Association, Howrah v. Kolkata West International City Pvt. Ltd. & Ors.*

21. Case No. 16 of 2010 Prints India v Springer India Private Ltd and Indian Academy of Sciences and eight Institutes of Science, Order dated July 2012, Majority Order, Order by Member Dhingra and Order by Member R. Prasad.
22. BCCI is a society registered under Tamil Nadu Societies Registration Act, 1975 with the primary objectives as stated in the Memorandum of Association (MoA) of controlling the game of cricket in India, promoting the game in India, framing the laws of cricket in India and selecting teams to represent India in Test Matches, ODIs and Twenty 20 matches played in India or abroad. It is a 'full member' of International Cricket Council ("ICC").
23. Sports, Antitrust Chronicle, Competition Policy International, APRIL SPRING 2020 VOLUME 1(2).
24. My concern has always been that both sector regulators and the Competition Commission of India have more civil servants than academia or business people. Heated debates in the Commission revealed our backgrounds with each side learning from the others experience.
25. As The NCAA's Antitrust Battle Intensifies, 2021 Could Bring Monumental Change To College Sports Karen Weaver, Forbes.
26. See the Order by M(T).
27. John Treble, Funny Peculiar: Modelling Sports League, Working paper in Economics, SBE-E/2006/07, Swansea.
28. Aghion and Bolton (1989), Horn and Wolinsky (1988).
29. Cusumana and Takeishi.
30. Posner and Bork.
31. My analysis of the case was first developed in Distinguished Lecture 2016 on "High Technology and Competition Law Enforcement", sponsored by Delegation of the European Union to India under "Capacity Building Initiative in the Competition Area under Trade Development Program in India", Delhi 2016 summarized later in Jenny F., and Y. Katsoulacos op.cit, Russian Journal of Economics, op.cit., first developed in my lecture.
32. Case No. 13/2009 Information filed on 16.11.2009 In continuation of order dated 25.05.2011, Date of order under Section 27 of the Competition Act, 2002: 23.6.2011, MCX Stock Exchange Ltd v National Stock Exchange of India Ltd. DotEx International Ltd.

33. Predatory pricing premises on the aspect of recoupment and is a strategy to win over customers and a larger market share. Lina Khan has brought it out effectively op.cit.
34. Geeta Gouri and Salinger M., Protecting Competition Versus Protecting Competitors: Assessing the Antitrus
    Complaints Against Google, The Criterion Journal of Innovation Vol 2, 2017. I have drawn heavily from this article.
35. Under Indian jurisprudence of 'innocent till proved guilty' shifting the burden of proof on to the defendant. Under competition law, any presumption on anti-competitive activities the burden of proof is shifted to the party. My colleague Commissioner Augustine Peter reminded me of this.
36. Op.cit Gouri and Salinger.
37. Ibid.
38. For convenience, I refer to search intermediate on agreement services as intermediary services.
39. Sebastian Wismer and Arno Raesk in Market Definition in Multi-sided markets, in a background note for OECD Directorate for Financial Enterprise Affairs Competition Committee, DAF?COMP/WD(2017)33/FINAL, Nov. 2017.
40. Google's reaction maybe a bit exaggerated and lack of familiarity with the use of the English language in India.
41. Geeta Gouri on Non market abuse.
42. See M. M. Sharma, CCI dismisses allegation of leveraging of dominance for Google Meet Application
    Vaish Associates Advocates, Case No. 39 of 2020, Baglekar Akash Kumar, Google LLC and Google India Digital Services Private Limited. Jan. 2021.

References

Geeta Gouri and Salinger M., Protecting Competition Versus Protecting Competitors: Assessing the Antitrust Complaints Against Google, The Criterion Journal of Innovation, Vol. 2, 2017.

Report of the Competition Law Review Committee, Ministry of Corporate Affairs, Government of India, July 2019.

Sebastian Wismer and Arno Raesk in Market Definition in Multi-sided markets, in a background note for OECD Directorate for Financial Enterprise Affairs Competition Committee, DAF?COMP/WD(2017)33/FINAL, Nov. 2017.

CHAPTER 6

Economic Analysis of Combinations Mergers, Amalgamations and Acquisitions

Maturing of CCI is most sharply discernible in decisions on combinations. The wider term combinations covers mergers, amalgamations and substantial acquisitions that are ex-ante assessment of possible future dominance or AAEC by the Competition Commission. Over the years and 700 merger clearances, the canvas has shifted from dominance to attracting investment for economic growth. In its wake concepts of control and ownership have evolved to provide varied perceptions on the practice of transacting business in different markets. Equally fascinating at least to me was the terminology that added color to legalese that emerged in every decision of CCI elucidating the business of investment. The Commission has over the years built up a vast repertoire of nuances in M & A, and these are incorporated in the regulations issued. The literature on the economic tools of analysis used in combination clearances has however been minimal. This chapter attempts to close the gap.

1 Framework of Analysis of Combinations

Section 5 and 6 of the Competition Act, 2002 (CA02) deal with Combinations. Section 5 sets out the transactions which are notifiable for clearance from the Commission. The Act stipulates that all Combinations have to be notified to the Competition Commission within 30 days of the decision to merge or a penalty would be levied.[1] Thresholds in

G. Gouri, *A Commissioner's Primer to Economics of Competition Law in India*, https://doi.org/10.1007/978-981-19-9476-0_6

terms of value of assets and turnover for the three categories of transaction mergers, acquisition and acquisition for control, define the nature of 'control' exercised by the acquiring or acquired entity and of 'group'. Section 6 is on the substantive test of combinations and competition "*No person or enterprise shall enter into a combination which is likely to have an appreciable adverse effect on competition within the relevant market in India and such a combination will be void*" a decision the Commission must take in 250 calendar days proposed to be reduced to 150 days.[2]

The notification time limit of 30 days stipulated in the Act is not a strict time limit with CCI allowing for a grace period within reasonable boundaries notifying a merger. This shifts the onus on quick and timely clearances on the merging parties as a forerunner to the Green Channel automatic clearances. Lower redefined thresholds for emergent market; understanding of 'control' and 'owner'; and the yardstick from 'decisive influence' to 'material influence' in tune with international practices are signs of a mature competition authority.

Sections 5 and 6 came into effect in June 2011 two years after the Commission was established and the other two sections notified. The non-exhaustive list of factors listed in Section 20(4) to assess a merger and its impact on timelines was cited as a major factor of delay in clearances and of concern to the corporate sector (Shroff and Uberoi 2012).[3] Time no doubt is a critical factor.[4] Market responses on the bourses can change the course of mergers in terms of valuation and of new contenders including white knights. The apprehension of law firms that a merger or acquisition can be stalled or delayed in running through the laundry list of Section 20(4) was perhaps a misplaced understanding of regulatory abilities, or maybe an excuse. CCI is systematic in considering all factors listed in 20(4) and in doing so have looked at concepts that fall outside the haloed list: concepts of non-compete clause, gun-jumping, standstill operations and catchment area to mention in tune with changing business in emergent platform markets.

The substantive test of creating dominance and AAEC in an ex-ante approach to cartels and of possible abuse of dominance was central to M&A clearances. Attracting investments in vital sectors of telecommunications, biotechnology, pharma and drugs sector the new frontiers of an expanding economy has seen a shift in emphasis from AAEC to investment and growth.[5] The emphasis is on quick clearances and trust in the merging firms which as we shall see in the next section is on merger regulations that are continuously modified from modifying thresholds to shifts from asset size to deal value, Green Channel, modifications to Form I and II are in this context. A further distinction has to be maintained on mergers of firms that have online and offline presence and those purely brick and mortar ex-ante merger analysis pre-platform markets and merger analysis of platform markets.

CCI does not issue Guidelines but Merger Regulations. Regulation (Procedure in Regard to the Transaction of Business relating to Combinations) Regulations, 2011 remains the basic framework. Modifications and changes were incorporated by way of amendments over the years and 700 merger filings. Section 20(4) lists out the factors for assessment of merger clearances.

Two basic issues will be examined in this chapter: How should a prescient decision of a merger be assessed ? What is the appropriate economic tool for mergers on platform markets, platform markets or for data markets? This chapter will analyze select set of decisions which have influenced the criteria of M&A clearances. Assessment of ex-ante decisions has two advantages as compared to ex-post analysis. Firstly, the parties have to provide the required information in the Forms that are part of regulations issued regularly. Additional information is also sought and provided to the Commission. Secondly, the parties to the merger are expected to do the rigorous economic analysis to prove that the possibility of future dominance is unlikely. Further information or economic analysis required for clearances are forwarded to the parties. Merger clearance do not normally get sent to the DG for investigation.

The Commission staff check on the information and data submitted by the parties. They verify if the information matches the requirements of the Forms appended to the regulations issued by the Commission. Verification and analysis submitted are subjected to critical assessment. This is a major exercise where global high-tech firms of international stature are involved as in platform markets. The possibility of naivete in assessment and even of "*Stockholm Syndrome*" is what the Commission is deeply concerned and discussed in the meeting before permitting a clearance.[6] Strong ethical standards are important for the Commission to be independent and fair and also appear to be so as in maintaining confidentiality of reports submitted. Public objections are also sought. Under regulation 13 (1-B), the summary of the combination not exceeding 500 words with details on the names of the parties, the type of combination and the market to which the transactions refer have to be submitted to the

Commission. The summary is to be published on the web site of CCI. These details are also published in four daily leading newspapers.

Law firms are 'gung-ho' about merger clearances as their reputation and of the firm they represent is built on the number of clearances they are able to achieve. In fact, articles on the subject in competition blogs such as Lexicon or Competition Review are mainly from law firms.

There have been two main revisions to thresholds which require notification to CCI, the *de minimis* condition of notification and the criteria for defining the threshold. Thresholds were initially fixed on the basis of asset size and turnover which are now deal-based transactions. The Central Government proposes to introduce an amendment that empowers it to fix threshold levels with CCI and in determining the criteria apart from that prevalent. The intent is to have judiciary and administrative control over mergers in the framework of 'control of data' and of 'specialized assets'. It is a proposal that shifts competition law into areas of data acquisition and privacy.

The debate on thresholds of raising the thresholds maybe even bypassing it and of changing the criteria in defining thresholds has been necessitated by high-value digital mergers These mergers are not asset based but have high value. In this context, the criteria of notification to CCI has undergone change depending on the market in which the merger is taking placing whether it is in the traditional product market or in emergent platform markets. Recent digital mergers cleared by the Commission have crossed the boundaries of competition law into control over personal data and '*upped the ante*' in introducing non-price competition as a factor for reckoning.[7]

Parameters such as parallel imports, failing business; scope for innovations, ownership and control are factors that are considered in evaluating mergers of emergent business. The anachronistic 'non-compete' clause once vigorously advocated by company lawyers is accepted only as an exception. Valuation of trade marks and brand value cross over to patent rights and of validity of international trade marks.[8] As on date, all mergers have been cleared. COVID-19 pandemic has seen greater urgency in the clearing of M&A with the issue of Green Channel Regulations relaxing the rules for clearing mergers. Often clearances are subject to structural and behavioral remedies as in the case of abuse of dominance. Structural remedies include divestiture of some part of the business before clearance is granted. In the Holcim-Lafarge merger, the Commission's clearance was subject to the divestment of two plants. In the Sun-Ranbaxy, merger divestment of some molecules was ordered. Behavioral remedies were suggested where it mattered as in the case of DT/PVR cinema halls.

2 Regulations

The Commission Regulations (Procedure in Regard to the Transaction of Business relating to Combinations) Regulations, 2011 is the basic structure for procedures and processes relating to the business of M&A. The Regulation lays down several forms of transaction and the related thresholds mandating clearances from CCI. Obligation to file and the mandated notice period accompanied with a summary of 2000 words covering details that are set out in Schedule II Forms I and II. Clearances go through two phases: Phase I if no abuse is discerned and Phase II for deeper and detailed analysis; Form I for phase I and Form II when the investigation proceeds to Phase II. The parties can choose to file either in Form I or Form II. Post the prima facie decision, the parties are required to publish the details of the proposed merger in newspapers. Request for confidentiality is permitted in conformity with Section 35.

Later regulations are amendments to the 2011 Regulation. There have been no significant changes in the required economic details of either Form I and II. An inclination toward quicker clearance of mergers under the sub-heading of "Green Channel" is important. The recent Green channel proposal goes on trusts and as the name suggest it is to facilitate quicker clearances for mergers. Under this process, the combination is deemed to have been approved upon filing the notice in the prescribed format. This system would significantly reduce time and cost of transactions and thereby contribute toward ease of doing business in India. Simultaneously, CCI has also revised its pre-filing consultation guidance note to extend its scope to include consultation to assist the parties to determine whether their combination is eligible for Green Channel. The Green Channel is aimed to sustain and promote a speedy, transparent and accountable review of combination cases, strike a balance between facilitation and enforcement functions, create a culture of compliance and support economic growth.[9]

Regulations on thresholds have come a full circle,[10] from setting a higher threshold on the basis of value of assets and turnover to looking at value of transaction deal and empowering CCI to examine all deals on the basis of flexible thresholds. In the literature on mergers, greater emphasis has been on the procedural details than on the economics of combinations that constitute a major part of the Forms in both Phase I and II.

2.1 *Forms–Group and Control*

Forms are designed to provide the required data and information sought by CCI to initiate a merger clearance. Let us at the outset look at the regulations of CCI with regard to merger clearances. In regard to clauses 6 and 7 of Form I details, the requirements have to be submitted for a Phase I clearance and meet the requirements of Section 5 of the Act on '*structure, ownership and control*' prior to and after the combination of parties (6.2.2). Section 5 defines two important concepts:'group' and 'control'. Section 5 lists out the transactions that are to be notified to CCI for clearance referring to group and control in CA02 (Section 5(b)(i) and (ii)).

Section 5

(a) *The acquisition of one or more enterprises by one or more persons or merger or amalgamation of enterprises shall be a combination of such enterprises and persons or enterprises, if—*
   a. *any acquisition where—*
   i. *the parties to the acquisition, being the acquirer and the enterprise, whose control, shares, voting rights or assets have been acquired or are being acquired jointly have*

(b) *acquiring of control by a person over an enterprise when such person has already direct or indirect control over another enterprise engaged in production, distribution or trading of a similar or identical or substitutable goods or provision of a similar or identical or substitutable service,*

(c) *any merger or amalgamation in which—(i) the enterprise remaining after merger or the enterprise created as a result of the amalgamation, as the case may be,*[11]

The criterion of group and control is detailed in *explanations* to Section 5. Group is where the reference is two or more enterprises which directly, or indirectly, are in a position to:

i. exercise twenty-six percent or more of the voting rights in the other enterprise;
ii. appoint more than fifty percent of the members of the board of directors in the other enterprise: or
iii. control the management or affairs of the other enterprise;

Control includes controlling the affairs or management by way of acquisition of shares that enables either jointly or singly control over another enterprise or group (i) that has already direct or indirect control over another enterprise or (ii) of acquiring control over the enterprise when two or more enterprise are involved; (iii) merger or amalgamation where reference is to the remaining merger or the enterprise created. The rights to control are veto rights, affirmative voting rights and sharing of information rights which can occur even without 26% shareholding rights with of course the rights of the ordinary shareholder. The concept of two or more enterprises' control over another enterprise limits the number to three enterprises which is no indication as the Review Committee of the Competition Law pointed out in its report.

Section 6 lays out the intent of clearing merger or acquisitions in regulation of combinations.—(1) No person or enterprise shall enter into a combination which causes or is likely to cause an appreciable adverse effect on competition within the relevant market in India and such a combination shall be void. There is an overlap of Section 6 with Section 3(3) which is on agreements that cause or likely to cause AAEC. Apart from substantial acquisition of shares and mergers, it is imperative in examining combinations to look at agreements signed by the two parties and the reference is to joint ventures.

The 20(4) list has been described as non-exhaustive. Section 20(4) lists 14 possible scenarios that need looking into and are basic to clearances of combinations.[12] Experience and business models change new dimensions of especially the forms that constitute Schedule II. Standstill obligations (Agreements), redefining both threshold levels and the criteria from an asset base to a transaction value based, are changing the contours of merger analysis. Theory of Harm and consumer welfare impinge on the substantiative test of Section 6 of AAEC to an expansive approach of investments on growth and on innovations.

2.2 *Regulations of Significance*

Regulation 6.2.2 of Schedule II Form I refers to the "*structure, ownership and control prior to and after combinations, of a) parties to the combination and b) for the enterprise whose structure, ownership and control will be directly or indirectly affected by such combination*". Regulation 6.6.2 of the same Form refers to "*justification for the non-compete provisions covering each of the elements mentioned above*" in regulation 6.6. In case such an agreement is executed, *non-compete* clause for justification for continuing the clause and in explaining the scope and coverage of the clause has to be provided.

Sector review is given in Regulation 7 where Regulation 7.4 is on horizontal and vertical linkages of the combination in the sector similar to Section 3(4) on vertical agreements. Presence of other parties horizontally or vertically to be provided requires detailing of market surveys.

Regulation 7.4:

> State whether any of the parties to the combination are engaged in any activity relation to the production, supply, distribution, storage, sale and service or trade in products or provision of services which is at different stage or levels of the production chain in which any other party to the combination is involved. If yes, provide the details.

The relevant market(s) cover the SNNIP test and the HHI index. A few of the regulations are given below, while the reader is referred to the regulations. In Schedule II Form I. Regulation 8.1 is a close approximation to the SNNIP test. It reads

> Provide an estimate indicating the relevant source and the basis of estimate of the total size of the market, in terms of value of sales (I rupees) and volume (units), of identical/substitutes/similar products or services produced/distributed/supplied in India.

Further, Regulation 8.4

> Provide details with regards to the sales in value (in rupees) and in volume (units) along with an estimate of the market share(s) of each of the parties to the combination for identical/substitute/similar products or services produced/distributed/suppled in India. In asee of a group, same information should be given for a the enterprises of the group.

Form II is for meeting the requirements of Section 6 of the Act. The Form is expansive and calls upon the skills of the parties to the combination to justify that the merger or amalgamation that will not lead to AAEC. Under Regulation 2, purpose of the Combination Regulation 2.2 captures the intent of a merger. The regulation reads: "*Describe the rationale of the combination and its impact on the economy, markets and consumers*".

Economics comes into the picture in Part VIII: Relevant Market. The relevant and geographic markets constituted by identical/substitutes/ similar products produced in India and similarly for the group are given in regulations 8.1, 8.2, 8.3 and 8.4. This definition of markets is in conformity with Section 2(r), (s) and (t). Regulation 8.6 is on market size and share of the merging firm both upstream and downstream with details of parties entering into a Combination. The commonly used test for defining the contours of the market is the SSNIP test. Herfindahl Hirschman Index (HHI) index and Lerner Index are the measures of concentration in the relevant market.[13] CCI has not used the SSNIP test but defined the market especially geographic markets in terms of catchment area or of maintainable distance as in the entertainment segment. The Elzinga-Hogarty test is the widely used measure.[14] Merger simulations and upward pricing power indices (UPPI) are other common simulation exercises and require large amounts of data. In this context, the market studies initiated by the Commission into e-commerce, telecom sector, health and now film distribution are attempts to fill the data gap.

Framework of economic analysis grounded in the traditional product market concept is limited for assessing mergers that could result in future monopolistic structures. Dependence on static economic tools of assessment such as HHI and SSNIP that are used in AoD analysis may not come to grips in defining the relevant market(s). The tendency toward legalese than of economics is noticeable in the modifications to the regulations. The former Chairman of CCI expressed concern that many of these small start-ups are targets for acquisitions by the dominant-tech companies (Dhanendra Kumar and Gupta, 2021) meriting lowering of thresholds.[15] The approach was of providing start-ups the backing of CCI. Another view points to higher thresholds as the gap in the clearance of Facebook/WhatsApp merger with CCI exercising restraint as the prescribed thresholds were not met (Tyagi, 2021). Importance of economics lies in understanding emergent markets predominantly platform markets.

3 Cases of Combinations from an Economics Perspective

How should a prescient decision of a merger be assessed? I look at merger decisions as falling into two categories. Mergers of traditional product economics which provided a wide range of phrases that define the scope for AAEC and mergers that fall into platform market mold. What is the appropriate economic tool for mergers in the two categories? Or for data markets? The initial stages Orders of CCI provided detailed analysis. Recent decisions that detailed Orders are awaited. In recent times, mergers in platform markets have come to the forefront with Amazon and Flipkart. Amazon's acquisition of More the retail arm of Aditya Birla Group was sold to Amazon Samara Capital.

3.1 Mergers Pre-Platform Markets

3.1.1 Drugs and Pharmaceutical Sector

Non-Compete Clause

Business transaction of Orchid Chemicals and Pharmaceuticals with Hospira India Ltd included a non-compete clause. The clause specifically stated that a non-compete clause will be operative for 8 years and 5 years relating to activities involving research, development and testing. The parties claimed that this was standard industry practice for effective business transfer and "allows the acquirer to obtain full value from the acquired assets". It was never explained in the filings as to the how full value is created after the stipulated period. A country with a large diverse population and a well-developed pharmaceutical base for generic drugs and out-of-patent drugs considers that Hospira does not possess any of the APIs required for injectable formulations in drugs such as Penicillin and Penem including Carbopenem. This capability was with Orchids. Hospira was the major buyer of injectable APIs resulting in limited market share of Orchids further limited by the non-compete clause. The merger from a horizontal agreement had the potential for vertical integration of Hospira.

The parties proposed reduction in the number of years for applicability of non-compete clause from 8 to 4 years and ensure that there is no overlap in geographical areas of business activity that would not result in AAEC. Mergers were not envisaged in terms of investment and growth but in terms of AAEC. It was undoubtedly a restrictive view of mergers and a regulators' intervention to define business strategies without looking at the underlying economics.

It was a merger that would benefit Hospira as an entry to the Indian market from the capability of Orchids while upgrading their research and development facilities.

Substitution Among Molecules

(Combination Registration No. C-2014/05/170), Sun Pharmaceutical Industries Limited and Ranbaxy Laboratories Limited a scheme of agreement. Sun has an investor agreement with Sanyo Daichi. An economist's report was submitted on the nature of the transactions. Sun-Ranbaxy is a manufacturer of branded generics manufacture and sale of APIs. Sun has a wide market range with presence in the US market. Their drugs and pharmaceuticals deal with a wide range of products related to the central nervous system. Ranbaxy on the other hand is a vertically integrated manufacturer of branded generics, APIs and intermediates. It has presence in many therapy areas that include pain management, in the central nervous system. Ranbaxy has equity participation in Zenotech Laboratories.

Public opinion was sought in this case, and the parties requested to place notices in leading newspapers.

The relevant market was defined as the market for molecules which are the basic ingredients of both enterprises and would permit substitutability. A given molecule consists of chemical properties. This enabled 49 molecule markets to be defined. Two other relevant markets for formulations were also identified. Alternative definition based on therapeutic value was inappropriate as the mechanism for intended applications notwithstanding that generic drugs competition takes place on the basis of molecules. Significant overlaps among the molecules was found. The incremental share of the parties in each market as a result of the merger; the number of parties in each market; and the respective market shares were calculated using the Moving Annual Total (MAT). In the process, the Commission was able to identify the markets in which the merger would result in AAEC.[16] It was also the first case suggesting divestment of some of the overlapping molecules.

The market share value was calculated using MAT using in this case the total value of sales over the course of the previous 12 months. MAT is a rolling yearly sum which helps analyze changes in sales volume at the end of each month with data from the new month added to the total and data from the first month of the period taken away. It is smoothening of the curve usually for removing factors such as seasonality.

The list did not include the National List of Medicines as they are subject to price control by the National Pharmaceutical Pricing Authority. The detailed analysis took into consideration products that were in the pipeline.

The molecule approach has been followed by the Commission in most of the drugs and pharmaceutical cases of merger to check for horizontal and vertical overlaps. This was also the modality used in drugs for animals and livestock as in Eli Lilly's Stock and Asset agreement in the acquisition of the global Novartis Animal Health (Combination Registration No. C-2015/07/289) in Intas Pharmaceuticals Ltd the acquisition of less than 5% shareholding by Canary Investments Limited and Link Investment Trust II, under Section 31(1). of the Competition Act, 2002 (Press Release No. 09/2020-21).[17]

3.1.2 *Clearance with Failure to Notify*

i. Combination Registration No. C-2015/01/241) General Electric Company, GE Industrial France SAS, Alstom and Alstom Holdings a combination cleared on grounds (Section 31(1) that the acquisition of GEC of Alstom and Alstom Holdings is unlikely to have an AAEC on competition. At the same time, penalty was levied on the acquisition for failure to issue notice within thirty days of having received clearance from SEBI. The Order should be read for the detailed analysis of the power sector. The linkages between generation, transmission, grid network and distribution of power as a total approach to investments in the power sector are important for economic growth. A similar case is of JSW Energy in a securities purchase agreement with two other parties' transfer of a 1000 MW operational coal-fired thermal power plant at Tamnar, Chhattisgarh ("Target Asset"), currently owned by Jindal Power Limited. The acquisition was cleared on similar grounds in 2016 (Combination Registration No. C-2016/05/399).

The present proposal of GE v Alstom related to the entire spectrum of the energy sector. It was an interesting combination where the focus was on the strengths of each of the parties. The first labeled as the Primary

Acquisition involved the acquisition of Alstom's thermal power, renewable power and grid businesses by GE and its group companies. The second part was with regard to the formation of joint ventures (JVs) comprising the Grid and Digital Energy JV, the Renewables JV and the Global Nuclear and French Steam JV, between GE and Alstom in which Alstom will hold a minority shareholding. The third portion of the acquisition was of the signaling business of GE by Alstom called the "**Signaling Transaction**". Different agreements for each section were signed on 4 November 2015.

The Order is a detailed technical analysis of the two parties with respective strengths in the energy sector by classifying the sector into (i) thermal power business; (ii) renewable energy business; (iii) grid business; and (iv) signaling business. In the thermal power area, both have overlapping capabilities in gas-based plants, and within this, the analysis examined generators, boilers and balance of power (BoP) equipment including pollution control. Alstom is active in the supply of boilers, BoP equipment and pollution control systems.[18] In the turbines business a wide range of capacity was available for GE and Alstom without overlaps. The merger would cover the range from levels from 5 to 476 MWs. Out of five OEMs GE, Alstom, Mitsubishi Heavy Industries Limited ("**MHI**"), Siemens and Ansaldo have the proprietary technology for generator turbines (GTs), Ansaldo is not present in the market for GTs in India. Thus, the power sector for generating equipment is very competitive. Interestingly, for large generators for those above 500 MW no expertise was available among the five listed manufacturers. The other major constraint was of the availability of natural gas in the country which limits the number of gas-based thermal power stations. Bidding was the mechanism adopted for selecting. Similarly, in the case of steam turbines, there was no overlapping between GE and Alstom. As bidding is the mechanism used in the electricity sector for placing Orders for turbine, CCI opined that the possibility of a dominant party asserting market power does not arise.

The Commission examined other areas of expertise that would add value to the combination and to the power sector such as Supply Machinery Protection and Condition Monitoring Solutions ("**MPCMS**") which are employed across a range of industries in plant asset management including power plants to measure the vibration levels of rotating and reciprocating equipment. It is useful in detecting changes in the condition of the machinery parts and to predict potential failures. The expertise and market share of both groups and their subsidiaries were estimated and found no cause for AAEC.

3.1.3 *Mergers–Platform Market*

Restrictions on Sales of Flipkart on Aditya Birla Fashion Retail (ABFR)

(Combination Registration No.C-2020/12/792) There was no hesitancy on clearing the acquisition of 7.8% by Flipkart of the apparel fashion wear firm ABFR. Both groups have interest in fashion apparel with market shares less than 5% even in a broader market definition of clothing. The market was not defined without any upstream or downstream linkages. On these considerations, CCI had no objections to the acquisitions considered not to create AAEC. It, however, issued an advisory that the platform of ABFRL could not be used by the Flipkart (Walmart) to get preference for their brands.

Flipkart is part of the Walmart group which hosts fashion brands such as Myntra and Jabong, ABRL. Flipkart is of the Walmart group e-commerce platform for fashion products. ABRFL also deals in another line of fashion products. CCI in their Order issued an advisory restricting the fashion brands as they may get preference on ABRFL e-commerce platform restricting intra-platform competition.

As a foreign direct investor, Flipkart under the rules is permitted B2B sales and not B2C. ABFRL as a domestic firm is permitted to sell both B2B and B2C sales. The advisory issued can be viewed as in conformity with government rules and regulations on the premise that some fashion brands will get more prominence and attempt to regulate online markets and consumer preferences. The Commission in fact considers these as investments and not as acquisitions. Perhaps it is also a move for clearing mergers as investment as long as no obvious horizontal or vertical overlaps exist.

Investment by Google in Jio Platform Markets

Notice (Combination Registration No. C-2020/09/775) was given by Google in relation to its proposed acquisition of approximately 7.73% of the equity share capital in Jio Platforms Limited (Jio Platforms), a subsidiary of Reliance Industries Limited (RIL). Jio Platforms also holds 100% of the issued and outstanding share capital of Reliance Jio Infocomm Limited (RJIO), a licensed telecommunication operator, providing mobile telephony services to users across India. Google will also have certain affirmative rights. These rights offer protection to Google's minority investment into Jio Platforms without conferring any rights over Jio Platform's commercial strategy.

The Order is a neat succinct summary of the telephony mobile system covering all aspects starting from Original Equipment Manufacturers (OEMs); OS (Operating Systems developers); App developers that use the OS; and Telecom Service Provider (TSP). The competition assessment in these dynamic markets has been undertaken in the Order. Google is an OS developer, while Reliance Jio is a TSP. The proposed investment was much wider in scope than mere acquisition of stock and shares by Google in the Jio platform. It was focused on helping RJIO develop a smartphone, cheap and useful for the growing Indian mobile market rated the third fastest mobile systems market in the world. The acquisition aimed at entering the OEM segments in producing a smart phone and of encouraging Apps on the mobile smart phone sets to the use of Android. It involved modifying the android software customized to reduce the cost of smartphone and suit requirements of Indian consumers.

There were therefore two components of the investment by Google: (i) a share in the Rio platform market and (ii) business collaboration or joint venture in the production of smart phones. The analysis would require assessing the vertical overlaps of the web services and OTT business of the two firms including the advertisement services and revenue on their respective platform market services. Analyzing the competition scenario in the mobile operating systems with Google being an important supplier with Reliance making an entry into this market, Both these integrated but separate businesses prompted the Commission to evaluate whether the two firms had the ability and incentives to discriminate between competitors in their respective businesses and to retain their individual comparative advantage.

Firstly, the advertising service on their respective platforms Google is a major player while Jio platforms' earnings from advertisement constitute only 1% of their revenue. This poses no competition threat. Second, there is however considerable overlap in the supply of apps and mobile services covering the entire range of mobile browsers, payment apps, music streaming, games, news, etc.. The market dynamics are continuously changing and the standard antitrust tool of market share has little significance. On this understanding, CCI observed that conditions of multi-homing and the ease of shifting from one web service on a particular platform poses no antitrust concerns. Thirdly, the android software of Google is posed against the KaiOS of Reliance.

It is an Order in the framework of 'internet of things' with the upgradation of the telephony mobile system to 4G emphasizing interoperability, data connectivity and the growing importance of 'Quad Play'. CCI examined whether the net neutrality of Reliance Jio would be affected by way of discriminatory tariffs. TRAI regulation Prohibition of Discriminatory Tariffs for Data Services Regulations, 2016, ruled this happening while the License condition of Department of Telecommunications rule out discrimination in content provision.

On access to data and sharing of data with both parties having their own privacy policies, it is interesting to note that CCI found that a share of 7.73% as too insignificant to raise concerns of competition or of data backed market power.

Mergers and Investment for Growth

The recent clearances in need for quick decisions await a long-detailed Order. As mentioned earlier, if no overlaps are noted the case can be reviewed a year later or further under Section 3 or 4. The acquisition of shares and/or voting rights by MacRitchie, Fort Canning and Ola Founder in ANI ("Proposed Combination") is an example of quick clearance on the grounds *"The investment represents a good opportunity for MacRitchie and Fort Canning to invest and participate in the long-term growth of the cab aggregator market in India". The investment represents a good opportunity for MacRitchie and Fort Canning to invest and participate in the long-term growth of the cabaggregator market in India.* MacRitchie and Fort Canning are investment holding companies, while ANI is a software technology company for autorickshaws, taxis, etc.

There are several acquisitions by investor holding companies investing in share and securities of up-coming ventures, start-ups signaling a new trend in merger control. The emphasis on control is not an issue in mergers but rather of investments.

Investment in Ports

A variant of control for efficient operations is the clearance vide share purchase agreements in ports and related infrastructure. Notice was given to CCI pursuant to the execution of Share Purchase Agreement ("SPA") inter alia between Adani Ports and Special Economic Zone the acquirer in Adani Krishnapatnam Port Limited (Target) in which it holds 75% of the shareholding with management control and Mr. Chinta Sasidhar and Vishwa Samudra Holdings Pvt. Ltd. With this share acquisition, Adani

Ports now has 100% control of the port. The acquisition was cleared treating it as a subsequent to the earlier acquisition that CCI had cleared ("Initial Acquisition") Combination Registration C-2020/02/726. For the Adani group, it completes the move to being a private multi-port operator, which provides integrated port infrastructure services equipped with the latest infrastructure capable of handling large vessels.

The Green Channel Regulation on Combinations was a follow-up on the approach that investment and growth are high on priority for clearances of mergers, amalgamations and acquisitions.

4 Conclusions

The economics of competition law in the combination cases has two phases: the first phase where the emphasis was on the scope afforded for a merger or an acquisition to emerge as a dominant holding to exert market power. This phase also saw concerns on the scope afforded by control through acquisitions of shares perhaps even less than the required 26%. The second phase shifts to looking at investments where mergers and acquisitions are tools to achieve this objective. The coming of age of the Indian economy prompts an equally open approach to mergers and acquisitions. The case on platform markets or of Google's acquisition of 7.73% of Jio platforms heralds emergent competition concerns on interoperability, data portability and privacy.

Notes

1. I use mergers to cover M&A and acquisitions. The decision could be a meeting of the Board of Directors, or a notice by the competent authority to initiate proceedings duly signed for submission to the commission.
2. Report of the Competition Law Review Committee, July 2019 Ministry of Corporate Affairs, Government of India.
3. Section 20(4) of the Competition Act reads:

   (4) For the purposes of determining whether a combination would have the effect of or is likely to have an appreciable adverse effect on competition in the relevant market, the Commission shall have due regard to all or any of the following factors, namely:—

   (a) actual and potential level of competition through imports in the market;
   (b) extent of barriers to entry into the market;
   (c) level of combination in the market;

(d) degree of countervailing power in the market;
(e) likelihood that the combination would result in the parties to the combination being able to significantly and sustainably increase prices or profit margins;
(f) extent of effective competition likely to sustain in a market;
(g) extent to which substitutes are available or are likely to be available in the market;
(h) market share, in the relevant market, of the persons or enterprise in a combination, individually and as a combination;
(i) likelihood that the combination would result in the removal of a vigorous and effective competitor or competitors in the market;
(j) nature and extent of vertical integration in the market;
(k) possibility of a failing business;
(l) nature and extent of innovation;
(m) relative advantage, by way of the contribution to the economic development, by any Combination having or likely to have appreciable adverse effect on competition;
(n) whether the benefits of the combination outweigh the adverse impact of the combination, if any.

Cyril Shroff and Nisha Uberoi have referred to Section 20(4) as the non-exhaustive longlist of factors that CCI will consider to assess whether a notifiable transaction has an appreciable adverse affect on competition (AAEC). In an article on Merger Review in Competition Law in the BRICS Countries, edited by Adrian Emch. Jose Regazzini and Vassily Rudomino, Walters Kluwer, 2012. Cyril and Nisha belong to a well-known law firm and their views reflect those of other law firms on the apprehension regarding quick clearance by CCI.

4. The Competition Amendment Bill (2007) stipulated a mandatory notice period of 30 days for filing of the proposed merger or amalgamation. Failure to do so would attract penalty up to one percent of the total turnover or assets. The Commission is provided a suspensory period of 210 days to arrive proposed to be revised to 150 days under the revisions suggested to the Act, extendable by but not more than 30 calendar days in case of rectification or need for providing additional information. Transaction is deemed to have been cleared if the stipulated period is over.
5. Combinations do not go to the DG for investigation unless advised by the Commission.
6. The Stockholm Syndrome which all of us are familiar from the famous James Bond Movie "The World is not Enough" refers to the psyche of the captor to side with those who imprisoned them and not with the party that rescued them. I use the term to refer to Commission's staffs possible gullibility and is a major behavioral trait we at the Commission take seriously. It undoubtedly has strong ethical overtones.

7. The CCI has exercised its suo moto powers and restarted investigations into the Facebook/Whats app merger after the Bundeskartellamt the German competition authority, in coining breach of privacy as competition concern.
8. In the automotive case, it was argued by the DG that protection of trade-marks under Section 3(5) was not applicable as these trademarks were not registered in India.
9. PRESS RELEASE No. 8/2019-20 Competition Commission of India (CCI) introduces Green Channel clearance for Merger & Acquisitions, accessed on 14 June 2021, https://www.cci.gov.in/node/4616.

   The list of mergers cleared and approved by CCI under the Green Channel includes:

   - Kyndryl Holdings LLC and Grand Ocean Managed Infrastructure Services Private Limited in relation to internal restructuring of IBM Corporation, and is deemed approved. 10 May 2021.
   - Acquisition of IDBI Asset Management Ltd. (IAML) and IDBI MF Trustee Company Ltd. (IMTL) by Muthoot Finance Limited (MFL) [filed on 16th December, 2019].
   - Acquisition of Adani Electricity Mumbai Limited (AEML) and Adani Electricity Mumbai Services Limited (AEMSL) by Qatar Holding LLC (QH) [filed on 19th December, 2019].
   - Acquisition of GVK Airport Holdings Limited (GVKAHL) by Green Rock B 2014 Limited (Green Rock), National Investment and Infrastructure Fund (NIIF) and Indo-Infra Inc. (Indo-Infra) [filed on 19th December, 2019].
   - Acquisition of up to 18.951% (Eighteen point Nine Five One percent) of the equity share capital of the Religare Health Insurance Company Limited (Religare/Target) by the Trishikhar Ventures LLP (Trishikhar/Acquirer) ("Proposed Combination"). 20 April 2020.
   - Acquisition of equity stake in Hero Future Energies Global Ltd and non-voting compulsorily convertible preference shareholding in Hero Future Energies Private Ltd. by Abu Dhabi Future Energy Company P.J.S.C.—Masdar, on 28th October, 2019. 30 October 2019.
   - CCI received the first green channel combination filed under sub-Section (2) of Section 6 of the Competition Act, 2002 (Act) read with regulations 5 and 5A of the Competition Commission of India (Procedure in regard to the transactions of business relating to combinations) Regulations, 2011 (Combination Regulations), 3rd October, 2019. The notification relates to the acquisition of the Essel Mutual Fund (Essel MF), a mutual fund registered under the SEBI (Mutual Funds) Regulations, 1996 (MF Regulations) by an entity forming a part of the Sachin Bansal Group. 7 October 2019.

- Motherson Sumi Systems Limited (MSSL), Samvardhana Motherson International Limited (SAMIL), Sumitomo Wiring Systems Limited (SWS) relating to an intra-group reorganization of the Motherson Group and is deemed approved. 27 May 2021.
- Acquisition by Aéroports de Paris SA (the "Acquirer" or "ADP") of equity share capital of GMR Airports Limited ("GAL"), and GMR Infra Services Limited ("GISL") 21 February 2020.

10. Revised Thresholds.

REVISED THRESHOLDS

On March 4, 2016, the Central Government issued notifications pertaining to the statutory thresholds for the purposes of "combinations" under Section 5 of the Competition Act, 2002 ("**Act**").

1. ***Increase in thresholds***: Pursuant to Notification No. S.O. 675(E) dated March 4, 2016, the value of assets and the value of turnover has been enhanced by 100% for the purposes of Section 5 of the Act. Accordingly, the revised thresholds for notification to the Competition Commission of India ("**Commission**") are:

THRESHOLDS FOR FILING NOTICE				
		Assets		**Turnover**
Enterprise Level	**India**	> 2000 INR crore	**OR**	>6000 INR crore
	Worldwide with India leg	>USD 1 bn with at least >1000 INR crore in India		>USD 3 bn with at least >3000 INR crore in India
			OR	
Group Level	**India**	>8000 INR crore	**OR**	>24000 INR crore
	Worldwide with India leg	> USD 4 bn with at least >1000 INR crore in India		> USD 12 bn with at least >3000 INR crore in India

2. ***Increase in thresholds of De Minimis Exemption***: Pursuant to Notification No. S.O. 674(E) dated March 4, 2016, acquisitions where enterprises whose control, shares, voting rights or assets are being acquired have assets of not more than Rs. 350 crore in India or turnover of not more than Rs. 1000 crore in India, are exempt from Section 5 of the Act for a period of 5 years. Accordingly, the revised thresholds for availing of the *De Minimis* exemption for acquisitions are:

THRESHOLDS FOR AVAILING OF DE MINIMIS EXEMPTION FOR ACQUISITIONS				
		Assets		**Turnover**
Target Enterprise	**In India**	≤350 INR crore	**OR**	≤1000 INR crore

3. ***Definition of Group***: As per Notification No. S.O. 673(E) dated March 4, 2016, the exemption to the "group" exercising less than fifty per cent. of voting rights in other enterprise from the provisions of Section 5 of the Act under Notification No. S.O. 481(E) dated March 4, 2011, has been continued for a further period of 5 years.

Page 1 of 1

11. Competition Ac, 2002.

Regulation of combinations Combination 5.

The acquisition of one or more enterprises by one or more persons or merger or amalgamation of enterprises shall be a combination of such enterprises and persons or enterprises, if—

(a) any acquisition where—

(i) the parties to the acquisition, being the acquirer and the enterprise, whose control, shares, voting rights or assets have been acquired or are being acquired jointly have,—

(A) either, in India, the assets of the value of more than rupees one thousand crores or turnover more than rupees three thousand crores;

(B) 7 [in India or outside India, in aggregate, the assets of the value of more than five hundred million US dollars, including at least rupees five hundred crores in India, or turnover more than fifteen hundred million US dollars, including at least rupees fifteen hundred crores in India; or].

(ii) the group, to which the enterprise whose control, shares, assets or voting rights have been acquired or are being acquired, would belong after the acquisition, jointly have or would jointly have—

(A) either in India, the assets of the value of more than rupees four thou sand crores or turnover more than rupees twelve thousand crores;

(B) 8 [in India or outside India, in aggregate, the assets of the value of more than two billion US dollars, including at least rupees five hundred crores in India, or turnover more than six billion US dollars, including at least rupees fifteen hundred crores in India; or].

(b) acquiring of control by a person over an enterprise when such person has already direct or indirect control over another enterprise engaged in production, distribution or trading of a similar or identical or substitutable goods or provision of a similar or identical or substitutable service, if—

(i) the enterprise over which control has been acquired along with the enterprise over which the acquirer already has direct or indirect control jointly have,—

(A) either in India, the assets of the value of more than rupees one thousand crores or turnover more than rupees three thousand crores;

(B) [in India or outside India, in aggregate, the assets of the value of more than five hundred million US dollars, including at least rupees five hundred crores in India, or turnover more than fifteen hundred million US dollars, including at least rupees fifteen hundred crores in India; or].

(ii) the group, to which enterprise whose control has been acquired, or is being acquired, would belong after the acquisition, jointly have or would jointly have,—

(A) either in India, the assets of the value of more than rupees four thou sand crores or turnover more than rupees twelve thousand crores or.

(B) [in India or outside India, in aggregate, the assets of the value of more than two billion US dollars, including at least rupees five hundred crores in India, or turnover more than six billion US dollars, including at least rupees fifteen hundred crores in India; or] (c) any merger or amalgamation in which—

(i) the enterprise remaining after merger or the enterprise created as a result of the amalgamation, as the case may be, have—

(A) either in India, the assets of the value of more than rupees one thou sand crores or turnover more than rupees three thousand crores; or.

(B) [in India or outside India, in aggregate, the assets of the value of more than five hundred million US dollars, including at least rupees five hundred crores in India, or turnover more than fifteen hundred million US dollars, including at least rupees fifteen hundred crores in India; or].

(ii) the group, to which the enterprise remaining after the merger or the enterprise created as a result of the amalgamation, would belong after the merger or the amalgamation, as the case may be, have or would have—

(A) either in India, the assets of the value of more than rupees four-thou sand crores or turnover more than rupees twelve thousand crores; or

(B) [in India or outside India, in aggregate, the assets of the value of more than two billion US dollars, including at least rupees five hundred crores in India, or turnover more than six billion US dollars, including at least rupees Fifteen Hundred Crores in India.

12. Op.cit.,
13. Ram Tamara puts forward the use of these tests in an article with Dhanendra Kumar. A behind the curtain look at CCI's analysis of M&A, Financial Express,
14. Ibid.

15. Dhanendra Kumar and Anish Gupta, Reshaping the Contours of Combination Threshold through the 2020 Draft Competition Amendment Bill—Meeting the Need with Digital Merger Control in India? Competition Policy International, February, 2021.
16. The detailed market share of each of the players and the number of players is given in the Order.
17. Press Release No 9 of 20-21, dated 30 April 2020. Detailed Order is awaited/
18. The reader should read the Order for the miniscule analysis undertaken. It does not help in reproducing the Order.

References

Cyril Shroff and Nisha Uberoi, Latest Indian Merger Control Trends Analysed, Euromoney Learning, Sep, 25, 2012

Dhanendra Kumar and Anish Gupta, Reshaping the Contours of Combination Threshold thorugh the 2020 Draft Competition Amendment Bill - Meeting the Need with Digital Merger Control in India, Competition Policy Internations, Feb, 2, 2021

Kalpana Tyagi, Big Data Mergers: Bridging the Gap for an Effective Merger Control Framework, Competition Commission of India, *Journal of Competition Law and Policy*, Vol1, Dec,2020 Pp 29-52

Press Releases of CCI on Combinations.

The Competition Commission of India (Procedure in regard to the transaction of business relating to combinations) Regulations, 2011 (No.3 of 2011)

The Competition Commission of India (Procedure in regard to the transaction of business relating to combinations) Amendment Regulations, 2019

CHAPTER 7

Interface Between Competition Commission of India and Sectoral Regulators

In Chapter 1, the dimension of regulation and competition was highlighted, and in this chapter, we explore the relationship between sectoral regulators and competition commission. Sectoral regulators preceded Competition Act, 2002 (CA02) as the process of reforms started with unbundling of public utilities. The operationalization of the Competition Commission of India (CCI) and the overlap between technological developments that lead to modular systems and decentralization have changed the boundaries of regulation and competition.

With several regulatory commissions and an overarching competition commission dotting the economic scene interface among regulators becomes critical. While the role of competition authority and sectoral specific regulator can be complimentary, at times, the interface between the two could also be a source of tension. Where the Commission is concerned sector-specific regulations, regulatory authorities bring distinct challenges to competition law and authority. The 'war of turfs' as coined by the media in reference to the spat between IRDA and SEBI draws attention to the sensitivity of boundaries between regulators. The Commission is sensitive to this issue. This is an exploratory chapter and important to the extent that too many regulatory commissions lead to *forum shopping* by enterprises either to avoid the higher penalty provisions of CCI or to escape detection of anti-competitiveness.

G. Gouri, *A Commissioner's Primer to Economics of Competition Law in India*, https://doi.org/10.1007/978-981-19-9476-0_7

The chapter will broadly cover defining the turf of sectoral regulators and of the changing interface between CCI and sectoral regulators. Emphasis will be on the electricity sector, telecom and the petroleum and natural gas sectors drawing reference to other sectors only to emphasize a point. Each sector has its own specificity of technical considerations with the underlying thread that all sectoral regulators are ex-ante regulators. As discussed in Chapter 1, the major difference is that sectoral regulators are ex-ante regulators while CCI is an ex-poste regulator except in the case of mergers. This major difference also defines the form and structure of regulation. Sectoral regulators are mandated to fix the tariffs of all regulated utilities and ensure that no losses are incurred by the entity. Public utilities are State Government instruments of bringing change more prominently in the electric sector. In the case of other utilities, larger social objectives of growth and development as in the telecom sector or in the laying of pipelines play a dominant role.

1 Drawing the Boundaries

CA02 was legislated in 2002 functional only after May 2009 when the Commission was established with full powers to adjudicate and levy fines. Competition Commission looks solely at competition and on forces and factors that prevent the market from operating competitively. It was a progressive approach toward markets and allocation or resources unlike as discussed earlier the extant MRTP Act. The MRTP Act exempted the governmental companies from its purview and focused only upon the private entities. The philosophy underlying the MRTP Act as observed was that governmental companies as legally created monopolies were for public interest in no need of regulation, a view that did not extend to the private sector companies.

1.1 Brief Overview of Legal Provisions[1]

The mandate of CCI is extraordinarily wide. ***It is also agnostic about sector-specific regulators***. The duty of the Commission is 'to promote and sustain competition in the interest of consumers'.[2] Section 18 of the Competition Act, 2002 states that

> it shall be the duty of the Competition Commission of India to eliminate practices having adverse effect on competition, promote and sustain

competition, protect the interests of consumers and ensure freedom of trade carried on by other participants, in markets in India

Competition is not the main focus of sectoral regulators although there is mention of promoting competition in some such as of the Electricity Act. CCI on the other hand can intervene if competition is restricted in any sector and permit filings on the same. This right is not vested with sectoral regulatory commissions. Specific provisions contained within the legislation demonstrate the probable basis of tension. Section 60 of the Act reads:

> The provisions of this Act *shall* have effect notwithstanding anything inconsistent therewith contained in any other law for the time being in force.

Section 60 of the Competition Act, 2002, is the usual *non-obstante* provision asserting the supremacy of competition legislation within the domain of competition enforcement. However, Section 62 of the Competition Act, 2002, encouragingly declares that competition legislation ought to work along with other enactments.

> the provisions of this act shall be in addition to, not in derogation of, the provisions of any other law for the time being in force.

Both Sections 60 and 62, ironically, are couched in mandatory language.

Further, Section 21 of the Competition Act, 2002, suggests that in any proceedings before statutory authority, if such a need arises, the statutory authority may make a reference to competition authority. Section 2(w) of the Competition Act, 2002, defines statutory authority as:

> any authority, board, corporation, council, institute, university or any other body corporate, established by or under any Central, State or Provincial Act for the purposes of regulating production or supply of goods or provision of any services or markets therefore or any matter connected therewith or incidental thereto.

While Section 21(1) states:

> Where in the course of a proceeding before any statutory authority an issue is raised by any party that any decision which such authority has taken or

proposes to take, is or would be, contrary to any of the provisions of this Act, then such statutory authority may make a reference in respect of such issue to the Commission.

Incidentally, even upon reference the opinion of the competition authority is not binding upon the statutory authority. The competition authority is, however, bound to deliver its opinion to the statutory authority within a stipulated time period of two months.

> Section 21(2) states: "on receipt of a reference under sub-section (1), the Commission shall, after hearing the parties to the proceedings, give its opinion to such statutory authority which Shall thereafter pass such order on the issues referred to in that sub-section as it deems fit".

Proviso to Section 21 states: "*Provided that the Commission shall give its opinion under this section within sixty days of receipt of such reference*".

The essence of the interface between competition authority and sector-specific regulators in India as can be seen from the above quoted Sections 18, 21, 60 and 62 of the CA02 is that the Commission can intervene to ensure markets function competitively; act concurrently with other authorities or independently of other authorities; and can advice or seek advice from other authorities. Competition authority could have potential interface with the jurisdiction of sector-specific regulators viz. public utilities Telecom Regulatory Authority of India (TRAI), Central Electricity Regulatory Commission (CERC) and Petroleum and Natural Gas Regulatory Board (PNGRB).

Upon a complaint the Commission on investigation comes to the conclusion that there has been Appreciable Adverse Effect on Competition (AAEC) on account of agreements or on account of abuse of dominant position it is empowered to levy fines to the extent of three times the turnover of the past three years in case of any enterprise. There is also the aspect of mergers where both sets of regulators have to take an ex-ante decision. In the bidding for bandwidth, the Supreme Court upheld the first right of the Telecom Authority and TRAI.

1.1.1 Electricity Act

The Electricity Act, 2003, is redolent of the conundrum caused by overlapping jurisdictions of regulatory authorities in India. The Electricity Act was passed on May 26, 2003, which is a good four and a half months after the Competition Act, 2002 was passed on January 13, 2003, but still, one of the objectives behind the Electricity Act is that of promotion of competition. The preamble to the Electricity Act, 2003 states:

> [a]n Act to consolidate the laws relating to generation, transmission, distribution, trading and use of electricity and generally for taking measures conducive to development of electricity industry, promoting competition therein, protecting interest of consumers and supply of electricity to all areas, rationalization of electricity tariff, ensuring transparent policies regarding subsidies, promotion of efficient and environmentally benign policies, constitution of Central Electricity Authority, Regulatory Commissions and establishment of Appellate Tribunal and for matters connected therewith or incidental thereto.

Indeed, the framers of the legislation also conferred power upon the regulator to deal with anti-competitive agreements, abuse of dominant position and mergers related to impediment to competition in electricity.

Section 60 of the Electricity Act, 2003 states:

> The Appropriate Commission may issue such directions as it considers appropriate to a licensee or a generating company if such licensee or generating company enters into any agreement or abuses its dominant position or enters into a combination which is likely to cause or causes an adverse effect on competition in electricity industry.

This is similar to the language used in Sections 3, 4 and 5 and 6 of the Competition Act, 2002, which pertain to anti-competitive agreements, abuse of dominant position and regulation of combinations.

Similarly, Section 42 of the Electricity Act deals with 'open access' the modus for competition in the electricity sector. The section per se does not mention the concept of competition. But non-provision of open access could be considered as an issue of AoD or vide agreements among distribution companies to restrict competition.

The regulator, while fixing tariff levels, is to be guided by the principle of competition and efficiency specifically, Section 61 of the Electricity Act.[3] In order to promote competition, it is open to the regulator Section 23 of the Electricity Act to issue directions to the licensees engaged in transmitting, distribution or trading in electricity.[4] The regulator has also been entrusted with the task of advising the government in competition within electricity sector (Section 79).[5] In this

Section 79(1)(a) that the power to fix tariffs of central generating stations is with Central Electricity Regulatory Commission (CERC) and is entirely within the purview of the Central Government to allocate or reallocate power from the Central Generating stations to the beneficiaries and the same being covered under regulation of tariff under Section 79(1)(a) of the Act cannot be subject to adjudication under Section 79(1)(f) of the Act by CERC nor is it within the frame of adjudication by CCI.[6] The regulator has been mandated to be guided by the lodestar of competition while evolving schemes for reorganization of provincial electricity boards that were under financial distress.[7]

The electricity regulator, too, has been armed with the *non-obstante* powers that stipulate that the electricity legislation trumps other enactments.[8] Like competition authority, the electricity regulator also finds itself constrained by a duty to act in aid of other regulators.[9] Unlike the PNGRB Act, the Electricity Act does not provide for the levy of fines in cases of anti-competitive Acts.

The Electricity Act has been amended and is awaiting clearance from Parliament. Broadly, the emphasis in the new Act is on open access involving private participation in a large manner. Technological developments in this sector where it is possible to consider small power stations of 1 MW based on renewable sources of energy such a solar and bagasse have changed the role of regulatory commissions in fixing of tariffs or of grid connection charges.

1.1.2 TRAI Act

The Telecom Regulatory Authority is the oldest among the sectoral regulator commissions with the Act legislated in 1997. It was the first sectoral regulator with a turbulent history on its role as a regulator coming into prominence in recent times with the allocation of spectrum and bandwidth. The entry of private service providers brought with it the inevitable need for independent regulation to regulate telecom services, including fixation/revision of tariffs for telecom services which were earlier vested in the Central Government. TRAI's mission is to create and nurture conditions for growth of telecommunications in the country in a manner and at a pace which will enable India to play a leading role in emerging global information society.[10] The importance of spectrum and bandwidth allocation and TRAIs domain over the internet and of broadcasting is to introduce competition among the varied services offered. Licenses for spectrum are issued by the Department of Telecommunications (DOT) which were auctioned. Debates on the introduction of floor prices or of differential prices are at the forefront. The unified license system is now moving toward a differential licensing system in line with the numerous services offered on the internet. Digital markets and services are always on the churn with bundled packages to Quad Plans (combining landline, mobiles and internet) under 4G and to 5G. The scope for horizontal agreements and of vertical convergence do raise competition concerns and are under CCI purview.

One of the main objectives of TRAI is to provide a fair and transparent policy environment which promotes a level playing field and facilitates fair competition. In pursuance of above objective, TRAI has issued from time to time a large number of regulation, orders and directives to deal with issues coming before it and provided the required direction to the evolution of Indian telecom market from a government-owned monopoly to a multi-operator multi-service open competitive market.

The directions, orders and regulations issued cover a wide range of subjects including tariff, interconnection and quality of service as well as governance of the Authority.

The TRAI Act was amended by an ordinance, effective from 24 January 2000, establishing a Telecommunications Dispute Settlement and Appellate Tribunal (TDSAT) to take over the adjudicatory and disputes functions from TRAI. TDSAT was set up to adjudicate any dispute between a licensor and a licensee, between two or more service providers, between a service provider and a group of consumers, and to hear and dispose of appeals against any direction, decision or order of TRAI.

TRAI in its attempts at repositioning itself issued a consultation paper on tariff fixation seeking public consensus on the new principle of "Forbearance" the Authority intends to adopt. Forbearance or 'self-restraint' is freedom to Telecom Service Providers (TSP) to design and price the packages they offer of voice and data on telephony, mobile, internet services and virtual networks. Telecom services now include OTTs service, telecom towers and infrastructure providers prompting CCI to launch a market study on the telecom sector. The attempt is laudable. What is however uncomfortable and in my opinion distracting in the repositioning is to seek a shift from being an ex-ante regulator to an ex-poste regulator without statutory backing and the requisite tools to be effective in the new position sought by TRAI. The argument that the new 'Forbearance Principle' is a first step in tariff reforms, the new regulatory principles enunciated is more interventionist than the earlier 'hard touch'.

The principle of forbearance is on restraint subject to compliance of regulatory principles in an effort to provide transparency in the tariffs announced. Measures such as capping the number of permissible packages with validity of 6 months; clear enunciation of the tariffs and of any promotional offers in language understood by laypersons; and due publicity to the packages etc. are well known measures of transparency. In this long list of compliance, TRAI has included two concepts of tariff fixing non-discriminatory pricing and non-predatory pricing as regulatory principles to be complied by TSPs when announcing their tariffs for the retails services they provide. My unease is with these two principles of tariff fixing. These are ex-poste outcomes even where discriminatory pricing is concerned. Any ex-ante intervention has the effect of creating entry barriers to the entry of innovative services by new firms. The expected enabling environment of development and innovation much required in internet and telephony services suggested in the 'Forbearance Principle' may not be forthcoming. Rather, all features of the new principle point to an overkill, advantage to the incumbent large firms. My unease stems from the fact that the Authority lacks both expertise and legal backing in economics of competition.

Economics of sector regulation stems from the theory of 'Principal-Agent' appropriate to natural monopolies. Market discovery of costs of operation (CAPEX and OPEX) does not happen as in a monopoly there is only one firm in a designated area. The regulator faced with information asymmetry the attempts to minimize the asymmetry in the design of tariff usually through a process of tariff filing and auditing of costs. Auction theory of networks is among the more advanced design mechanisms under conditions of information asymmetry. In contrast, retail tariffs are subject to price discovery by the market defined by consumer choice. Application of natural monopoly principles largely cost-plus to retail tariffs fixed by the regulator enables incumbent firms to recover their costs. Retail tariffs so fixed encourage inefficient incumbent firms to continue while discouraging new entrants with innovative packages of voice and data. Process for a regulator empowered to fix tariffs cannot be justified leading to interventions that are sub-optimal. Inefficiency of operations under such conditions are ultimately borne by the end consumer.

Reference to tariff fixation in the entire TRAI Act only to Section 11(2). This is not surprising as recourse to tariff fixation by the Regulator is only to the licensed activity which under normal circumstances constitutes the natural monopoly segment limited to cost discovery of the Agent. There are no sections pertaining to predation and discrimination under the Act which cites no principles for tariff fixation. The Competition Act has no provision for tariff fixation. Prices are left instead to firms and market forces. The Competition Commission intervenes only if markets are not functioning as in allegation of abuse of dominance with respect to discriminatory pricing or of predatory pricing are made. Recourse is then to economic theory of oligopoly and monopolistic competition for assessing the alleged anti-competitive activities of firms. The consultation paper draws its analytical framework entirely from the Competition Act posing a set of questions on defining the relevant market (product and geographic) and defining market share and market power.

TRAI and Abuse of Dominance

Proxy reliance on the Competition Act by TRAI raises two pertinent issues; (i) can an ex-ante regulator develop capacity building for ex-poste outcomes; (ii) provide statutory backing for effective enforcement.

Let us take up the first issue of capability as regards assessing abuse of dominance in a sector subject to continuous technological development of networks and on bursts of innovative products that have emerged in the tail end services. Developments and innovations have been so rapid in the last ten years with speed gaining momentum in shorter intervals that the existing contours of the telecom sector are no longer relevant. We are looking at the information highway constituting the network or service provider and the apps available on the internet. Platform markets two sided or multi-sided are within the tariff framework of tariff fixation and of forbearance. The digital space has no boundaries between products and services. The traditional parameters of monopolization and abuse of dominance in terms of price-cost are constantly under review in the current literature on antitrust. Anti-competitive effects in networks and of platforms do not lend themselves easily to the established price-cost vortex that defines competitiveness. This complicates matters raising concerns on definitions themselves such as: (i) how to define the relevant product market when the product is free? (ii) how to demarcate geographic boundaries for viral networks that do not follow national boundaries; and (iii) what constitutes predatory pricing or discrimination when prices are not charged purely on account of the fact that marginal costs are negligible. The shift from price to non-price competition and the importance of data that platform markets generate. These are some of the issues that Competition authorities are grappling with unable in many instances to establish unequivocally dominance of large players and of abuse. CCI is currently looking into agreements between sellers and platforms such as Amazon and Flipkart both on nature of the agreement and terms of condition. An offshoot is the enquiry into privacy and competition renegotiating the contours of competition law, a subject matter for the next chapter. Both US and European Commission on renewed antitrust investigations into the Big tech platforms have not been able to convincingly establish abuse of dominance by the GAFAM.

To borrow existing structures of the Competition Act as TRAI attempted when the sector is continuously disruptive while the Competition Act is exploring ways of accommodation TRAI would be doing injustice to a sector that defies all standard approaches to abuse of dominance or of abuse. Consumers are the ultimate losers. A more appropriate approach for an ex-ante regulator is to leave predatory and discriminatory pricing to the market regulator. The debate is on antitrust outcomes of firms in the high technology and in balancing the positive gains to consumers as against possible negative effects of entry barrier that incumbents attempt to erect two important criteria are required:

1. Consumer Sustainability Dimensions
2. Lead-Laggard Argument

Technical or rather technological expertise available in the telecom sector can instead be effectively utilized by CCI. The approach is of synergy.

In 2018, TRAI passed the Telecom Commercial Communications Customer Preference Regulations (2018), mandating telecom companies in the country to adopt blockchain technology (permissioned and private/consortium). The communique as per TRAI was to ensure regulatory oversight in commercial communication and to move to smart contracts. The suggestion was to extend the use of block chain technology on all data including consumer data base including complaints of past 3 years. The blockchain also enables interaction and exchange of information between relevant entities in a safe and secure manner. The regulation also talks about the possibilities of setting up regulatory sandboxes for the blockchain solutions. CCI also initiated a study on competition issues in the use of blockchain technology.

Table 1 Requisite elements for effective enforcement in the telecom sector

	TRAI Act and its focus	*Private enforcement*	*Damages*	*Consumer welfare*
Discrimination Tariffs Predatory Pricing	Section 11(2) relating to tariff fixation has no reference to discrimination It is framed in the context of fixing tariffs for natural monopolies Reference to discrimination in tariff fixing is clause 2(k) of TTO and not of the Act	No equivalence of Section 19 of CA02	No equivalence of Section 27	Price discrimination is often welfare enhancing. As the Act does not mention consumer harm, welfare outcomes are not in the purview of TRAI

Lastly, and perhaps in my opinion, the most important consideration in the attempt of TRAI to see consensus on defining ex-ante predatory pricing and discrimination with regard to tariff fixation is that the TRAI Act has no provisions for enforcement. There are two other aspects viz that of private enforcement and damages which define the regulatory scope for effective intervention. The Commission unites the power of private enforcement with the claim of damages and hence can ensure healthy consumer welfare. Often private individuals have better information about infringement of legislative provisions. No matter how powerful an economic regulator is, it cannot possibly replicate the mélange of information accessible to individuals. A look at the Table 1 indicates this lacuna.

The lack of statutory backing to levy fines and rectify damages in a sector dominated by large incumbent firms, there is always a tendency for forum shopping. In issuing subordinate legislature in the form of TTO or Regulations, large firms will prefer to approach TRAI as there is provision for levy of penalty.

1.1.3 *Petroleum and Natural Gas Regulatory Board Act, 2006*

In spite of the Competition Act, 2002, already on statute book, one of the objectives behind the Petroleum and Natural Gas Regulatory Board Act, drafted as recently as March, 2006, is "to promote competitive markets" and "protect the interest of consumers by fostering fair trade and competition amongst the entities". The Preamble to the Petroleum and Natural Gas Regulatory Board Act, 2006, reads:

> Act to provide for the establishment of Petroleum and Natural Gas Regulatory Board to regulate the refining, processing, storage, transportation, distribution, marketing and sale of petroleum, petroleum products and natural gas excluding production of crude oil and natural gas so as to protect the interests of consumers and entities engaged in specified activities relating to petroleum, petroleum products and natural gas and to ensure uninterrupted and adequate supply of petroleum, petroleum products and natural gas in all parts of the country and **to promote competitive markets and for matters connected therewith or incidental** thereto.

Section 11(a) of the Petroleum and Natural Gas Regulatory Board Act, 2006 states that the

> Board shall protect the interest of consumers by fostering fair trade and competition Amongst the entities.

The Petroleum and Natural Gas Regulatory Board ("PNGRB") is mandated to be mindful of competition while dealing with access to common carriers or contract carrier as well as distribution networks.

> Section 11(e)(i) states that the "Board shall regulate, by regulations, access to common carrier or contract carrier so as to ensure fair trade and competition amongst entities and for that purpose specify pipeline access code".
>
> Section 11 (e) (iii) of the PNGRB Act states that the "Board shall regulate, by regulations, access to city or local natural gas distribution network so as to ensure fair trade and competition amongst entities as per pipeline access code".

Specifically, if PNGRB is interested in declaring existing pipeline or distribution network as a common carrier, it still needs to be guided by the principles of competition (Section 20(5)).[11] Subject to an entity's right of first use, the entity's excess capacity is to be distributed by PNGRB in accordance with 'fair competition'.[12] Further, while determining transportation tariffs,[13] PNGRB is expected to keep considerations of competition and efficiency at the back of its mind.

> Section 22(1) states: "Subject to the provisions of this Act, the Board shall lay down, by regulations, the transportation tariffs for common carriers or contract carriers or city or local natural gas distribution network and the manner of determining such tariffs."

The provisions for a common carrier as maybe noted are similar to the Electricity Act, 2003.

Interestingly, the PNGRB Act borrows the concept of 'restrictive trade practice' from the Monopolies and Restrictive Trade Practices Act, 1969, and not of unfair practices in the context of Abuse of Dominance by a dominant player under Section 4(2).

In order to deter the infringers of the enactment, a la other regulatory enactments, contravention of the directions given by the Petroleum and Natural Gas Regulatory Board attracts civil penalty. A complaint based upon the entitled 'restrictive trade practice' ensures that penalty is enhanced by five times.[14] However, unlike the electricity regulator, the PNGRB Act does have any overriding, *non-obstante* provision.

2 Private Enforcement and Damages

There are two other aspects viz that of private enforcement and damages which define the regulatory scope for effective intervention. CCI unites the power of private enforcement with the claim of damages and hence can ensure healthy consumer welfare. Often private individuals have better information about infringement of legislative provisions. No matter how powerful an economic regulator is, it cannot possibly replicate the mélange of information accessible to individuals.[15]

CA02 lays down a private right of action to the extent of mandating the Competition Authority to act upon complaint under Section 19(1) by any person.

> Section 19(1) of the Competition Act, 2002 states: "The Commission may inquire into any alleged contravention of the provisions contained in subsection (1) of section 3 or sub-section (1) of section 4 either on its own motion or on – (a) receipt of a complaint, accompanied by such fee

> as may be determined by regulations, from any person, consumer or their association or trade association; or (b) a reference made to it by the Central Government or a State Government or a statutory authority."

This is in contrast with the older MRTP regime that conferred a right of complaint to a 'consumer' only in cases of 'restrictive trade practice'. As mentioned unlike in the advanced competition authorities, the right to private action is a limited right. It confers the right to an individual to knock at the doors of the Competition Authority. It does not necessarily constitute any special allurement to initiate action. Coupled with possibility of damages, private right of enforcement confers upon a potential plaintiff an incentive to sue.[16]

Possibility of damages become critical in order to compensate a victim for the loss suffered owing to infringement of competition law. A compensatory damage merely makes a victim of anti-competitive conduct as a whole. It does not necessarily deter the conduct of an enterprise. Anti-competitive conduct on several occasions could be quite sophisticated. Since there is a very low possibility of detection, compensatory damages only mean that *if* an enterprise is found violating competition legislation, it would have to restore the victim in its position prior to the infringement.[17]

In order to punish or deter violators of competition law, certain jurisdictions traverse beyond compensatory damages and include recovery of illegal gain or exemplary or punitive damages. One of the categories, in England for instance, warranting exemplary damages is 'wrongful conduct which has been calculated by the defendant to make a profit for himself which may well exceed the compensation payable to the claimant'.[18] Specifically, under competition law regime, if there is a cost benefit analysis by a violator that illegal gains would outweigh potentially payable damages; an action for exemplary damages may lie.[19]

CA02 incorporates a provision for award of compensation by the competition authority for any loss or damage suffered by any victim.[20] Though there is no specific provision for punitive or exemplary damages, since the provision speaks of 'loss or damage caused… as a *result* of any contravention' rather than 'loss or damage caused… *arising out of* any contravention'.

Further once the competition authority has found contravention of the competition law, victims in a group would be able to file for compensation claims from the competition authority. This is only a 'representative

Table 2 Elements of Sector Regulatory Acts

	Private enforcement	*Damages*
Electricity Act, 2003	No	Limited
TRAI	Yes	Yes
Petroleum and Natural Gas Regulatory Board	Unclear	No
Competition Act, 2002	Yes	Yes

action' and not 'collective action', 'class action' or 'public interest litigation'. It is instructive to compare the mechanism of right of private action coupled with damages with the legal framework available under sector-specific regulators. Table 2 summarizes the position.

From the above chart, it is clear that the sector-specific regulators are *parens patriae* regulators, where regulator dons the mantle of protection of consumer interest. Besides competition authority, electricity regulator is the only sector-specific regulator having provision for, albeit limited damages. Nonetheless, damages recoverable through the electricity regulator are confined to violation of specified standard of performance or payment of excess tariff. There is no possibility of recovering damages for causing an adverse effect on competition in the electricity industry.[21]

In the case of the telecom sector, complications of interface between TRAI, DOT and CCI arise from the allocation of spectrum, licensing of TSP, of platforms and OTTs and with traditional landlines referred to as the 'Quad Play',[22] the presence of horizontal agreements and vertical arrangements. Issues of bundled packages, zero pricing on voice with data prices in different packages offered by the telecom firms as technology progress, raise several competition issues.

The right of private action under petroleum regulator is unclear. Subject to the existence of any arbitration agreement, the petroleum regulator has jurisdiction over dispute 'between an entity and any other person'.[23] The regulator also has right to 'receive any complaint from any person'. Nevertheless, complaint by *individual consumers* maintainable before consumer disputes redressal forum is exempt. The most bizarre aspect of this enactment is that unlike Competition Act, 2002, it does not define a 'person'. There is also an absence of any guidance under the enactment to construe 'person'.

Even if one gives a liberal interpretation to 'person' and construes a right of private enforcement under petroleum regulator, there is no possibility of recovery of any damages for anti-competitive conduct.

2.1 *Rethink over Sectoral Regulators*

From the legislative intent of the sectoral regulations and of the competition law, a general rule followed is that sector-specific regulation identifies a problem *ex-ante*, within a particular sector and the regulator builds an administrative machinery to address behavioral issues before the problem arises. Competition policy addresses the problem *ex post* and the Commission examines cases in the backdrop of market conditions. The exception is mergers and acquisition where cases dealt are ex-ante.

Competition law seeks to promote efficient allocation and utilization of resources, which are usually scarce in developing countries. A good competition law lowers the entry barriers in the market and makes the environment conducive to promoting entrepreneurship.

Regulations, on the other hand, are public constraints on market behavior or structure. They usually refer to a diverse set of instruments by which governments set requirements on businesses and citizens.

Regulations can be categorized as under:

(a) Economic Regulations—Those which intervene in market decisions such as pricing, competition and entry/exit.
(b) Technical Regulations—Those which regulate the technical aspects which are distinct and unique to the sector
(c) Social regulations—Those which protect public interest such as health, safety and environment.
(d) Administrative regulations—administrative formalities through which government collects information and intervenes in individual economic decisions.

The objective of a sectoral regulator is to provide good quality service at affordable rates, but the promotion of competition and prevention of anti-competitive behavior may not be high on its agenda or the laws governing the regulator may be silent on this aspect. If the utilities are under government ownership entities in all likelihood considerations of tariff fixation are more biased toward meeting the requirements of the fisc than by considerations of encouraging competition.

It is not uncommon for sectoral regulators to be more closely aligned with the interest of the firms being regulated, which is also known as 'regulatory capture'. Then, where would consumers as a class be it end consumers or producers seek redressal for denial of the expected benefits of competition. A sectoral regulator may not have an overall view of the economy as a whole and may tend to apply yardsticks which are different from the ones used by the other sectoral regulators and definitely very different from the yardsticks of competition applied by the completion. In other words, there is a possibility of the lack of consistency across sectors.

3 Overlapping's of Jurisdictions: Commissions Approach

The conflicts between CCI and the sectoral regulators could be caused by legislative ambiguity or jurisdictional overlap or legislative omission. Interpretational bias of the bureaucracy involved could further aggravate the conflicts. Conflicts between two may be generated by the market players and legal arbitrators for obvious reasons. Conflicts are bound to hurt consumers and the uncertainties that go with them can increase risk of investment. Conflict resolution by a court of law may perhaps be time consuming, and therefore, be only the last alternative.

There are innumerable instances of ostensibly overlapping jurisdictions on questions of competition. Allocation of specific areas of work for sectoral regulators does not appear to have been done very carefully. To illustrate the areas of overlap and of conflict, a few judgements of the Commission relating to the above sectors are given. CCI in all cases of judicial overlap follows two procedures:

(a) Before taking a prima facie decision and referring the case for further investigation, the Commission refers to the concerned Sectoral Regulator for opinion and if required a decision;
(b) Decisions of the Commissions as regards violations of the Act are taken purely on merit considerations of being anti-competitive and constraining market functioning detrimental to consumer and to trade.

3.1 *Electricity Sector*

Case 1

In ***Shri Neeraj Malhotra, Advocate vs. North Delhi Power Ltd. & Ors. [Case No. 6/2009]***, in which the anti-competitive behavior of the electricity distribution companies was alleged, there was clear confusion regarding the jurisdictional authority in competition related issued. The Discoms alleged before the CCI that only the Delhi Electricity Regulatory Commission (DERC) under the Electricity Act, 2003 had jurisdiction to deal with the issues relating to anti-competitive behavior of electricity distribution companies. However, this regulator appears to be in favor of leaving the competition-related issues exclusively in the hands of the competition authority and retaining the responsibility of deciding on the technical issues with themselves. The DERC in the said case categorically stated in its communication to the CCI that although all matters pertaining to electricity tariff have to be decided as per the provisions of the Electricity Act and DERC Regulations, allegations of anti-competitive behvior, including abuse of dominant position by the Discoms, fall within the jurisdiction of the CCI.

Case 2

Information was filed under Section 19 of the Competition Act by **Anila Gupta against Brihan Mumbai Electric Supply and Transport Undertaking (BEST)** alleging contraventions of Section 4. The informant, a consumer of electricity of BEST, made an application to Tata Power Co (TPCL) for supply of electricity which would entail migration from the current supplier BEST. TPCL responded by appraising her that her request could not be acceded to on the ground that rules for changeover from one supplier to another were not applicable to BEST, it being a local government body. The informant subsequently filed a case before the Maharashtra Electricity Regulatory Commission (MERC) against TPCL praying for an order for commencement of supply by TPCL. BEST opposed the informant's request on the ground that it being a local authority had exclusive territorial jurisdiction to supply electricity with BEST's area of supply. TPCL, on the other hand, expressed willingness to supply electricity to the informant. Allegations by the informant against BEST included the following:

- That the stand taken by BEST against its consumers is illegal.
- BEST has blatantly indulged in gross and flagrant abuse of its dominant position by denying permission to avail 'open access' from the second distribution licensees TPCL.

The issue before the Commission was whether BEST has abused its dominant position in the relevant market in light of the legislative intent of Section 42(3) of the Electricity Act and Regulation 19 of MERC which in the framework of the Electricity Act accords a special status to local authorities.

The Commission defined the relevant market as the distribution and supply of electricity in the Island town and island city of Mumbai, bound by the Mahim Creek on the western side and Sion on the eastern side, which is licensed to be serviced by two electricity distribution licensees BEST and TPCL. The relevant market is defined by the licenses issued to 'BEST and TPCL by MERC. The license issued by MERC to BEST also grant the status of local authority to the distribution company enabling it to be classified under Section 42(3) of the Electricity Act. The licensed area of operation of TPCL extends beyond the jurisdiction of local authority of the Mumbai Municipal Corporation.

The Commission was of the view that a finding on the issue as to whether BEST has abused its dominant position as per the provisions of the CA02, would depend entirely on the extent of protection available to BEST under Section 42(3) of the Electricity Act, 2003 by virtue of being a local authority. The Hon'ble Supreme Court in Civil Appeal No. 2458 of 2011 has asked the Central Electricity Tribunal to decide the case on merits. The finding of the Hon'ble Central Electricity Tribunal will have a direct bearing on determining the extent of protection available to BEST under Section 42(3) of the Electricity Act, 2003. In view of these facts, the Commission did not give a finding in this case at that stage. However, it made it clear that the informant can again approach the Commission, if she so desired, after a final view is taken was taken in the matter pending before the Electricity Tribunal.

Case No 3

Tata Power Distribution Company vs NTPC Case No. 20 of 2017 which is an excellent treatise on sectoral interface through the provisions of long-term PPAs. PPAs earlier designed on 'take or pay' concept left very little scope to renegotiate except through the Central Government as the allegations pertained to high tariffs charged by NTPC a Central Government-owned generating company.

The dispute regarding termination of PPAs having been thus decided by the CERC, the Informant approached the Commission alleging abuse of dominant position by the OP by virtue of having included such onerous terms and conditions in the PPAs that the Informant does not have an option to exit the long-term PPAs. In this regard, the Commission takes note of the submissions of the OP whereby it has been stated that although the Informant and other procurers are bound by the terms and conditions of the PPAs, they can approach the Ministry of Power, Government of India, for reallocation of power to any procurer in case they do not wish to take power at any time during the operation of the long-term PPAs. The release of procurer from the PPAs is, however, subject to the Ministry of Power, Government of India, being able to reallocate the power to any other procurer and limited to the period for which such reallocation fructifies. The boundaries of sector regulators and CCI were clearly drawn as can be observed in the Order:

> Agreements entered into between the parties of their own volition for commercial purposes cannot be said to be an abuse of dominant position. (para 17 Case 20of 2017)

3.2 Telecom Sector and TRAI

All merger and acquisitions are mandated to seek clearance from CCI. The turf wars between TRAI and CCI are in the allocation and auctioning of spectrum and bandwidth.

Case 1

Reliance Jio Infocomm-Right to Use Spectrum of RCOM and RTL (Combination Registration No.C-2017/06/516) Notice given by Reliance Jio Infocomm Limited pursuant to an inquiry under subsection (1) of Section 20 of the Competition Act, 2002 ("Act") to acquire right to use of certain spectrum, from Reliance Communications Limited ("RCOM") and Reliance Telecom Limited ("RTL"). It is a case of acquisitions.

In this regard, the National Telecom Policy, 2012 envisaged moving toward liberalization of spectrum to enable use of spectrum in any band to provide services in any technology as well as to permit spectrum pooling, sharing and later, trading to enable optimal utilization of spectrum through appropriate regulatory framework. In this regard, DoT issued various guidelines from time to time, including guidelines for Trading of Access Spectrum by Access Service Providers vide Communication No.: L-14006//05/2015-NTG dated 12.10.2015 ("Spectrum Trading Guidelines").

At present, the spectrum holding in a licensed service area is subject to cap of 25% of the total spectrum assigned and 50% of the spectrum assigned in a specific band. ("Spectrum Caps").

The Commission noted that the competition assessment in such cases need to focus primarily on concerns that may emanate from spectrum holding of the acquirer and that of other telecom service providers ("TSPs").

The Commission noted that RJIO's spectrum holding, post-acquisition (of spectrum) pursuant to Trading Agreement and options exercised pursuant to RCOM is within the Spectrum Caps prescribed by the DoT. Commission is, however, of the view that the assessment of the Combination would need to be based on factors as given in sub-section (4) of Section 20 of the Act, independently of such guidelines/Spectrum Caps. Accordingly, the Commission examined spectrum holding of different TSPs in all telecom circles relevant for the Combination. The Commission is of the opinion that spectrum holding of RJIO in 800 MHz band and its overall spectrum holding, post-acquisition, when examined along with the spectrum holding of other TSPs, is not likely to result in an appreciable adverse effect on competition in any of the markets that may be affected by the Combination. In its assessment, the Commission also considered spectrum which may be acquired pursuant to exercise of RCOM/RTL Option Agreements. However, in this regard, the Commission is of the opinion that given the significant uncertainty surrounding the exercise of further option rights, capability of each spectrum acquisition transaction to affect market dynamics and fast changing competition dynamics, the approval of the Commission is subject to the condition that any future acquisition(s) of the spectrum under the RCOM/RTL acquisition(s) of the spectrum under the RCOM/RTL Option Agreements not completed within one year from the date of the decision of the Commission would require fresh filing, if applicable under the provisions of the Act.

Considering the facts on record, details provided in the notice and assessment of the Combination on the basis of factors stated in subsection (4) of Section 20 of the Act, the Commission is of the opinion that the Combination is not likely to have an appreciable adverse effect on competition in India and, therefore, the Commission, hereby, approves the Combination under sub-section (1) of Section 31 of the Act, subject to the condition regarding future acquisition(s) of spectrum under the RTL/RCOM Option Agreements as stated above.

3.3 Gatekeepers and Platform Markets

Case 2

Google and Reliance Jio Merger
(Combination Registration No. C-2020/09/775) Notice under Section 6(2) of the Competition Act, 2002 filed by Google International LLC for acquisition of share capital of 7.3% in Reliance Jio Platforms a subsidiary of Reliance Industries vide an Investment Agreement and Commercial Agreement to collaborate and develop new low-cost smartphones and operating system for such devices.

Cases in the telecom sector that have come to the Commission pertain to allegations of markets on the platform market. A major ongoing case is of the Delhi Vyapar Sangh and later by the All India Online Vendors Association on Flipkart (Case No. 20 of 2018). Their allegations pertain to discount pricing, preference to some sellers by major platforms. The line of reasoning is convoluted. Flipkart buys goods at a low price and sells to WS Retail a Content Delivery Network which then sell it to Flipkart Internet. All of this low pricing is possible on account access to VC funds. As sellers are chosen entry is restricted. Predatory pricing and differential barrier also create entry barriers.

The presence of competition on platform markets was clearly perceived in the e-commerce study and the fact that apps have become the favorite mode of shopping on the net which has created competition (Gouri, 2021).[24] Persistence from the All India Online Vendors Association has seen two major competition issues formalized. First, the nature of agreement between sellers and platform markets. Are these agreements unfavorable forcing sellers to sell at discounted prices perhaps predatory compared to their off line stores. Second, the importance of data and issues of privacy. These are emerging competition concerns and will be discussed in the next chapter.

3.4 Petroleum and Natural Gas Board

Case 1

Information was filed under Section 19(1)(a) of the Competition Act, 2002 by South Gujarat Textile Processors Association (GTPS) against M/s Gujarat Gas Company (GGC) Ltd whereby the informant alleging abuse of dominance by the Gas Distribution Company in terms of arbitrary and unfair conditions of supply and fixation of monopoly prices.

GGC is enjoying a position of monopoly in the transmission and distribution segment of CNG and Natural Gas in the geographical area of Surat District. The Commission on examination found that:

(a) There is nothing on record to indicate that GGC is charging alleged unfair or discriminatory price of gas from the GTPS and other consumers.
(b) The Informant GTPS has also not given any data which suggests that the price being demanded by the GGC is excessive, unfair or discriminatory.
(c) The price of gas is uniformly applicable to all the consumers of the GGC.
(d) Similarly, the other alleged terms and conditions which have been imposed upon GTPS are uniformly applicable to other buyers/consumers.
(e) From examination of other gas distribution available on public domain, it was found that GGC was not indulging in pricing policies that were enabling higher profits
(f) Thus, it is not discernable from the record that how the alleged amended conditions in the agreements can be termed unfair or discriminatory.

The Commission was of the prima facie opinion that the conduct of GGC was not abusive in terms of the provisions of Section 4 of the Act and that there was no prima facie case made out for referring to the DG for investigation under Section 26(1).

4 Suggested Future Actions

Having settled for some sort of framework overseeing business conduct, the Indian policy makers are faced with the dilemma of choice between sectoral regulation and competition law. In order to organize the division of labor between sectoral regulators and competition authorities, there are three board options available:

(a) *Clear separation of competition enforcement functions from technical functions:*
Sectoral regulator may be vested with powers of *ex-ante* control and the competition authority may be given the *ex post* authority. For example, fixation of electricity tariffs may be left to the electricity authority constituted under the Electricity Act unless the prices are claimed to be excessive or predatory which then may require an *ex post* review by the competition authority.

(b) *Competition authority substitutes sectoral regulator*:
Another option is to make competition authority responsible for both sector-specific regulation as well as overarching competition enforcement. This approach is advantageous as this reduces the problem of multiplicity of regulators and accumulates sectoral expertise. Indeed, Australia has taken this approach to settle for an economy-wide economic regulator that integrates technical and competition regulation.[25] This may lead to complex bureaucratic structure combined with the lingering danger that the regulator may prefer using direct regulatory power over indirect competition enforcement powers.[26]

(c) *Concurrent existence of competition authority and sectoral regulator*:
Institution-building is a complex, time-consuming exercise. At a pragmatic level, sector-specific regulators are here to stay as it would be practically impossible to abolish the authorities that have already come into existence.[27]

Further, experiences of other countries aren't of much assistance. There is a wide diversity in models that are available. While Australia on one hand, privileges competition authority, the UK grants explicit concurrent powers to sectoral regulators.

The optimal, *sui generis* model must be rooted in contextual legal milieu. To be sure, both sector-specific regulator and competition authority have unique core competencies to offer.

Nevertheless, there are pragmatic, descriptive as well as normative justifications why Indian competition authority ought to trump sectoral regulators.

Descriptively, the compelling justification behind primacy of competition authority is that unlike legislations governing sector-specific regulators, competition legislation grants private right of action along with provision of damages. The twin rubrics of private enforcement and damages ensure a qualitatively higher standard of consumer welfare which is unavailable under the legislative framework of any sector-specific regulator.

5 Conclusion

The seemingly uneasy interface between the two is evident from the legislative framework. A closer examination of the interface requires exploratory as well as normative insights. Unlike sectoral regulators, competition authority combines the twin powers of private enforcement with right to claim damages. In the absence of the two, sector-specific regulators cannot possibly serve as an effective instrument for promotion and protection of consumer welfare. Competition enforcement is a sophisticated, complex process. Therefore, in order to reduce transaction cost and efficiently enhance legal certainty, the realm of competition law enforcement ought to be left in the hands of the competition authority.

This does not necessarily mean that the sector-specific regulators must wind up their shops. However, clarity about the jurisdiction of the sectoral regulators and the competition authority is must for the smooth functioning of both.

Notes

1. My young legal intern at the Commission Neha was very helpful and picked out the relevant sections of the Acts for this topic without whose help a detailed legal analysis would not have been possible.

   An early version was given as an invited lecture to the Administrative Staff College, Hyderabad whose Director Late T.L. Sankar (IAS) was among the early pioneers of reforms and sectoral legislation under whose tutelage my work on regulatory economics saw its beginnings.
2. The preamble of CA02 states:

> An Act to provide, keeping in view of the economic development of the country, for the establishment of a Commission to prevent practices having adverse effect on competition, to promote and sustain competition in markets, to protect the interests of consumers and to ensure freedom of trade carried on by other participants in markets, in India, and for matters connected therewith or incidental thereto.

3. Section 61 in, relevant parts, state: "The Appropriate Commission shall, subject to the provisions of this Act, specify the terms and conditions for the determination of tariff, and in doing so, shall be guided by the following, namely,:-… (c) the factors which would encourage competition, efficiency, economical use of the resources, good performance and optimal investments; … (e) the principles rewarding efficiency in performance…". Further, the second proviso to Section 62(1) states that "in case of distribution of electricity in the same area by two or more distribution licensees, the Appropriate Commission may, for promoting competition among distribution licensees, fix only maximum ceiling of tariff for retail sale of electricity".
4. Section 23 of the Electricity Act, 2003 states: "If the Appropriate Commission is of the opinion that it is necessary or expedient so to do for maintaining the efficient supply, securing the equitable distribution of electricity and *promoting competition*, it may, by order, provide for regulating supply, distribution, consumption or use thereof."
5. Section 79(2), in its relevant part, states: "The Central Commission shall advise the Central Government on all or any of the following matters, namely: - (a) (ii) promotion of competition, efficiency and economy in activities of the electricity industry…". See also, Section 86(2) (i) that stipulates for the counterpart provincial regulator that "[t]he State Commission shall advise the State Government on all or any of the following matters, namely … promotion of competition, efficiency and economy in activities of the electricity industry…".
6. Order of CCI in Case Case No. 20 of 2017 Tata Power Delhi Distribution Limited and NTPC Limited. To quote "*the judgment dated 16.02.2017 passed by the erstwhile Hon'ble Competition Appellate Tribunal (COMPAT) in Appeal No. 33 of 2016 in the case of Anand Prakash Agarwal v Dakshin Haryana Bijli Vitran Nigam Limited, wherein it was inter alia observed that the Electricity Act, 2003 is a self-contained, comprehensive legislation that vests the appropriate commission under that Act power to fix tariff, which includes Fuel Supply Agreements and that there is an implied immunity from the competition law in matters of electricity tariff approved by the appropriate commission in terms of the Electricity Act, 2003*".
7. Section 131(5) (a) states that: "[a] transfer scheme under this section may … provide for the formation of subsidiaries, joint venture companies

or other schemes of division, amalgamation, merger, reconstruction or arrangements which shall promote the profitability and viability of the resulting entity, ensure economic efficiency, encourage competition and protect consumer interests...".

8. *See*, Section 174 of the Electricity Act, 2003 states: "Save as otherwise provided in Section 173, the provisions of this Act shall have effect notwithstanding anything inconsistent therewith contained in any other law for the time being in force or in any instrument having effect by virtue of any law other than this".
9. Ibid.
10. Accessed from the TRAI website trai.gov.in, hosted by National Informatic Centre, August 17, 2021.
11. Section 20(5) of the PNGRB Act states that "for the purposes of this section, the Board shall be guided by the objectives of *promoting competition* among entities, avoiding infructuous investment, maintaining or increasing supplies or for securing equitable distribution or ensuring adequate availability of petroleum, petroleum products and natural gas throughout the country and follow such principles as the Board may, by regulations, determine in carrying out its functions under this section".
12. Section 21(1) of the PNGRB Act states: "The entity laying, building, operating or expanding a pipeline for transportation of petroleum products or laying, building, operating or expanding a city or local natural gas distribution network shall have right of first use for its own requirement and the remaining capacity shall be used among entities as the Board may, after issuing a declaration under Section 20, determine having regard to the needs of *fair competition* in marketing and availability of petroleum and petroleum products throughout the country".
13. Section 22(1) states: "Subject to the provisions of this Act, the Board shall lay down, by regulations, the transportation tariffs for common carriers or contract carriers or city or local natural gas distribution network and the manner of determining such tariffs."
14. Proviso to Section 28 states that "... in the case of a complaint on restrictive trade practice, the amount of civil penalty may extend to five times the unfair gains made by the entity or ten crore rupees, whichever is higher".
15. Section 25(1) of the PNGRB Act, 2006 states: "A complaint may be filed before the Board by any person in respect of matters relating to entities or any matter arising out of the provisions of this Act" However, the proviso adds, "Provided that the complaints of individual consumers maintainable before a consumer disputes redressal forum under the Consumer Protection Act, 1986 shall not be taken up by the Board but shall be heard and disposed of by such forum". (emphasis supplied).
16. Steven Shavell, Foundations of Economic Analysis of Law, Harvard University Press, Cambridge, 2004, p. 390 (where he asserts that the

"plaintiff will sue when his cost of suit is less than his expected benefits from suit").

17. Commission Staff Working Paper, Annex to the Green Paper, "Damages Actions for Breach of EC Antitrust Rules", SEC(2005) 1732, para. 114, p. 34.
18. Lord Devlin in Rookes v. Barnard [1964] AC 1129.
19. B. Rodger, "Private Enforcement and the Enterprise Act: An exemplary system of awarding damages", [2003] ECLR 103.
20. Section 34(1) of the Competition Act, 2002 states: "Without prejudice to any other provisions contained in this Act, any person may make an application to the Commission for an order for the recovery of compensation from any enterprise for any loss or damage shown to have been suffered, by such person as a result of any contravention of the provisions of Chapter II, having been committed by such an enterprise". 18 Section 34(2) of the Competition Act, 2002 states: "The Commission, may after an inquiry made into the allegations mentioned in the application made under sub-section (1), pass an order directing the enterprise to make payment to the applicant, of the amount determined by it as realizable from the enterprise as compensation for the loss or damage caused to the applicant as a result of any contravention of the provisions of Chapter II having been committed by such enterprise".
21. Section 12(1) of the PNGRB Act, 2006 states: "The Board shall have jurisdiction to – (a) adjudicate upon and decide any dispute or matter arising amongst entities or between an entity and any other person on issues relating to refining, processing, storage, transportation, distribution, marketing and sale of petroleum, petroleum products and natural gas according to the provisions of Chapter V, *unless the parties have agreed for arbitration*" (emphasis supplied).

    Section 12(1)(b) of the PNGRB Act, 2006 states: "The Board shall have jurisdiction to – (b) receive any complaint from any person and conduct any inquiry and investigation connected with the activities relating to petroleum, petroleum products and natural gas on contravention of – (i) retail service obligations; (ii) marketing service obligations; (iii) display of retail price at retail outlets; (iv) terms and conditions subject to which a pipeline has been declared as common carrier or contract carrier or access for other entities was allowed to a city or local natural gas distribution network, or authorization has been granted to an entity for laying, building, expanding or operating a pipeline as common carrier or contract carrier or authorization has been granted to an entity for laying, building, expanding or operating a city or local natural gas distribution network; (v) any other provision of this Act or the rules or the regulations or orders made thereunder."

22. The study on Telecom Sector by ICRIER commissioned by CCI is very comprehensive on the sector and on the areas of competition concern. Available on the website of CCI.
23. Section 12(1) of the PNGRB Act, 2006 states: "The Board shall have jurisdiction to – (a) adjudicate upon and decide an,y dispute or matter arising amongst entities or between an entity and any other person on issues relating to refining, processing, storage, transportation, distribution, marketing and sale of petroleum, petroleum products and natural gas according to the provisions of Chapter V, *unless the parties have agreed for arbitration*" (emphasis supplied).
24. Geeta Gouri Platform Markets: The Antitrust Challenge in India, Competition Policy International, March 12, 2021.
25. "Subgroup 3: Interrelations between antitrust and regulatory authorities", Antitrust Enforcement in Regulated Sectors Working Group, International Competition Network, Report to the Third ICN Annual Conference, Seoul, April 2004, pp. 20–23.

    "Subgroup 2: Interrelations between antitrust and regulatory authorities", Antitrust Enforcement in Regulated Sectors Working Group, International Competition Network, Report to the Fourth ICN Annual Conference, Bonn, June 2004, p. 9.

    See generally, Department of Trade and Industry and HM Treasury, "Concurrent Competition Powers in Sectoral Regulation", May 2006, URN 06/1244.
26. Antitrust Enforcement in Regulated Sectors Working Group, International Competition Network, Report to the Third ICN Annual Conference, Seoul, April 2004, p. 5.

References

CCI—Journal of Competition Law and Policy.
Competition Policy International.
Reports of International Competition Network.

CHAPTER 8

Conclusions: Challenges for Competition Policy and Law

Areas of public policy are reshaping the contours of competition policy and of competition law. In its implementation this emerging consciousness suggests that several terms of the law need redefining. Who is the consumer? How is consumer welfare to be assessed? The debate in earlier chapters on the historical emphasis of defining welfare in terms of increasing the number of competitors in the field and the hesitancy to accept welfare in terms of consumer benefit is now sharper. In defining the parameters of welfare several fresh challenges have emerged for competition as offshoots of the internet and of platform markets. Investigations have been initiated in two areas by CCI: (i)What is a fair agreement or contract? (ii) Privacy and competition. Apart from these two areas, the Commissions assigned a study on blockchains and competition that have raised concerns in the area of public health facilities. **Inclusive Agenda** is emerging as yet another major challenge of competition policy in terms of gender and migrant labor and employment in the implementation of law. As the concluding chapter, it is conceptual with the intent to draw attention of emerging challenges to competition.

G. Gouri, *A Commissioner's Primer to Economics of Competition Law in India*, https://doi.org/10.1007/978-981-19-9476-0_8

1 Privacy and Competition

Privacy as a competition issue has come to the forefront with the contention of EU that access to personal data without consent is the price consumers pay for accessing the platform markets of the Big Five firms on the internet. The categorization of privacy as 'non-price competition' presents a challenge to the existing competition law framed in terms of price competition, of predatory pricing; of differential pricing and of unfair pricing. It also presents a challenge on how privacy of data hinders competition.

In the judgment of Bundeskartellamt the German Competition Authority prohibited Facebook privacy policy for the collection and processing of data which gave it exclusive control of the data gleaned from consumers.[1] The Dusseldorf Higher Court took a different viewpoint. The Higher Court stated that any violation of data protection law did not constitute a per se violation of competition law. If harm to data protection law also damages to competition, it would constitute a violation of competition law. Therefore, in our case, even though Facebook imposes abusive data processing policy, it would not directly violate competition law.[2] Proceeding on the argument the Higher Court was not able to link the connection between collecting and collating personal data of users on the platform service of Facebook or WhatsApp causing any economic harm. The user may lose control of his data but with the presence of effective competition among social media competition is unlikely to be affected considering all platforms would resort to the same control over data accessed by them. On these considerations, the Higher Court opined that the judgment of the lower court based their assessment on principles of data protection law and not on protection of competition and its law.

Following the EU decision, CCI initiated a Suo moto investigation into the Amazon (Facebook) and Walmart (Flipkart) in examining the dimension of privacy as a competition concern. In the earlier chapters, I had looked at the business model of network industries on 2-sided or multi-sided markets emphasizing the necessity of using different functionalities to attract consumers and advertisers. All social media platforms collect data and as I had argued this data is a facilitating factor in building consumer profiles and in offering new services to attract more consumers. The competition dimension is that access to data is always a facilitating factor in business development acting as an entry barrier to new entrants or of leveraging their position to entry into another market.

The data collected by these firms has raised the present concerns of privacy. Facebook is in a dominant position in terms of data and has its own privacy policy if you wish to access Facebook or WhatsApp as the data is shared between the two of them. Is the personal privacy law over and above the legislated privacy law of the country. What is privacy and its protection in India? The Sri Krishna Committee Report on personal data protection and the K. Gopalrishna Committee report on non-personal data (NPD) have yet to be enacted. NPD is more aggressive in equating dominance in data as dominance in competition hinting that perhaps CCI is protecting these dominant enterprises. Till the investigation by CCI is completed the links between data policy and competition policy remain diffused.Data is always important for any business. Personal data is collected from everyday services in the form of Know Your Customer (KYC) or from Aadhar data. The data is sold to other business clear evidence is the irritating phone calls made in the middle of the afternoon by companies selling a product or insurance schemes. As discussed in the earlier chapter data markets are emerging with data sold as a good. Access to personal data of the big tech companies is leveraged to customize new services. Substantive evidence was, however, not available in the Google and Bharat Matrimony case.[3] Privacy jurisdiction in the absence of a Data Protection Law is now pending with the Supreme Court. The Supreme Court recognized the right to privacy as a fundamental right. The CCI Telecom Report raises similar concerns without substantiating their arguments but leaving it to the Commission to examine the scope for exclusionary behavior due to low privacy standard, leveraging the data advantage across various services provides the following illustrations of abusive conduct: (a) a low privacy standard implying lack of consumer welfare; (b) lower data protection, which could also indicate exclusionary behavior; and (c) leveraging a data advantage across various services.

In Case No. 99 of 2016[4] *Vinod Kumar Gupta v. WhatsApp Inc.*, on CCI had held that breach of Information Technology Act did not fall under its ambit nor of privacy considerations. Approach of CCI on privacy was clearly enunciated in Case No. 99:

> However, the contention of the petitioners is that the proposed change in the privacy policy of WhatsApp amounts to infringement of the Right to Privacy guaranteed under Article 21 of the Constitution of India. Even this cannot be a valid ground to grant the reliefs as prayed for since the legal position regarding the existence of the fundamental right to privacy is

> yet to be authoritatively decided {**Vide: K. S. Puttaswamy (Retired) and Anr. v. Union of India &Ors., (2015) 8 SCC 735**}. Having taken note of the inconsistency in the decisions on the issue as to whether there is any "right to privacy guaranteed under our Constitution, a three Judge Bench in K.S.Puttaswamy (supra) referred the matter to a larger Bench and the same is still pending

A reversal in position is noticed in the Suo moto investigation on WhatsApp perhaps prompted by the Telecom Report.[5] The Report itself acknowledges the primacy of Consumer Protection Act. Moreover, the Delhi High Court single judge found no constitutional dereliction of Facebook and its group (Instagram, WhatsAPP) but left it open to CCI to investigate the competition dimension.

In this debate on privacy and competition, I think of privacy law as the right to be forgotten. This is an area of low concern as of now in India and for Indian consumers. But if sensitive data is accessed say on health and contagious disease anonymity is the prime consideration. Is such data available from social media and whether privacy law of WhatsApp (Facebook) is a guarantor for privacy?

Is the consumer ensured greater privacy under Data Protection Law and whether it prevents a social media group to use cookies remains unanswered?

Is the data advantage unsurmountable as often innovations are not from quantum of data accessed but from observations of selected data?

The persistence of price conscious Indian consumers in finding a good deal is well known raising questions on the Google v Bharat Matrimony and CUTS on the allegations of MakeMyTrip (Gouri and Salinger, 2018)[6] endorsing that competition promotes competitors is the welfare objective of Indian competition law. Possibility or perverse outcomes could occur with CCI's intervention in privacy laws of say Amazon by losing out on better quality products and services. The emphasis in all advertisements a central theme is price even for durable consumer goods such as motor vehicles, fridges etc. The cultural ethos of a consumer is an important factor.[7] In a paper for Competition Policy International, I had observed that:

> My unease with the universality of these antitrust abuses is that the diversity of economic systems, and, more importantly, the diversity of consumers and consumption patterns, risk being painted with an overly broad brush.

> This unease, which began with the first CCI Order in the Google case in 2017, continues to apply in relation to current competition issues in platform markets.

A recent study by Pinar Akman, a law professor at the University of Leeds, confirms the price concern of Indian consumer. Her observation is that as much as 40% of Indian consumers believe that "free" services offered by platforms are a good bargain.[8] There is a privacy paradox in the Indian context has been voiced by me suggesting the need for more studies on the subject. Privacy as a non-price metric for competition may be a distorted measure.

Finally, as per the prima facie Order the imposition of unfair terms and conditions on consumers suggesting a theory of harm is the issue raised in recent allegations field with CCI on unfair terms of contract between a seller and a big tech platform.

2 Agenda of Inclusive Growth

Several questions have emerged in recent times of how competition authorities must also assess the effect of market operations in terms of inclusive growth. Competition is about markets and market functioning should empower the less privileged. It is about creating a level playing field which is the core of competition policy. I raise a few areas of concern only to sensitize the reader.

2.1 Unfair Contracts

The concern that markets on platforms are fixed by the big players and competition is not on merits is a concern voiced by several players to CCI. It is a difficult proposition to decided what is a fair contract as most of the players are also brick-and-mortar enterprises. A big grocery shop offers its wares on Amazon, on its own web site and offline. The DLF case on real estate discussed in an earlier chapter detailed the nature of 'unfairness' in buyers agreements. In that case consumer interest was well perceived.[9] In the Delhi Vyapar Sangh complaint to CCI on steep discounts offered by some sellers to Flipkart and Amazon (Case no. 40 0f 2019) enabling these platform market to attract and lock-in consumers may have prompted the enquiry into contracts. Public interest remains undefined in competition policy and whether the allegations of Delhi

Vyapar Sangh on steep discounts offered by select vendors to Flipkart and Amazon are pro-consumer leaves the argument ambivalent.

Contracts are always defined by the dominant party. Who is the dominant party in platforms markets depends on the measure of dominance applied? Size and volume of transactions as is the criteria of dominance currently applied is inappropriate. The dependence of attracting consumers and creating depth by way of network effects does not suggest that large platform markets of Amazon are in a position to always dictate terms of a contract. Small niche player important for attracting consumers can also alter the terms of the contract. It may extend to other sellers as they always have the choice to choose their manner of sales. Competition on platforms is necessary to provide choice to sellers and consumers.

In this context, the use of smart contracts in the case of blockchain technology does raise competition concern on account of the nature of the technology. The CCI commissioned a study on blockchain technology by Ernst & Young. The study has been insightful in terms of application of the technology and raised several definitional issues for competition law such as defining 'an agreement', and of blockchain as an association of enterprises in lieu of collective dominance. Blockchain technology and its use in fintech firms and of bitcoin gaining currency, however, reveal the opacity of this collective grouping for cartel detection or in assessing dominance. It does emerge as a challenge to competition. The challenge is to find anti-competitive behavior in these closed portals.

2.2 Gender and Migrant Labor

Gender concerns and migrant labor and the need for inclusive growth is a dimension that competition policy must concern itself. At CCI the emphasis is on broad anti-competitive forces without drilling down to the affected groups. These are considered as macro policies outside the realm of competition policies. Gender and migrant labor are for trade unions to intervene perhaps definition of a level playing field. A suggestion that is now being debated is to include these dimensions into AI and algorithms could be a dimension hitherto ignored in competition policy. For instance in looking at algorithmic collusion and cartels a gender perspective of the cartel is available. I include gender with migrant labor as COVID-19 forces portrayed against growth rates were at variance with inclusive growth.

3 Conclusion

Competition law is not a stagnant subject. Emerging challenges briefly touched in this concluding chapter suggest the need for a competition policy and competition law sensitive to different dimensions of market functioning. Consequently, emerging tools with emphasis on behavioral economics and game theory gain credence in assessing competitiveness.

Notes

1. Kemal, Mehmet, Social Media Platforms' Rush on Personal Data and Competition Law: Facebook Decision of German Federal Cartel Office, Competition and Innovation, May 2019.
2. CCI's Order under Section 26(1) of the Competition Act in In Re: Updated Terms of Service and Privacy Policy for WhatsApp Users, Suo Moto Case No. 01 of 2021, dated March 24, 2021 as available at https://www.cci.gov.in/sites/default/files/SM01of2021_0.pdf; the WhatsApp Suo Moto Order has been since taken before the High Court of Delhi as a writ petition on the ground that the CCI is overreaching its jurisdiction by investigating a matter on privacy which is pending before the Supreme Court and the High Court of Delhi. The Delhi High Court dismissed the appeal for lack of merits to interdict the CCI investigation.
3. Protecting Competition v/s Protecting Competitor: Assessing the Antitrust Complaints against Google," co-authored with M. Salinger, The Criterion Journal of Innovation, Vol 2, 2017, p 531–558, also at http://ssrn.com/abstract=2787343.
4. Case No. 99 of 2016 Vinod Kumar Gupta v. WhatsApp Inc.,
5. CCI sponsored Telecom Report, ICRIER.
6. Op. cit.
7. Geeta Gouri, Platform Market: The Antitrust Challenge in India, Antitrust Chronicle, Competition Policy International Special Edition, Winter 2020.
8. Pinar Akman, Akman P. 2019. Competition Policy in a Globalized, Digitalized Economy. Antitrust Chronicle. Competition Policy International (CPI) (December).

References

Competition Policy International.
Conference papers of ICN Network.

Index

G. Gouri, *A Commissioner's Primer to Economics of Competition Law in India*, https://doi.org/10.1007/978-981-19-9476-0

CPSIA information can be obtained
at www.ICGtesting.com
Printed in the USA
LVHW021804090423
743867LV00005B/882

9 789811 994753